Kayaking the Great Circle Trilogy:

Down the Mississippi River, Around the Intracoastal Waterways and Across the Great Lakes

by Randy Bauer

and edited by James J. Bauer

ISBN: 978-1-7363148-4-5

Published by North Orchard Press, LLC.

www.northorchardpress.com

Graphic Design by Earl Sorenson

Cover Art by Kristen Rasmussen

First edition published in 2010 by Educational Media
Corporation, Copyright © 2010 by James J. Bauer, LLC.
Republished with permission after rights to the first
edition were released to North Orchard Press, LLC.
ISBN: 978-1-930572-57-7

Special Thanks to:

Jessica Bauer
Jon Bauer
Molly Bauer
Sara Ohotto Bauer
Amy Vatne-Bintliff
Kristen Rasmussen
Susan Foley

Contents

Brothers Randy (left) and Jim Bauer (right) at the Ohio farm.

About the Author

Randall R. Bauer was born in Long Prairie, Minnesota, on August 15, 1949. When Randy was three, his family moved to Cleveland, Ohio in order for his father to find work. Following a short stay in Cleveland, the family moved to an old farm site near Chardon, Ohio. This is where Randy's sense of adventure and curiosity about nature first was noticed.

It was at Christmas time, during the third grade, that Randy received a chemistry set and his first microscope. It was, however, a third grade teacher who truly facilitated Randy's interest in science and nature.

In 1958, the family moved back to Minneapolis, where Randy attended St. Lawrence Parochial School. Randy's interest in science and nature continued to be nurtured by another teacher who recognized his gifts.

In the early summer of 1959, the family made a final move to Coon Rapids, Minnesota. Located across the street from their new home was an undeveloped wooded area. This is where Randy spent much of his leisure, expanding upon his adventures. Randy meticulously saved his allowances, birthday money and so forth in order to make purchases at an army surplus store, located in nearby Anoka. This is where Randy purchased such items as: surplus army packs, canteens and numerous other objects, which aided him in his adventures.

Scouting was a natural for Randy and his interests. He was a member of Troop 419 in Coon Rapids, Minnesota. On September 27, 1965, Randy was awarded "Eagle Scout."

Randy attended De LaSalle High School located on Nicollet Island in Minneapolis. De LaSalle High School is located only a few yards away from the Mississippi River, St. Anthony Falls and the lock and dam. Randy spent much time observing the river, its magnificent falls and the human attempts to harness it. This is where I feel that the seeds for the "Trilogy" adventure were first planted.

Following his high school graduation in 1967, Randy attended The University Of Minnesota, St. Paul Campus where he pursued a degree in, what else, but "Wildlife Management." During this time Randy also took part in other canoeing and kayaking adventures. This included a short little trip from Lake Itasca to New Orleans, as well as a kayak trip to Hudson Bay.

Following his college graduation, Randy received a written invitation from the United States government beginning with, "Greetings! You have been selected...." This invitation selected Randy to participate in a two-

year all expense paid trip to Alabama and on to Europe with a lovely olive green uniform included. Shortly after his induction, the military discovered Randy's gifts in science. He was then sent for additional training where he became a "nuclear arms expert." During his basic training in Alabama, Randy began plans for a trip, which would circumnavigate the United States. When Randy's obligation to the military was met, he requested what was known as a "European Out," where he ventured through Europe with only a backpack and camera.

After returning home from Europe, Randy launched the Trilogy Adventure, which you are about to experience in his own words. When the Trilogy Adventure was finished, Randy returned to school at St. Cloud State University where he obtained a teaching certificate in biology. Teaching was another adventure for Randy. He taught at the Grand Marais, Minnesota High School, International Falls Community College and three years in Costa Rica.

Randy also sprinkled his adventures with employment through the National Park Service. He provided services at Grand Portage National Monument, Voyagers National Park and Mammoth Cave National Park.

It was when Randy returned to Minnesota and obtained a teaching position at Crossroads Alternative High School that he truly found a place to anchor. The Anoka Hennepin Independent School District #11 was wise in allowing this unconventional person to teach in an unconventional manner to students who learn unconventionally. In 2003/2004, the students at Crossroads Alternative High School elected Mr. Bauer "Teacher of the Year."

In 2004 Randy was diagnosed as having a cancerous tumor in his leg. The cancer eventually metastasized to his kidney, liver and pancreas. Following a heroic endeavor with conventional treatments that produced little success, Randy chose to enter an experimental treatment. Randy's willingness to enter into this new adventure of treating cancer helped to blaze a new trail into the understanding of cancer and its eventual final cure.

In early August 2007, with medications and wheel-chair in tow, Randy and his soulmate Susan Foley entered an adventure of an Alaskan cruise. Shortly after his return home on August 29, 2007, Randy's soul left his body and entered a final unknown adventure.

One of Randy's final requests was for this manuscript to be published.

James J. Bauer

Randy Bauer

Introduction

Adventure is timeless and so is true friendship. On September 8, 1974, Randy Bauer, Jerry Mimback and Tom Anderson began an adventure known as the "Trilogy." The "Trilogy" refers to three bodies of water: the Mississippi River, Coastal Waters of the United States and the Great Lakes—over 7,500 miles by kayak. These three individuals initially met in the 1960s as members of Boy Scout Troop 419. This is where the seeds of confidence, camaraderie, skills and ability think outside the box were first planted.

The book opens with the Trilogy crew being approached by two youths in a fishing boat, who inquired as to their adventure. "Peace and harmony" was the later deciphered answer. "Peace and harmony" runs as a theme for the entire adventure, even through exhausting and seeming impossible times.

The "Trilogy" was a risk for everyone involved. However, it was not a wild risk but a calculated risk. Many years of planning and training went into this trip. It is not recommended that anyone enter such an adventure without proper knowledge, skills and planning.

James J. Bauer

Chapter 1

The Trilogy Begins

"My house says to me, 'Do not leave me, for here dwells your past' And the road says to me, 'Come and follow me, for I am her future.' And I say to both my house and the road, 'I have no past, nor have the future. If I stay here, there is a going in my staying; and if I go there is a staying in my going. Only love and death change all things.'"

Kahlil Gibran

Randy Bauer

It was calm all day and the miles sailed by as we cruised the mirrored surface of the bay. Paddling was automatic, effortless. It was a moment we had experienced many times before, where kayaker and kayak were one in the same. The afternoon sun was in our faces when we rounded the ten-mile straightaway between Glenora and Deseronto and headed southwest. In the glare we could see a fishing boat rowing across our path a hundred yards away. On board were a sixteen year-old and his younger brother. We talked for a while in the golden light explaining where we had been and what we still hoped to accomplish. Our conversation was approached at first with disbelief, then with wonder and finally with a smiling reply: "You know, you guys have found the answer, you've really found the answer!"

At dusk, we were comfortably set up in an open wooded area surrounded by oak trees and a few cow pies. I stared into the embers of the glowing campfire and wondered about the statement we had heard four hours earlier.

"What have we found the answer to?" I asked myself aloud.

"Peace and harmony," Jerry replied. "Peace and harmony."

He was right. What we did and who we were just a few years before now seemed alien and light years away.

It was hot and sticky that day in Alabama in 1972. I could smell the chives in the sparse grass between the barracks as I sat on my bunk… sweating. My thoughts were far away. A kayak trip to Hudson Bay the year before was fresh in my mind and I longed for the water, the freedom and sunlight of the trail.

"Hey buddy, there you are!" Denny's voice shattered my daydream. "You wouldn't believe what Sergeant Strawbridge has got us doing for the big inspection…. By the way, I got a cassette tape from home. You want to hear it?"

Denny and I walked over to his barracks. The sun was behind the hills but it was still hot. We listened to the tape amidst the barrack noise we had learned to ignore long ago. Fumbling through a disorganized stack of magazines and papers, I pulled out a map of the Eastern United States and began studying it.

"You know Denny, it would be possible to go completely around the Eastern United Stated by boat—the Mississippi River, the Intracoastal Waterway and the Great Lakes."

"Yeah, I suppose it would be, if you wanted to go around that way by boat," Denny said.

"No, I really mean it. I would like to do it once I get out of the army."

Soon, I was in Germany, keeping in touch with a dream through a trickle of letters from friends I had grown up with. By the time I came home, two years had passed and Jerry and Tom were building kayaks they had ordered. In contrast, with the start of the journey less than six weeks away, I still needed a craft… until my Mother happened upon what I was looking for at a rummage sale.

Forty dollars bought a two-person kayak plus sailing accessories. The boat itself, a high school shop project, was fifteen feet long with a thirty-six inch beam. Essentially, it was a wooden frame boat covered with painted canvas and weighed close to a hundred pounds.

The frame was in excellent condition. Its keel was two and a half inches wide, fitted with three-quarter inch plywood keel-ends. Four, three-quarter inch plywood crossframes fastened themselves to the keel; and three ash ribs (longerons), on either side of the keel, fastened to the crossframe and keel-ends forming the hull. Ash gunwales were bent along the upper part of the cross frames and deck struts ran across the center of the crossframes to form the deck. The cockpit was huge and the frame's deteriorated covering reminded me of an eggshell because it was cracked and punctured easily. In the weeks ahead, the craft would be re-designed to hold one person and would be recovered with a hull and deck considerably tougher than the original.

In the meantime, Jerry and Tom worked on their kayaks. Both had ordered kits from a boat company in South Carolina. Family garages were transformed into kayak factories. When Jerry was done with his boat, he estimated it took one hundred and fifty hours to build.

"Laying the keel was the most tedious part of construction and making sure the frame was 'true' when the ribs were put on," he said.

Jerry and Tom's kayak frames were held together by wood glue and corrosion resistant brass screws and protected with several coats of varnish. A fabric skin was then stretched over the frame. When viewed from a distance, the kayaks looked as though they were covered with fiberglass. In reality, the rigs were covered with a tough cloth-backed vinyl.

The hull went on in two layers. The first, a thinner fabric than the outside layer, was stretched over the frame "inside out," the shiny side of the fabric facing the inside of the boat and the cloth side facing the outside. The first layer was stretched and then tacked and stapled to the inside of the gunwale. The second layer or outside hull, was glued onto the inside hull with its cloth back against the cloth back of the inside hull. When complete, the hull was a kind of vinyl sandwich with shiny fabric on both sides.

With my own boat, most of the frame had been reworked. The fore and aft cross frames were originally solid pieces of plywood. I cut large openings in each to allow ventilation to the bow and stern and packed the ends with solid pieces of Styrofoam for flotation. The large cockpit had been reduced to half its size by adding two new cross frames made from conduit pipe bent and welded to the proper size and shape.

The vinyl fabric I selected came from an upholstery shop. I bought the deck material at the same place, as well as material used for covering grain trucks to make a spray apron. Altogether, twenty yards, forty-five pounds and sixty dollars worth of fabric were needed for the job.

During the metamorphosis, a canary yellow, punctured, two-person boat transformed into a single person kayak with a dark blue hull and cream yellow deck. A blue racing stripe with black borders ran from stern to bow on the deck and the gunwales were bordered with cedar strips.

I considered the craft beautiful, although it was a battleship compared to the sleek design of Jerry and Tom's kayaks, both boats were half a foot longer (15 1/2 feet) and two inches narrower at the beam (32 inches). They were an inch shorter in total height than mine and had less hull area.

Work on the kayaks was integrated with other preparation details. We felt the journey should be somewhat scientific in nature and collected a meager assortment of material and tools to meet those ends. We'd be hauling down the river a Beckman Dredge, which was borrowed from the University of Minnesota, film canisters for collecting river bottom specimens, alcohol for preserving them and a sieve for separating the specimens from the mud. Tom threw in his dissecting kit with its assortment of scalpels, forceps, picks and scissors. And I picked up a journal for recording our findings. We also would pack a maximum-minimum thermometer, barometer and Secchi Disk for measuring water turbidity.

Food sources varied. By now, the journey had become a joint effort on the part of all three families. Jerry's mom made huge batches of cocoa and granola for us, my mother set aside food in the pantry that she figured we would need and there was a growing stack of food items at Tom's folk's house earmarked "trip."

There was also food from our relatives and friends. My cousin left a stack of instant soup and pudding at the house one day with a note attached: "Randy, here are some dry goods for your journey—Sue."

Likewise, a very good friend of ours left a box of candy bars for each of us one night with the message: "I hope these will last part way down the river, Larry."

My great aunt loaded us down with an assortment of canned goods. "You need this... and this..." Barbara said. "Better take some of these.... Do you think you'll eat these or is it too much?" She also told me she regretted not traveling in a time long past when she had the opportunity and—most important of all—her health. Those same words would be repeated to us many times on the journey.

We also bought a few groceries: oatmeal, rice, sugar, tea and other basics. We really didn't know what we would actually need. Our potpourri of donated and store bought supplies would sustain us on our "shakedown" cruise from Lake Itasca to Minneapolis. By then, we figured we would know what we preferred and needed in foodstuffs.

I bought a small gasoline-backpacking stove and together we purchased a three person nylon wall tent. Resourcefulness provided us with many things. Pots and pans came from home, water jugs were recycled bleach bottles, a tin can candle lantern provided a general light source inside the tent and discarded ice cream buckets and restaurant food jars became food containers.

Other shared equipment included matches, toilet paper and several small can openers. We kept matches on ourselves in watertight plastic bags and also scattered throughout our equipment. Toilet paper, besides its obvious use, proved invaluable for cleaning pots and pans before washing.

Tom and Jerry's "Fiberfill II" sleeping bags were modified mummy styles. Each had a hood, which could be drawn tightly around the user's head and both were tapered. Each bag was also equipped with a double, full length, nylon zipper. The bottom of the bag could be opened to maximize ventilation; it could also be used as a blanket by opening it fully.

My sleeping gear consisted of a double sleeping bag: the outside one a cheaply made Fiberfill II bag and the inner one an army issued goose-down bag. I'd use the double bag on cold nights and a single bag during warmer weather. The sleeping bag was warm but unlike Jerry and Tom's, did not fully open, was not adequately ventilated and was cramped at the foot end. I also had to keep it wrapped in plastic or in a rubberized bag to insure the down would not get wet and lose its insulating value.

For raingear we started with the inexpensive and later bought the best we could find. During our journey, staying warm and dry became paramount. The cheap raincoats leaked and didn't hold up under constant use. Their hoods did not sufficiently cover our heads and they lacked adequate elastic cuffs to prevent water from seeping into the inner sleeve when the paddle blade was raised.

Each of us also carried an army field poncho, which were used as raincoats, windbreaks, kayak covers, ground and tablecloths, sails, padding and for collecting rainwater.

In total, we carried six sets of kayak paddles, one spare set in each boat.

I made a survival kit from a welding rod can. It contained matches, a compass, glass mirror, hard candy, two large garbage bags, fire starters made from paraffin soaked cardboard, signal flares and smoke canisters.

All of our equipment was either impervious to water or wrapped in recycled plastic bread bags. We learned very quickly to distinguish "waterproof" from "water repellent."

Departure was less than a week away. The Friday before, Jerry followed through with one of the most difficult decisions of his life, he quit his job. For two years he had worked as a pellet mill operator in Minneapolis saving some money for the trip and spending the rest, for the most part, on having a good time. "I was caught in a trap and wanted a chance to change," Jerry recalls. "The money would come and I'd spend it as fast as I could. I felt financially secure but I really wasn't happy. I now look back at that time and see how much was just wasted."

The "old timers" at work couldn't understand why Jerry was planning to quit. They thought it was just idle talk, the same thing many of them said five, ten, even fifteen years before but were too scared to try. When Jerry's quitting time rolled around most of them were shocked. From that day, a reincarnation for Jerry began.

For Tom and I, the transition to kayaker would be less traumatic. Tom was a student working on a degree in biology. His jobs were either part time or temporary. For the past three years the end of summer meant change and instead of going back to school, Tom would launch a kayak.

For me, the transition was easy as far as life style. I had no permanent employment since I left the army. Therefore, I didn't have a job to quit that would give me an immediate sense of loss or insecurity. The kayak trip to Hudson Bay and one down the Mississippi five years before, also gave me confidence in what I was undertaking. However since I had been home for such a short time, the feeling of being cheated by leaving so soon bothered me. How precious people became in those last weeks, especially my parents, brother and his wife. The note saying: "Take the boiled eggs in the frig and the peanut butter cookies in your bedroom—Mom," became a special reminder of the love and concern felt by those who would wait for our return.

Chapter 2

A Narrow Beginning

"Look deeply into nature and then you will understand everything better."

Albert Einstein

The pick-up sped north as disconnected thoughts flashed through my mind. Our journey would be called "Trilogy" because of its three phases: the River, the Ocean and the Great Lakes. I wondered what would happen in the days ahead. I wondered if we would be able to function effectively as a team and I wondered if our circle would be able to follow the circle of seasons and be completed in a year.

By 7:00 p.m. all of us were at the Douglas Lodge parking lot, Itasca State Park— our pre-determined rendezvous point. Jerry's folks left shortly afterward and his kayak was placed alongside mine on top of the truck. Jerry and I slept in the truck that night while Tom, his family, and my brother and his wife slept in the lodge.

Three kayaks waited in the September moonlight for what they had been made, the water. Tom's kayak, with orange deck and blue hull called "Endurance;" Jerry's "Mississippi Queen," with its light blue deck and dark blue hull; and mine, the blue and yellow kayak named the "Molly-B," after my sister-in-law.

Elk Lake flowed into Lake Itasca via a short creek and was our embarkation point.

A man asked what we were doing and later replied with a statement which became a standing joke for the rest of the trip, "Must be nice... all you do is just sit and drift."

"Aren't you leaving a little bit late in the year?" someone else asked.

"No," I said. "We planned it so we'd avoid the hurricane season along the Gulf Coast."

More questions about our endeavor started to irritate me and apparently made Jerry anxious. Once we were in open water, Jerry madly raced to the north end of the lake. In the meantime, the "launch crew" drove down to the headwaters (about three miles away) to help lift the boats over the stepping-stones. Of course Jerry arrived fifteen minutes ahead of us and Molly heard him remark,

"Boy, those guys better hurry up... we'll never get to New Orleans this way!" It would take Jerry until New Orleans to slow down.

We read the inscription on the wooden marker, "Here 1,475 feet above the ocean the mighty Mississippi begins to flow. On its winding way 2,552 miles to the Gulf of Mexico." We carried our boats around the rocks, walked them into deeper water and were gone.

For a while we continued to wade and lifted our kayaks over several low footbridges. Here was the infant Mississippi, a clean, winding stream with a gravel bottom. In one place, the Father of Waters ran through a culvert no more than four feet wide.

The boats slid through a winding channel choked with waterweeds and bordered with ripe wild rice five to six feet tall. The walls of rice stems bent and separated as we passed through and then closed behind us. In the process, hundreds of ripe kernels landed in the water, on the decks and inside our kayaks. The area was a feeding ground for waterfowl and we flushed wood ducks and mallard by the dozens. In open areas, where the lily pads and floating vegetation didn't obstruct the view, I could easily see the riverbed.

"Here in the rice swamps we can plainly see the Secchi Disk as it sits on the bottom of five to six feet of water. I'm sure we could read newsprint if a paper were lying on the bottom of the young Mississippi." rib

We stopped at Anlagen Landing, the first of several campsites the Forest Service maintained on the ninety miles of winding river from Lake Itasca to Bemidji and got a late start the next morning. A major time consumer involved the repacking of the kayaks. Our equipment was a hodgepodge. We were unaccustomed to it and it would take awhile before our packing efficiency improved.

We were also unaccustomed to each other. Even though we had known each other for a long time, it would take time and patience before we'd be able to effectively cope and accept each other's strengths, weaknesses and idiosyncrasies.

Our bodies would also be required to change. Our sleeping, eating and exercise habits were in the process of being molded for a new way of life. We would need more rest and food to compensate for the increased exercise. The exercise itself would require some getting used to. Our general conditioning was excellent, but it would be a while before the twinge of sore paddling muscles would go away. Just sitting in the kayak would require the use of new muscles.

We figured we'd easily make it to Coffee Pot Landing by nightfall. The day's objective however, was not part of the Master Plan. It would be the trip's first lesson in "take things as they come."

"After leaving the camp we came to an old logging sluice way. We portaged around it and filled our water jugs at a nearby flowing well. The River changed after the sluiceway and we found ourselves running through a series of small boulder fields. I would have enjoyed the boulders if it weren't for the soft bottom of my boat. It was leaking slowly when we left the fields. Then, I tried to run a beaver dam. Tom and Jerry slid their boats over without problem. I did the same and crawled back into my kayak to discover, to my horror, the Mississippi rushing in. The sharp sticks of the dam punctured the hull like a pincushion. I floundered up to shore and by the time I was done repairing the leaks I had patched eighteen holes in the hull with duct tape. My kayak is fit for the dump!" rrb

I was outraged. The material on my hull was no-where near as tough as the other two kayaks and I was finding out the hard way. When reaching the next three beaver dams, I lifted my boat over. It was a difficult task considering waste deep water on the upstream side, muck on downstream and sharp sticks in the middle.

When nightfall came, we found ourselves in a deep river, nine to twelve feet wide, meandering through a tor-turous semi-dry swamp. In one area we passed under the same power lines three times. We pitched our tent over hummocks in the swamp and ate a tent supper of crackers, tuna fish, banana chips and hot chocolate. The entire day had been ridiculous (including our sleeping quarters, which required sleeping sideways, over and around the bumps on the floor) but we were in good spirits. We were able to laugh about the incidents and our unusual mattress. In so doing the objective of the day became unimportant, the misery of the day seemed far away and our campsite was a little more comfortable.

During the next two days we passed many tributaries as the Mississippi continued to grow. The weather, for the most part, was miserable...cool, heavy overcast, with a typical fall mist in the air. At one lunch break, we pulled onto the steep banks of a hardwood forest where Jerry and Tom built a roaring fire while I unloaded my boat and re-patched it with vinyl and contact cement. At another break, Indian people, driving up in a car, who asked if we had gone through any good ricing areas, greeted us.

Now and then we paddled by a farmhouse along heavily wooded shores only to recede back into rice swamps with their huge meandering curves. In the swamps, the River would virtually lay back on itself. Tom and I would often see Jerry holding his paddle blade above the reeds when he'd hear us talking. He'd be a quarter mile ahead of us by water, but if we wanted to we could have shook hands over the reeds.

Water in the swamps was low, so the possibility of wandering off into a side channel wasn't as great as during other times of the year. However, if one didn't pay attention to which way the submerged reeds bent the possibility of "getting lost" or very mixed up remained high. Consequently, it was fairly easy for Tom and I to imagine what went through Jerry's mind when the channel suddenly ended.

Jerry had been out of sight in the huge swamp for at least three hours. It was getting late in the afternoon and the prospects of a dry campsite looked dismal. Suddenly, his kayak exploded from behind a bend, as he raced like a mad man toward Tom and me. There was a look of panic on his face, even though Jerry tried to appear undisturbed.

"Channel dries up completely, comes to a dead end," he said. "We'll have to find another way."

We sat for a moment and then decided to investigate. It took twenty minutes to reach the "dead end." At first glance, the channel did appear to end abruptly. However, upon closer examination, the submerged reeds indicated a current and the shallow water didn't look too difficult to reconnoiter. Charging ahead, we pushed and pulled through ten feet of tall reeds and floating mat to find us once again in open water.

Clouds thickened to darker shades of gray as night approached. At last, the structure we had been anticipating the past several hours appeared. Iron Bridge meant an end to the swamp and a campsite for the night.

Fall was on its way in the northland and we talked about it as we cooked supper in the tent.

"I've noticed the mallards and greenwing teal in the swamps are all bunching up in groups of five or more," Jerry said.

Tom replied: "How about all those hundreds of blackbirds flocking together, that's a sure sign."

"The leaves in many places are rapidly reaching their peak," I added.

"When we left Itasca, most of the dogwood was green. Now, most of what we were seeing has turned red. Of course, that's because we're paddling north to go south." Tom went on to say.

Oddly enough, the last part of his statement was true. For the first one hundred and twenty miles, the Mississippi flowed north and then, near Bemidji, it bent to the east and south, forming a large question mark. We were going south by paddling north.

Jerry and Tom were asleep. Rain had settled in for the night and a strong wind roared through the pines and rustled the tent fly. The candle flame flickered now and then from the changing drafts. I thought about the message inscribed on the outhouse wall: "Here we stand in the pouring rain, our brand new tent leaking like a sieve!"

I thought how lucky we were to be in a dry shelter and wrote:

"This tent is at least twenty degrees warmer than the outside air temperature. Even though crowded, it is a welcome oasis in the dark, wet, cold world of tonight."

Soon after Iron Bridge, the Mississippi flowed through hardwoods all the way to Bemidji. We called it the enchanted forest. Red maples, green ash, box elder, oak and highbush cranberry reflected their fall splendor in the clear river water.

Hunger spurred our boats across Lake Irving and we feasted on steak dinners at an in-town restaurant. Bemidji gave us a chance to replenish our food stocks, which were rapidly being devoured by our monstrous hunger. We added bread, macaroni and cheese, oatmeal, powdered milk, sugar and tea to our miscalculated supply.

It was nearly dark when we crossed Lake Bemidji. The compass pointed to a patch of reed where the outlet of the river was supposed to be. An hour later in the dark, we reached the reed bed and followed the long arm of water six miles to the Ottertail Power Dam.

We paddled past cabins and resorts in blackness, checking our location now and then with the glow of the flashlight on map and compass. After taking a bearing, we'd paddle toward a far off light or the silhouette of a tall tree.

The colors of the day, along with the rush of the wind, had been replaced by the shades of night and quietude. The most dramatic element of the evening was the silence. As we approached our resting place for the night, the dip of paddle blades, the slap of a beaver's tail on the water, the hooting of an owl, the drone of our conversation and finally the hum of the hydro dam were music to our ears.

The Mississippi had changed from a winding stream to a waterway linking a series of large and small lakes. We had crossed Lake Bemidji and now paddled past high sandy hills on a river with a gravel bottom, a few boulders and deep holes. Oftentimes, we could see perch and walleye swimming beneath us in the clear water.

From high atop one of the pine ridges, we ate lunch and viewed the countryside. Below us, the river meandered another half mile or so to join Wolf Lake, Ambrosia, Cass Lake with its islands and Winnibigoshish.

Wolf and Andrusia lakes were no problem. Cass Lake, though, required a little more effort. We traversed the seven miles of the lake in a series of hops. Portage and Star islands offered us protection for the first four miles. Afterward, we quartered stiff southwest winds across the remaining miles of open water to the dam.

Ten years before, the three of us had camped together at Knutson Dam as scouts. We were in the same troop but hardly knew each other. How strange it was to be back at the same place.

I remembered swimming in the water and going over Knutson Dam in an air mattress. It was much too cold for that now. In the gathering twilight, we piled more wood on the fire and bundled up. I put on long underwear, an insulated jacket, a pair of wool gloves and stocking cap.

Chapter 3

Dirty, Miserable
Stretch of Water

"Everybody needs beauty as well as bread, places to play in and pray in, where nature may heal and give strength to body and soul."

John Muir

Randy Bauer

The river flowed through nine miles of swamp to connect Cass Lake with Lake Winnibigoshish.

We understood why Indian People named the Lake "Dirty, miserable stretch of water" when it broke on our horizon from behind a wall of reeds. We made camp on the lakeshore and would catch the lake in the early morning when it would most likely be in a more tolerable mood.

"Electrifying excitement shoots through all of us. We can see our goal on the east side, a point ten miles distant. The three kayaks sit side-by-side; they are ready for the crossing... the lake itself is a relief from the closeness of the River shoreline. I imagine it's much like the ocean and the Great Lakes will be. Blue and pink ripples on the water now, the wind has died. Many boats on this side, some are anchored and some are trolling... all are fishing. My eyes follow the shoreline and come to rest on a white pine ghost tree fifteen feet from shore. I can see geese flying south tonight." rrb

The flashlight burned my eyes as I looked at my watch. It was four o'clock. I poked my head out of the tent and could clearly hear the wind sough high in the pines. The sky showed no stars. It was overcast. None of us said very much. It was too early to say what the weather would do. By the time we had spooned down a breakfast of raw oatmeal mixed with sugar and powdered milk, the sky was clearing and the wind subsiding.

Most of our gear was already packed. The remainder—tent, sleeping bags and a few eating utensils—were stowed and we carried our kayaks around stumps, rocks and trees to the lakeshore.

Jerry and Tom put their rigs in at the public access. I launched my soft-bottomed boat from the dock for fear of tearing new holes in the hull. As a result, I had to set my boat into the water empty (it was much too heavy to launch when fully loaded from the dock) and then repack it. The task was painstakingly time consuming but I was left reasonably assured that I would not see water pouring into my boat from a new hole or ripped off patch when I was halfway across the lake.

By five-thirty, we were on our way. We paddled toward an invisible point of land ten miles and three hours distant. The evening before we had taken a compass bearing and now we fixed the same bearing to a low star above our destination.

When we reached the middle of the lake, the water had turned choppy. With the breeze at our backs, we realized the waves would continue to grow until we reached the protection of the point.

"I wonder what would happen if one of us did swamp out here?" I asked myself during one big wave. Reluctantly, I answered: "We'd probably freeze to death."

We stopped at a long sand spit near Tamarack Point for a few minutes before paddling the three miles to Plug Hat Point and the dam. We were safe now and looked with relief at the body of water we had crossed. The wind was increasing and the open lake was getting rougher by the minute.

Lake Winnibigoshish lay in the heart of the Chippewa National Forest and the Leech Lake Chippewa Indian Reservation. Below Winni's Dam, the river resumed its winding course through brush covered swampland, although it was evident, some of it had been straightened and dredged years ago.

As we passed underneath a highway bridge, we heard Indian children speaking their native language. Around a bend, Jerry spotted a Bald Eagle perched on a tree branch high above the water.

There was thirty miles of swampy river in between our campsite at Gambler's Point and Pokegema Dam near Grand Rapids. It's serpentine route, described by one fisherman as "crookeder than a barrel of guts" eventually lead us to the Corps of Engineers Campground adjacent to the dam after a long day of paddling.

The following afternoon, a dramatic change occurred in both topography and water quality above and below Grand Rapids. We couldn't think of anything more peaceful than drifting along the quiet pool above the town, surrounded by the seasonal beauty of flaming reds and yellows.

Likewise, we couldn't think of anything more ugly and disgusting as what we saw a mile after the paper mill truck portaged us around the Blandin Dam.

The river changed from a clear waterway flowing through rice swamps and sandy, lake country, to a fetid, gray stream winding through mud-banked forest. The change in topography we could understand. Grand Rapids marked the shoreline of glacial Lake Aitkin. Obviously, the river below the moraine would prove unappealing to almost any river traveler who had been on the other side. However, the change in water quality we could not understand. As we paddled along, we passed a giant outfall pipe spewing thousands of gallons of gray water into the Mississippi. For miles below, the Mississippi River resembled used wash water. The whole place smelled like a sump pump well and I almost vomited while taking a Secchi Disk reading.

Above the outfall pipe, the disc disappeared four feet below the surface. Below the outfall, the disc disappeared six inches under the water!

The river had turned from a clean, beautiful paradise to a polluted, ugly, gray nightmare in almost a wink of an eye. We raced down the stinking waterway as fast as we could and paddled into darkness before we set up camp.

None of us ate anything for breakfast. We sponged the heavy dew from the tent, wiped off the mud, crawled back into the kayaks and were happy to leave. The riverbanks revealed more disgusting sights: Piles of rusty tin cans; a smashed television set; the hulk of a junked car half submerged in the water.

"The 'universal sink' attitude is certainly working here," Tom said.

Maybe the very fact that the water was polluted added to an apathetic feeling toward the river. Miles went by before the Mississippi returned to a coffee color again.

Our spirits rose when Jerry surprised us with food he had bought in Grand Rapids.

"I don't know about you guys but I ain't gonna starve on this trip," he said.

He pulled a head of lettuce, salad dressing and four cans of pork and beans from a shopping bag in his kayak. We added the larder to our peanut butter and jelly sandwiches and consumed the whole works in our ongoing adjustment to find a balance between food, exercise and the elements.

After lunch, the world seemed a little brighter. In the late afternoon, we paddled by an old homestead. The tiny house was abandoned, its old sideboards weathered gray by the elements. A twisted jack pine poked up from the cleared ground in front of the house. And an overturned rowboat unused for years, its keel looking much like a swayback mule, completed the scene. The sun's low angle, the unbroken backdrop of sky, the silence and the "untouched for years" appearance enveloped the still life in a feeling of peace.

Darkness found us helping fishermen load their boat and motor at a public campground a few miles above Jacobson.

The next day, Jerry, Tom and I seldom saw each other until nightfall. Tom was far behind the entire day, Jerry was full of energy and I was in the middle. Once in a while I'd catch a glimpse of Jerry as his kayak blades would flash and then he'd disappear around another bend.

As the day progressed, it seemed we were in some kind of ridiculous race. It was unfortunate I thought not to be together to share what lay along the riverbanks: a wayside park smashed to pieces by a tornado; an abandoned railroad trestle upriver from Jacobson; pilings along the riverbank, possibly the remnants of the old steamboat days in between Grand Rapids and Aitkin; and a family of raccoons Jerry had seen washing their food along the bank.

It was a beautiful fall day. The river was alive with small sets of rapids here and there and the wind couldn't reach us between the corridors of trees. Sometimes, I'd sit back and relax for a few minutes, watching the bright collage of colored leaves rustling in the treetops. Elms, maples, basswoods and aspen drifted by. A strong gust would send showers leaves from the heights to join hundreds more floating on the water.

Come suppertime, I found Jerry waiting near the mouth of the Big Sandy River. He had been waiting about five minutes. We caught our first glimpse of Tom about thirty minutes later. In the meantime, I paddled up the Big Sandy River to see if I could find a restaurant for us at the town of Libby.

Tom and Jerry's conversation ran something like this:

Jerry: "What took you so long?"

Tom: SILENCE

Jerry: "We want to get something to eat here and then paddle the rest

of the night so we can get to the post office at Aitkin before it closes on Saturday."

Tom: "Oh no we're not! I'm damn tired right now. Yeah, they should call this the Trilogy kayak race."

A fight could have occurred, but it didn't. The confrontation spoke of transition from individuals to a cohesive group. It would be the first of several uncomfortable and oftentimes painful growing pains on the journey.

I didn't find a restaurant, but did find a Corps of Engineers Campground a half-mile up the Big Sandy River at the dam.

Tempers cooled after supper and we agreed the next day we'd rest. I'd hitch hike to Aitkin to pick up the mail.

During our stay at Big Sandy, we learned the camp had previously been the site of a fur trade post and Indian village. Back at the turn of the century, when Aitkin was the railroad head and steamboats made regular runs to Grand Rapids, the dam was equipped with a lock system to link Big Sandy Lake with the water highway.

The old timers on Big Sandy remembered one such steamboat called the "Oriole." Eventually, the Oriole became a lakeside dance hall and finally was torn down. Most of the other steamboats on the river met similar fates. Some sank, others burned. The "Andy Gibson," the largest steamboat on the Grand Rapids to Aitkin run, used to clip the sides of the riverbanks as it rounded the bends. It now lies sunk just below Aitkin. Its stately running light ended up being used as a hog trough.

Chapter 4

Paradise in Cold Weather

"Adopt the pace of nature: her secret is patience."
Ralph Waldo Emerson

SNOW! Snow on the tent and sprinkled on the ground. It was a harbinger of what was to come and a cool incentive to keep going.

Just below Palisade, a twenty-minute blizzard hit with stinging snow pellets. We nicknamed the town "Paradise" in honor of the weather and thawed out in the "Paradise Café." With "furnaces" stoked, our renewed vigor placed our sites on the town of Aitkin twenty-five river miles away.

Darkness came. At first it was fairly easy to see. The sky had cleared and a half moon hung low over the riverbank. We could see the orange glow and sparks from nearby grass fires and in the distance, the white pulsating glow of northern lights. Then the moon set and the magical mood started to wear off.

We paddled and paddled and it grew colder and colder. I turned on my flashlight to discover ice on the kayak deck and ice forming on parts of the paddle shaft. The river was full of dead heads. I hit some and skirted close by others. I prayed that I wouldn't hit a sharp log that would tear a wide hole in the boat filling it with icy water.

A chilling, ice fog settled over the river making visibility even worse. The tips of my toes felt like they were frozen. Jerry's feet were numb. Tom said he was "completely frozen." The northern lights, which had delighted me earlier, now made me angry. Their glow kept teasing me into thinking Aitkin was just around the bend.

At last, we made out the faint image of a bridge. We now knew we were in Aitkin and that the public campground was somewhere on the left bank— but where?

We were cold, tired, hungry, irritable and confused. Everything was dark and the high banks gave no hint of where it would be.

"Let's just find a place to camp," I groaned. "Any place."

Jerry climbed out of his boat, put one foot on the slippery clay, then the other foot and fell flat on his face. He slipped and stumbled three more times before getting back into his boat.

"Can't camp here," he said.

We continued to search, this time below the bridge. Tom crawled to the top of a bank and yelled, "We can set a tent up here, but I don't know how we'll get it up here!"

I know we could never have dragged our gear up that slope under normal conditions. It was just stubborn, frozen determination. The mercury dropped to twelve degrees, while we slept like logs.

At first light, Jerry got up to make sure the river wasn't frozen. Then he looked over a small rise to see picnic tables and fireplaces. We were on the boundary of the town's campground and the public access was only a stone's throw down river.

Fifteen miles below Aitkin, we passed the Aitkin drainage ditch outlet. The seven-mile long ditch bypassed twenty miles of river meandering through the flood plain and supposedly rid Aitkin of almost annual flooding.

After the ditch's outlet, the river was much straighter with gravel, rock strewn banks, typical of a glacial till plain. Bur oak, birch, aspen, Norway and white pine were common in the area. The change was certainly refreshing and the sighting of two more Bald Eagles enhanced it.

Some people told us about a sports equipment class from a local school, canoeing a few hours ahead of us. We found the group camped atop a high sand hill about twelve river miles from Brainerd and decided to join them for the evening. The canoe trip was a class requirement. We found an interesting contrast between them and us.

"For the sports equipment clan, and I guess it holds true for most people, the out-of-doors is for fun and recreation. For

us, the out-of-doors, at least on this journey, is our home, we live here!" rrb

As a result, we were upset over the sad sight atop the hill. Our home had been ravaged. The campsite we shared was supposedly a wayside park. When I first saw the place with its huge piles of tin cans, broken bottles, paper and other refuse, I thought we were camped at the Brainerd dump.

Brainerd too was a depressing place for us. The paper mill dam portage was an obstacle course of glass, sticks, jagged metal and huge logs embedded with spikes. The river below the dam flowed through a ravine giving us the view of unkempt banks and drain pipes. To make matters worse, unfriendly kids pelted us with huge rocks, chunks of concrete and profanities as we passed under a highway bridge.

We were glad to get to Crow Wing State Park twelve miles downstream. The park incorporated the town site of Crow Wing, a one-time fur-trading center, located at the junction of two important trade routes—The Mississippi River system and the Red River Ox Cart Trail. We looked at the markers and depressions where buildings had been and tried to imagine what the place looked like.

Nearby, a buck bounded through the meadow and disappeared behind a rise. A short while later, we stood on another rise— the same place where Chippewa Indians ambushed their Sioux adversaries in 1775. The dispute involved hunting and gathering rights in the area and illustrated the consequences of early arms trade. The Chippewa, displaced from the east, had trading contact with Europeans before the Sioux did. Contact met an exchange of trade goods, which meant firearms for the Chippewa and subsequent displacement of the Sioux farther west into the prairies.

"The thirty-five mile stretch of the river from Brainerd to Little Falls has an overall character I hope can somehow be preserved in years to come. The west side of the river borders

a military reservation and the east side has not yet felt major development. The river is clear, wide and often flows through a latticework of islands and gravel bars. It was alive with hundreds of Canadian Geese when we paddled through." rrb

In the thirty-six miles of the river between Little Falls and St. Cloud, we portaged four dams, beat into strong winds and ran through a long boulder field at Sauk Rapids.

The newspaper at Little Falls gave us opportunity to express publicly our feelings about the river we had lived on and our increased sensitivity toward it and the environment.

"Pollution, for many, is detached from ordinary life; but, when you see, feel, touch and taste it, it's quite different," Tom said.

At the Lindbergh Center immediately south of Little Falls, the director told us of Charles Lindbergh's personal fight against environmental deterioration.

"If I had to make a choice, I'd rather have birds than airplanes," the famous aviator is quoted as saying.

In St. Cloud, we overheard a radio commercial about harnessing the power of the great Manitoba Rivers by building hydroelectric dams— "power for the nation from northern Canada." The commercial rang with pioneer attitudes of "taming" and "subduing" the land and countered recollections of the running wild, singing rapids on the trip to Hudson Bay. What was once a memory of peace and great joy for me was now one of anger and sadness.

Chapter 5

Best So Far by a Dam Site

"One touch of nature make simple world can."
William Shakespeare

The roar of the St. Cloud Dam faded away as we slipped downstream in the twilight. We would paddle till midnight to insure ourselves of getting to Minneapolis' northern suburbs by the next night. The timetable wasn't important to us, but it was important to our families and friends down stream. So, we paddled a third of the fifty-three miles in the dark. The night was filled with groundings on gravel bars, a broken longeron in Tom's kayak and ghostly grass fires.

The smudge from one huge fire burned along the riverbank. Its patches of flame resembled fires from someone's camp; and the illusion brought on the thought of being invited in for hot coffee by "the campers."

By the next evening, we had traversed the first 450 miles of the Mississippi in twenty-one days.

The rest in the Twin Cities gave us time to restock our food supplies and time to add and subtract and repair equipment. Jerry found two large cooking kettles, a cast iron griddle "from the cabin up north," and a condiment box. We left behind the canoe paddles we used for negotiating the tight meandering curves on the Upper Mississippi. And Tom's worthless pocket radio was replaced by Jerry's AM/FM/Weather Band model.

A few days later, we launched nearly empty kayaks from the Champlin landing and paddled five miles to a portage sight at the Coon Rapids Dam where re-outfitted goods waited for us. Prior to our departure, Minnesota had its earliest freeze in history. Now, with the temperature in the forties and the sky threatening rain or snow, winter seemed close at hand. Most of the onlookers realized that a cold ride down the river would be in store for us.

The kayaks were stuffed when we left the dam. We had learned about nutrition and were loaded down with rice, macaroni, oatmeal, peanut butter, fifty pounds of canned goods, seven pounds of homemade granola, ten pounds of cocoa mix and a case of beef jerky. Minor repairs had been made on all the craft. My rig wore a new spray apron, had been re-patched and had the forward deck strut repaired. I also sat on a new seat made from a sheet of plywood instead of slats. Jerry replaced the stern strip on his boat with better fabric and Tom glued in the longeron section that had broken out of his kayak the week before.

The heavy kayaks were sluggish and hard to handle. I attempted to swing clear of a submerged boulder only to find myself running over the top of it.

An early start would have assured us Fort Snelling by nightfall, but now such a prospect was out of reach. The navigation channel began a few miles downstream. There were locks to go through and we were entering a heavily populated urban area. The only place in the thirty miles of river that looped through the Minneapolis-St. Paul metropolitan area that offered a safe camp, besides Fort Snelling, was the huge island we were approaching.

Our camp on Burman Island was less than ten miles from the Champlin landing and less than that from our homes, but it just as well could have been a thousand miles! The camp was our home for the night and we didn't expect to see our families until Christmas, if even then.

The campfire crackled and dried the cold mist falling from the sky almost as soon as it touched our clothes. I thought how our campsite home was "unstuck." The scenery changed, yet the camp remained basically the same. In my mind's eye, I could look out from the camp and see a huge rice swamp, if I wanted to. Then I might look down into the fire and raise my head to see a great pine forest. Then I might do the same thing again to reveal a wooded campsite and rows of houses on the riverbank.

From that riverbank, I thought I heard someone whistling. My ears strained to hear the sound. There it was again! This time, I thought it was a bird. The third time I heard the sound I was sure it was a bird. By the fourth time I looked close enough at the houses to realize someone was trying to get our attention!

"Are you the guys paddling around the United States?" the man asked.

"We sure are," I told him.

"Heard all about you in the paper and on TV yesterday! We're having a party here, if you want, you can come over in an hour or so!"

Dick and his wife were having a house warming and end-of-the-year business party. We ended up being the celebrities.

Of the people there, Gene stands out in my mind. He had planned an adventure similar to ours, but it was a different time then. Before his dream could be realized, he was off fighting World War II. Now, in a way, his dream lived through us as we traveled the waterways.

The misty rain didn't bother us after we left the party. We rode our kayaks back to camp with bags of barbecued ribs, ham sandwiches and chicken wings. We were sound asleep by 3:00 a.m.

Tom's parents tagged along with us through Minneapolis. They met us near the head of the navigation channel, at one of the locks and again along the University of Minnesota's River bottom flats. They kept asking if we were cold; they were quite concerned about our safety as they watched us being lowered forty-seven feet into the echoing caverns of the Upper St. Anthony Lock. To them, I'm sure, we looked like three toothpicks in a bathtub of dirty water.

Tom's parents, Tom and Jerry had never experienced "locking through" before. It was a much simpler procedure than portaging around the eleven dams upriver. All we had to do was pull a cord on the lock wall so the lockmaster would know we were around. Then, if the traffic light flashed green, we could enter the lock chamber, grab hold of a line on the wall, or a floating bulkhead and take a water elevator to the downriver level.

Chapter 6

Leaving the Cities Behind

"I believe that there is a subtle magnetism in nature, which, if you unconsciously yield to it, will direct us aright."

Henry David Thoreau

Despite the cold, gloomy, oftentimes misting weather, we encountered many types of pleasure craft just downstream from the third set of locks. The boats sped frenetically up and down the river— all of them except one. It apparently was broken down and the occupants were attempting to paddle downstream with water skis. That day, we proved the kayaks' supremacy over mechanical propulsion by slowly towing the runabout to the boat landing at Fort Snelling.

In the early eighteen hundreds, Fort Snelling was a military outpost. The fort and environs meant shelter and protection from a hostile wilderness. The night we camped on Pike Island; Fort Snelling offered us the same feeling of shelter and protection. The "wilderness" was still there; it had merely changed from water, rocks and forest to concrete, asphalt and glass.

Pike Island was situated at the mouth of the Minnesota River. Even though the Mississippi had become cloudy, it was nowhere near as muddy as the Minnesota. A distinct line formed where water from the northern forest watershed met the silt-laden water of the fertile Minnesota River Valley.

We passed through St. Paul and found ourselves amidst a maze of buildings, power plants, bridges, barges, towboats, trains, cars, planes and wires. Compared to the orderliness of wooded shoreline, everything seemed to be chaotic. We were subjected to auditory and olfactory bombardment. Individual sounds couldn't be distinctly sorted out. They could only be lumped into a category that we called "the noise from the spinning wheels of progress."

The smells though, were quite distinct. A sour, putrid scent enveloped an area near the South Saint Paul stockyards. In other places there were the smells of burning eggshells, the waft of fresh sewage, the strong odor of hot oil and the stench of exhaust fumes.

The river slowly leads us through the area to an ideal campsite on a large, hard packed sand spoil overgrown with willows. The camp sat directly across the river from what appeared to be a rendering plant— at least it smelled like one. With those two things in mind, I concluded the day's entry with the message: *"We have traded 'poor' campsites and clear water for good campsites and dirty water. We have gone from waterfowl to foul water!"*

Comparatively speaking, the Mississippi River below the Minneapolis-St. Paul metro area was not nearly as dirty as I found it five years before. At that time, I paddled my kayak through a liquid that looked more like ink than water. Time and the passage of environmental laws were definitely making slow but sure progress in improving the river's quality.

The St. Croix joined the Mississippi's flood to the sea at Prescott, Wisconsin. Its waters were clear and its shores protected by the Wild Rivers' Act. When we paddled by the confluence and saw the clear water mixing with the mud, it was as if the St. Croix was reminding the Mississippi of what it once had been.

Towboats pushing barges moved up and down the river. Cruisers and houseboats passed us and now and then, a fisherman in a runabout would greet us with a friendly salute. We were in a multi-purpose river used for commerce, industry and recreation.

The Prairie Island Nuclear Power Plant stood on the right bank. We could see the double reactors and the cooling towers. There were a lot of people concerned about the plant— like the ones we met. They were attempting to determine whether or not the warm water discharge was having a positive or negative effect on the fish population in the immediate area. We met one group the evening before working a fish shocker and now, we met a solitary figure conducting a creel census for the state. He roared by in his boat and told us to stop in for coffee at his camper parked at the Redwing marina four miles downstream.

Dick was a blue-eyed, grizzled, one time market hunter whose toothless smile and jokes made us laugh until tears came to our eyes. He was a kind hearted, sour dough character, whose coarse language went hand in hand with his coarse appearance. Originally, from Quincy, Illinois, he'd call anyplace along the Mississippi River Valley his home, as long as he could hunt and fish. Dick was our unofficial welcoming committee into the Hiawatha Valley.

Limestone and sandstone bluffs started a few miles above Redwing, but the most spectacular lay in the hundred-mile stretch of river between Redwing, Minnesota and Prairie du Chien, Wisconsin. Redwing was also the gateway to Lake Pepin. An hour after leaving the town, the long expanse of water lay before us. The lake was calm in the late afternoon. Soon, we found ourselves on a broad sheet of glass bordered by a velvet frame twenty-three miles NW to SE and two miles wide. The dip of the paddle blades into the unblemished surface seemed somehow sacrilegious.

Daylight faded and a flashing navigation light guided us the last three miles to Lake City. The night was warm—something our bodies had been unaccustomed to for several weeks. In the relaxed atmosphere, we ate supper in a nearby cafe and decided to sleep without the tent. The lake, now a huge reflecting pool, caught the twinkling lights from towns along the distant shore. The faint honking of southbound geese gave hint to their location in the star-studded sky.

At dawn, the wind was blowing lightly from the southeast and would continue to increase throughout the day. Since the lake was shallow and winds funneled over its surface, the last eight miles seemed five times the distance we had paddled the day before. Our invisible enemy hit us hard. It bounced us in chops and soaked us with breaking waves. It aggravated us with its roar and made us weary.

The town of Wabasha marked the end of Lake Pepin and we rested there a few hours before pushing on. Afterwards, we were able to use evasive action by ducking behind islands and running side channels where the wind's fingers couldn't reach us.

Along with headwinds, the lack of current was also frustrating. We looked for it below the dam at Lock Number 4, as well as Locks 5 and 5A— there was none. The gates were nearly shut tight to insure water depth for navigation.

We were also concerned with decreasing day length and the traffic jams at locks. Towboat companies were attempting to ship goods to and from the Upper Midwest before freeze-up. Because towboats had priority over all craft on the river, except military and emergency vessels, oftentimes, we had to wait several hours before we could lock through.

The headwinds, lack of current, short daylight hours and traffic jams wouldn't have concerned us earlier in the season. But now, when ice-free days were numbered, we were nervous. To cope with the situation, we had to force ourselves to take one day at a time. We'd put in as many miles as we could during the day, rest when we needed to and hoped for a late freeze.

Above Winona, there was wind but it was light and at our backs. The river towns we passed were picturesque. Alma and Fountain City looked surrealistic through the river haze. Later, such scenes would prove invaluable in our memory chests, allowing us to detach ourselves from the onslaught of the elements.

Bill didn't know we would be paying him a visit— neither did we. The situation just turned out that way. Three kayaks pulled into Prairie Island Park on the north side of Winona at 7:30. Within two hours, Bill had our kayaks safely stowed with campers, cooked supper for us and arranged our sleeping quarters. The Winona County game warden originally worked near our homes and we had gotten to know him through scouting. He arranged a newspaper and radio interview and agreed with us that anyone who paddled into the threatening weather conditions the morning we left the park had to "definitely be out of the ordinary."

It was cold and dark and the rain at noon came as no surprise. All of us dealt with its onset with a certain amount of detachment until cold water seeped through critical areas of our rain gear.

"We'd better hole up before we really get soaked," Jerry said. The spell was broken.

Tom jokingly blamed the weather on a book he was reading by Jane Goodall.

"Right now, I'm on a Chapter called 'The Rains'," he said.

We asked him what the next chapter was called.

"The Chimps Come to Camp," Tom replied.

The wind blew hard from the northwest in the morning. It was cloudy, but not raining. Our campsite was scattered with equipment drying on tree branches, a picnic table and later, after we launched, the decks of our kayaks.

Commercial fishermen visited the camp at daybreak. They drove in, launched a skiff and returned to fill wooden boxes in the back of their pickup with carp and catfish. To the fishermen the Mississippi meant a living, to us it was a water highway. Presumably to the houseboat mariners that nearly crushed Jerry's kayak, it was a place for recreation.

Wind was rapidly pushing us to a lock and dam when the incident occurred. Jerry was about a hundred feet ahead on the guide wall when the houseboat roared in beside him. The boat's horn was blowing and someone on board was yelling, "Get out of my way!" Jerry saw the boat at the last second and with a few quick paddle strokes was able to escape before the houseboat collided into the concrete guide wall. We never did understand what the Mississippi meant to the people who had ruined the spoil island a few miles below La Crosse.

"The island is a complete dump," I wrote. "Beer bottles and cans, pop cans, broken glass, the shambles of a picnic table, the entrails, feathers, heads and feet of about thirty or forty mud hens, paper, burnt logs and more."

We were glad when darkness covered up the mess and I thought about what Bill had told us: "One of the sheriffs in these parts used to sit on one of the bluffs with a powerful telescope. When he spotted boaters littering, he'd send a speedboat to the location and cite the violators!"

The dew was scraped off the tent in the morning. Our kayaks were also covered with thick frost. It was sunny and crisp, a beautiful fall day and we filled up with hot oatmeal as we packed up.

In the afternoon, we received a hint of the vast amount of waterfowl the Mississippi flyway carried. In Pool Number 8, just below Brownsville, Minnesota, the sky was black with mallards, Canadian Geese, herons and blue and snow geese. There were thousands of birds in the air and many more on the water. We were witnessing the great gathering—the great migration that had gone on for centuries. It took us two hours of paddling before the rush of wings, honks, cackles and squeaks faded into the distance.

It was a fitting farewell. We had left 650 miles of water tracks in Minnesota and that night slept on boat cushions and life jackets to protect us from the icebox effect of cold Iowa clay.

Chapter 7

Iowa and Wisconsin

"Man's heart away from nature becomes hard."
Standing Bear

In Lansing, Iowa, the townspeople greeted us with a cheerful hello or good morning and the waitress at the cafe gave us all the coffee we could hold.

Limestone bluffs were now shrouded in fading autumn colors and wrapped in gossamer. Into such a tranquil setting, we spied what appeared to be a Corps of Engineers dredge rounding a downstream bend. As it drew closer, we could see flags hanging from its top deck as well as a couple of tall smokestacks.

"It's the *Delta Queen!*" I yelled when the stern-wheeler passed us.

Tom said he felt as if we had been inserted into a chapter of Mark Twain's *Life on the Mississippi*. By coincidence, Jerry picked up ragtime music on his radio and we listened to it as the living past disappeared behind a wooded bluff.

The wooded campsite we stumbled upon, just as we left the lock at Lynxville, was pleasant. Earlier campers built a fireplace, table, a gear platform and rustic latrine. Ironically, the place shocked us because it was not trashed.

We watched the river traffic from our "ring side seats." Two tows with barges passed each other immediately in front of our camp. From our point of view, it looked as though the two giants would collide in the narrow channel. The southbound tow sounded two air horn blasts, to indicate a starboard-to-starboard pass and the northbound tow acknowledged with two more blasts. All we could see were the dark shadows of the barges and three flashing bow lights. The tows were bordered with running lights and their "insides," except for the pilot-houses, glowed white. When the tows rumbled past, one of the searchlights lit our campsite. At the same time, we saw five feet of river bottom momentarily laid bare exposing sticks, rocks, mud and the top of a wing dam, as the huge props sucked water in and pushed it out. A few seconds later, the water surged back like a tidal wave, grabbing and clawing at anything near the river's edge. We were glad our kayaks were far up on shore safe from the towboat wake.

(During my first trip down the river, I had made the mistake of sleeping too close to shore. During the night, a towboat rumbled by, immediately followed by something that resembled far off cannon fire. Just as I realized the noise was the tow's huge wake marching up the shoreline, I was hit by waves that nearly pulled my kayak and me into the river—never again!)

The quiet night, punctuated by the soft thump of leaves striking the tent, lead me through a dream. I told Tom and Jerry about it the next day.

We met two people paddling kayaks in a setting similar to the area near Grand Rapids. Both kayaks had thin poles sticking up from them. In the dream, I interpreted the poles as sailing masts, although there were no sails to be seen on the kayaks.

The dream wasn't strange, although it was vivid enough for me to talk about and for the majority of the day, it was forgotten.

We were looking forward to visiting Effigy Mounds National Monument. Thousands of years ago, Indian people built burial mounds high atop the Mississippi bluffs in this area of northeastern Iowa. Some mounds were typically conical or cylindrical; others were formed into animal effigies. The Great Bear and the Little Bear Mounds had to be pointed out to us by signs; otherwise we would have missed them. We weren't able to visit the Marching Bear group in the south unit of the park (each about three feet high and eighty to one-hundred feet long). But likewise, the forms would have been difficult to discern, even from an airplane.

Why the mounds were built high atop the bluffs is unknown. Why the effigies are only distinguishable from the air also remains a mystery. The riddle of the mound builders civilization may never be solved. They had lived for hundreds of years along the bluff tops and now they were gone. I wondered if they felt the same sense of timelessness as we experienced. Surely, some Indian person had stood on the edge of Fire Point and watched, as we did, the colored leaves swirl and tumble in the updrafts. From a three hundred foot perch, they had seen the island dotted Mississippi Valley's many moods.

From our kayaks, the river looked incredibly narrow. The ridge top view, however, had revealed a bluff bordered valley almost a mile wide, literally clogged with strips of islands, backwaters and sloughs. It was now called The Upper Mississippi Wildlife Management Area and it stretched one hundred and fifty miles from Wabasha, Minnesota, to Davenport, Iowa.

On our way down, we took a shortcut through a steep, shallow valley covered knee deep in oak, shagbark hickory and ironwood leaves. The walk immediately reminded me of the second part of the dream. "Rattlesnakes," I said. "In my dream we found quite a few in an area just like this." Fortunately, if there were serpents hidden in the leaves or rocks we didn't encounter any.

When we pulled out of our landing area, I looked behind to check for towboats and saw a huge white canoe bearing down on us. As the craft drew closer, we could see a "mast" sticking up from amidships. Jerry stopped paddling and stared. Although slightly different, the canoeists were basically the same people I had seen in my mind the night before.

"We're sailors from Norfolk paddling down the Mississippi for Muscular Dystrophy," they told us. "Lost one canoe in that bad weather on Lake Pepin, so we had another donated to us at Wabasha."

I pointed to the mast. "Oh, that's our two way radio antenna," one of them answered.

What the travelers, Mike and Mike, were doing seemed noble. But the more we talked with them, the more we realized what their hearts possessed their heads lacked. Their goal and philosophy of travel were incongruous. They were attempting to paddle one thousand eight hundred and fifty miles from Minneapolis to New Orleans in thirty days. In itself, the feat was nearly impossible. Mixed with their own heavy rations of "wine, women and song," the feat seemed incomprehensible. Furthermore, one of them hated camping. As a result, night stops conveniently coincided with naval recruiters in riverside towns. That evening, we "celebrated" with the sailors at Prairie du Chien and a couple more times thereafter.

It rained hard during the night. Now and then mist drifted into the sheet metal covered marina where we slept. Come daybreak, the clouds were gone and we breathed the clean air of a rain washed sky. So it was—day after day—rain and cold weather. The mercury frequently dropped into the low twenties. Frost covered kayaks were as common a sight to us now as river travelers were to local residents. At a place called Lee's Coffee Cup in Cassville, Wisconsin, we added our names to a long list of travelers using everything from luxurious yachts to water skis to navigate the river.

Near Dubuque, Iowa, we anticipated catching a glimpse of one such craft called the *Cindy Marie*. The seventy-five foot boat had taken a local farmer six and a half years to build and its maiden voyage would include an around the world cruise. Our hopes dimmed, however, when radio announcements revealed "a wheel had fallen off the trailer en route to the launch site," and were abandoned after the report: "*The Cindy Marie,* launched safely from a Dubuque marina, has become grounded on a wing dam. The Coast Guard is checking the craft for requirements. The voyage will be delayed until spring."

Jerry turned his radio off. Lunch was over and we prepared to leave the resort's dock. The Belleville Lock was within sight and its downriver gates were opening.

"Here come the sailors!" Jerry yelled.

We never did leave Belleville until the next day. What sleep we did get was punctuated by wakes bouncing, squeaking and shifting the floating dock to which our boats and the sailors' canoe were tied.

We roused ourselves in the morning darkness, hardly refreshed, with the haze of beer and loud music hanging heavy in our brains. There was never really a true dawn; the blackness merely thinned to a hazy gray. An uncanny stillness enveloped the entire day and the air had the faint smell of sour corn flakes.

The sailors were on a tight schedule. Their VW microbus support unit had set up a radio interview in Savanna, Illinois. Jerry, Tom and I followed Mike and Mike into the studio and suddenly found ourselves on a live program directed at raising funds for Muscular Dystrophy. We didn't want to "steal the show," so we left the studio with the announcer and listening audience believing there were five people traveling the River for M.D.

"Now to get to Clinton, Iowa, before dark!" the sailors said.

The town was twenty miles away. Mike and Mike wanted to get there because it meant a place indoors. We wanted to get to Clinton because it would mean paddling through Pool Number 13 when it was unusually calm. The pool was immediately upriver from Clinton. It was five miles wide, ten miles long and extremely shallow. The slightest breeze could make it "one mean stretch of water."

The five of us paddled through acres and acres of smooth water dotted with hundreds of duck blinds. Some were built on stilts, others sat on sand spoils. The heavy air muffled periodic shotgun blasts. Distant shots traveling over the pool's vast expanse were distorted and sounded like steam bubbles rising from boiling oatmeal or slow perking coffee.

From what we gathered on the Navy's two-way radio, a newspaper reporter was waiting at the Clinton Lock to interview the canoeists. Mike and Mike were a quarter mile ahead when they entered the lock chamber. When we arrived, we figured the interview would be over.

"And where are you guys going?" the reporter hollered.

We hesitated and then told him about our 7,000-mile kayak trip.

"Hey you guys, come here!" he yelled.

Before, we knew it, Mike and Mike were left dangling with their story and the reporter was interviewing us.

Few words passed between canoe and kayaks as we paddled into Clinton. Their VW van was waiting at the Clinton marina. The sailors had made their objective. They had gone from "Point A" to "Point B." It was now time for them to find a room for the night and to forget about something they really didn't like doing in the first place.

We also found a place for the night: a quiet camp, tucked away on a wooded shore. It was the last time we saw the two-man Navy. Lifestyles dictated sooner or later we'd part. They either succumbed to their wild ways, or the Navy, perhaps to avoid public embarrassment, "pulled the cork" on them.

Clouds of white particles swirled in the small eddy currents made by our paddles. The shore was commercially developed and the connection was obvious. At one time, this section of the river had felt huge rafts of logs floating down from the northern forests, as well as the bite of the shallow draft, paddle wheel, packet boats bringing goods and passengers to and from prospering river towns. Now, the river felt the discharge of growing industry along its banks and the throb of huge towboats pushing deep draft barges up and down a dredged waterway, bypassing many of the small towns.

One such river town was Cordova, Illinois. Dave and Dani, a family who had a feeling for the town's past, introduced Tom, Jerry and me to Cordova.

"From the water, Cordova looks huge. Like most old river towns, it stretches along the Mississippi's banks for almost two miles— but it's only two blocks wide!" Dave said. "There's the old sheriff's office and over there is where the hotel used to be."

He also showed us where the livery stable and the blacksmith shop once stood.

"Time's all changed that now. Town almost folded up when the steamboats quit stopping," he said. "Today, Cordova's life blood depends on the chemical, machinery, food and power industries of the 'Quad City' area."

When we slept at Dave and Dani's home, we were partaking in the town's living heritage. The packet boats were gone, but the feeling in the people was still there. River travelers in kayaks are just as grateful for food, shelter and hospitality as the transients of a hundred years ago— maybe even more so.

The rain that night went completely unnoticed until we dumped the collected water from the ponchos covering our kayaks. An hour later, we were three miles downriver. Our kayaks were moored to a dock and we were having lunch with Connie, the editor of the Port Byron Globe.

The tiny Globe office had stood for over a century on the main street of Port Byron. In a time when thousands of small town newspapers were going out of business due to runaway operating costs and consolidation, Connie had taken over the enterprise. She had been there for over two and a half years and was determined to be there many more.

History lay in the yellowed, dust covered files of the Port Byron Globe. "Buildings and public records give us roots to the past," she said. "A town without old buildings is like a person without a memory. Hopefully, through the records of this paper, we'll learn not to repeat the mistakes of the past."

Paddling progress was slow through the Quad City area. Oftentimes the horizon was draped in hazy, red smog. In one area, a grain seed operation filled the sky with stinking smoke and the Mississippi with wastewater from three huge outfall pipes. At camp, the ugliness, which had seeped into our subconscious minds with the aid of fierce headwinds, poisoned our appetites. None of us ate very much. We found the approaching darkness an antidote for what we had encountered on an industrialized river. As Illinois marker lights winked twice and our Iowa side of the channel answered with one quick flash, the reminders of modern society eventually became lost on a river bathed in moonlight.

Crickets and katydids sang all night. We heard their chorus a few days earlier during another mild night. The unseasonably warm weather was a welcome relief; I slept comfortably in one sleeping bag instead of the double one I had been using and Tom and Jerry used theirs merely as blankets.

The Mississippi downstream from Rock Island, Moline and Davenport ran nearly straight west for twenty miles and then turned abruptly south at Muscatine. The river seemed to be compensating for a broad eastward sweep, which caused the bulge on Iowa's border. We crossed the tip of the bump near Clinton, Iowa, where the Mississippi reached its eastern most point surveyed at 90 degrees 25 minutes.

In other areas were reminders that the river's border had felt the tracks of those carrying transit, chain and compass. In New Boston, Illinois, near the old landing, we found a brass marker set in 1898 by the Mississippi River Commission. Later we learned Abraham Lincoln did the original survey of the town in 1834. In a way, the river, for us, was a sort of time tunnel. It wouldn't have surprised us to see a young Lincoln step from the town's weathered hotel.

Chapter 8

Illinois

"I prefer to dream of the future to the history of the past."

Thomas Jefferson

We thrashed our way down nine more miles of windblown river before darkness gave an excuse to stop. The wind continued to bother us the rest of the night. It kicked sand into our soup and knocked down the tent at 3:00 a.m. By morning, clouds had moved in and it was threatening rain.

The major deluge held off until we were long underway. By the time the downpour was in full swing, we were in a covered boat stall at Oquawka, Illinois. We didn't like the rain, but it did have a redeeming factor— it was quite warm and posed no immediate threat from hypothermia. The cloudburst was nearly over and I sponged the last puddles of collected water from my boat, while Jerry and Tom walked to a nearby coffee shop to dry out.

At Oquawka we heard more about a so-called sugar shortage. Sugar prices had been going up three times faster than the nation's recent inflation spiral and many people soon figured it would be a dollar a pound. Most restaurants had taken sugar off their tables and were "rationing" the "white gold."

"Lots of small bakeries have simply gone out of business," we were told. "We were lucky here; we stocked up on sugar before the price hike. I hope we can last until it comes back down."

Here was a cry of help from someone just trying to get by in life. Whatever the cause of the high sugar prices, we didn't know; but the undercurrents of organized greed manipulating the nation's people haunted us.

That night we replaced leaking patches covering old war wounds left by upper Mississippi beaver dams on the Molly B's hull. I spread the glue on with my fingers and slapped the new patches in place. All of us were frustrated over problems with short day length, long waits at locks, wind, rain, slack current and equipment repairs. It seemed we were waging a battle with "Old Man River" and to "beat" the river before it froze up meant putting in more miles per day. We kept reassuring ourselves: "When the locks end at St. Louis, we won't have to wait and the current should be swift!" We rested with that hope, directed our thoughts toward mail pickup at Burlington and the meeting of friends in Keokuk.

The mail boosted our morale. Again, we discussed "getting to New Orleans."

"Whether or not we get to New Orleans before Christmas, I don't know. But I know we'll get there," I said. "It just depends on how much we want to endure. The biggest obstacle to our success lies between the space up here and..." I pointed to my head. "The biggest obstacle to our success lies in our own minds."

In the rain we passed rows of duck blinds built on stilts. Burlington was seven miles behind us. Our bodies were stoked with energy and our thoughts with the letters we had received. Suddenly, a voice rang out from one of the blinds: "Hey! You must be crazier than I am... bein' out here in this weather. Stop in for some coffee!"

We paddled around a flock of bleach bottle decoys and a few minutes later we were sharing the domain of a four hundred pound duck hunter named Jess.

"Boy, you guys are the last thing I expected to see out here," he said.

Jess didn't ask us why we were going down the river—he just knew. We didn't ask Jess why he was out here —because we knew. If Jess shot a duck today, it would be a bonus to the real reason he was here.

The river was peaceful after the rain stopped. At sundown we paddled through a fairyland of heavy mist and sunshine. Somewhere ahead of us was the Fort Madison Bridge. Normally, it would have been visible five miles away, but the fog and rapidly fading light made it difficult to pick out even at a quarter mile.

"The river is very different when it is like this. It's a spooky, weird feeling. You can hear things but you can't see them until they get next to you. One can imagine a lot of things out here," Tom recorded in his journal. *"The bridge terrified us when it broke through the fog. It resembled the huge bow of a barge about to run us down."*

Our spirits were high with anticipation. Five years before, I met river folks at Keokuk who took in a weary, sun burnt, solo kayaker for a few days. Now, those same folks waited for the arrival of three tired kayakers to offer them the same hospitality. I told Dick and Pat we'd be in Keokuk by five o'clock. So, we'd have time to explore the sixteen miles of pool between Fort Madison and Lock Number 19 at Keokuk.

The three hours we spend at Nauvoo was relatively short, but it impressed on us again the need for preserving the historical past. We walked through the restored village with its brick homes and split rail fences. We found it inconceivable that a sea of hate once covered such a tranquil place. Yet seven years after Mormons settled Nauvoo in 1839, festering prejudice exploded, killing prophet Joseph Smith and forcing his followers to leave.

We arrived at Keokuk on Halloween, the same day J.J. Finnegan's spirit was supposed to appear at Rand Park. According to local legend, J.J.'s secret rendezvous with his lover was never fulfilled— he drowned on his swim across the river. We were too tired to join the welcoming committee at the park but just as well, the ghost never showed.

That night and the next were spent with Pat, Dick and their three children. We relaxed, wrote letters and shared ideas in their Keokuk home located high atop a river bluff. By the time we were set back on the river, we were well-stocked, refreshed and sad to leave.

The family spent a lot of time sailing up and down the huge pool created by the Keokuk Dam. If their sailboat hadn't been stowed away for the season, we too would have joined them for a ride.

From experience, Dick knew Lock Number 19 opened only on the hour for pleasure craft. Realizing the problem three small kayaks might have in obtaining a lockage during the closeout of the shipping season, he raced down to the lock and convinced the lockmaster to open the gates for us.

Inside the great twelve hundred foot lock, one of the biggest on the river, our kayaks must have looked like chips of wood in a swimming pool. In a final farewell gesture, Pat lowered us a paper bag containing three cans of beer. By the time we drained the cans, the lower gates cracked open to reveal towboats waiting impatiently to lock through.

"Current! We finally got some current!" Jerry yelled.

We covered two locks and twenty-four miles of river in five hours. Compared to ten-hour days and distances half as much, it was like traveling at the speed of light.

Somewhere during the run, the one thousand mile mark passed underneath us. If there had been a line stretched across the water at that point, Jerry's rig would have hooked it. Once again, the stern strip had peeled from his boat. It was dark by now and we poked our flashlights around the shoreline of old spoil islands until we found a suitable campsite to make repairs.

Launching the next morning was like walking out of a minefield. The darkness had covered up a riverside strewn with logs and sharp sticks. Miraculously, we weaved through the obstacles the night before without ramming any of them and landed no more than twenty feet upstream from a huge wing dam. The dam extended a full one hundred yards into the river from the sandbar. We couldn't see it but could tell its sharp riprap lie barely beneath the surface by the way choppy water danced over it. The trick was, each one of us had to be nimble enough to push off from shore, steer around the maze of drift and at the same time maintain a paddling speed strong enough to clear the wing dam before the current and strong north wind dragged us onto it. Luckily, all of us maneuvered back into the main channel without difficulty.

Our week of Indian summer was over and we shuddered at the thought of what the north wind would bring. At La Grange, we discussed the whole matter over several cups of coffee. The picture windows of the Marina Cafe offered us an unobstructed view of our kayaks and the river.

The river near shore was choked with clouds of runoff from the night's rain. The wind swept in huge fan patterns across the water and the sky offered no hint of ever being blue again. The only thing I could see which offered hope to an otherwise cheerless scene was a sweet gum tree.

"Look at that sweet gum," I said. "We're getting into a warmer climate zone for sure now."

For an instant, our minds were off the weather while we dispelled each other's misgivings at becoming stuck in the "deep freeze."

"I don't think this bad weather will be around for long. Remember the Osage orange we saw the other day? Then I saw some ginkgo trees too. They all grow where it's mild. If the current keeps up, we'll be able to outrun winter anyway."

The final words of the commentary held some credence, for we covered the last five miles of the day in forty-five minutes! Unfortunately, we had to rest for the night— the weather did not.

Chapter 9

Cold Weather and Warm Hearts in Missouri

"No man ever steps in the same river twice, for it's not the same river and he's not the same man."

Heraclitus

The morning temperature was forty-four degrees at our camp. By the time we reached Hannibal, Missouri, some ten miles downriver, the mercury had settled to thirty-six degrees. It was cold and drizzling—definitely not a day to be paddling on the river or sightseeing in the boyhood home of Mark Twain.

We pulled into a marina where the old steamboat landing used to be and walked to the nearest cafe to "drown our sorrows" in food. The nourishment brightened our attitudes considerably but the weather was the same when we left the café— probably even a little worse.

While at the Becky Thatcher House and Book Store, one of the people we had met at the local museum came in and asked if there was anything we needed in town.

"Well, we'd like to hit a bakery before we leave," Jerry said.

"Okay, I'll take you there," he said.

"Paddling on the water all day gives us a craving for baked stuff," I told one of the ladies, as she wrapped up a few doughnuts and sweet rolls for me.

Just before we left, one of the women said: "Here, take these too—on the house!" And she handed us a huge bag of rolls, Bismarcks and bread. "My son traveled down the river on a raft a few years ago and he always told me how good the folks were to him," she said. "I'm just trying to give back some of the kindness. Good luck!"

We climbed into the car for a ride back to the museum. The driver's name was John Winkler; he was the president of the Mark Twain Boyhood Home Foundation. He left us off to continue our explorations, but soon appeared again as we made our way down from Cardiff Hill. This time he wanted to take us to lunch.

The drizzle continued outside as we ate. From our place we could see a flashing time and temperature sign. It was thirty-four degrees now!

"It's almost cold enough to snow," Jerry said. "It *is* snowing!"

I think John knew the weather forecast all along.

"If you guys want to see the Mark Twain Cave, I'll take you there," he said. "Then you have the choice of staying either at the Mark Twain Hotel or my home."

We meandered through the cool, limestone passageways, saw the "Post Office," "The Foot," "Straddle Alley" and "The Grand Piano." We "squeezed" through "Fat Man's Misery," stood at the "Five Points" and saw the chamber where Tom and Huck found the gold under the "Sign of the Cross." John turned off the lights for a few moments.

"Now you have some idea of what Tom Sawyer and Becky Thatcher must have felt when they were lost down here," he said.

There were no seasons in the cavern. The environment was constant and comfortable compared to the mess outside. The snow was coming down harder than ever now. We were lucky to be staying indoors this night.

The car turned up a long drive lined with carefully trimmed shrubbery.

"Now this may look expensive to you but Stella and I call it home," John commented.

We spent the evening paging through books and listening to records of Hannibal and "Mark Twain Tonight." John showed us the only motion picture of Mark Twain made in the early nineteen hundreds by Thomas Edison and we talked and talked and talked.

The inclement weather had been a godsend. During our stay in Hannibal, Mark Twain came alive to us through John Winkler. Likewise, for John, Mark Twain's characters were alive too— they were sleeping upstairs in his home.

The hills were covered with snow south of Hannibal and it was cold. The temperature never rose above forty-three degrees and we were looking for a place to camp. In such a wintry landscape, Louisiana, Missouri, seemed to be the proper place to bed down for the night. It was dark when we arrived and no one at the boat club saw us until we opened the door.

No more than five minutes passed before we were sitting amidst a group of friendly people, warming up and drinking beer. They tried to coax us into sleeping in the clubhouse for the night but we convinced them that the security hassle would be too great and we'd be just as comfortable sleeping under the overhang outside. Our conversation started out with river travel, wandered into queen bees talking with honey bees and ended with a discussion condemning the Corps of Engineers for destroying prime hunting and fishing areas through situation, dredging and draining. We could understand their feelings. Many of the people from the small town of Louisiana had a close affinity with the outdoors. To them, the outdoors was part of their life. Obviously, they would violently oppose any action, especially by the government, which would threaten their world.

Like the folks at the boat club, Jerry, Tom and I also disagreed with many of the things the Corps was doing. However, there were aspects of the Corps which total condemnation tended to overlook— flood control, low cost interstate commerce via navigation waterways and so forth. We tried to resolve the matter while at supper in a nearby restaurant. Our collective conclusion: "Protection of the earth must be humankind's primary objective, for in the long run, it would benefit the greatest number of people."

Back at the clubhouse, we proceeded to unpack the boats in the dark. A car pulled up with its headlights shining into our partially prepared sleeping quarters.

"Here comes a night watchman or a cop," Tom said.

"Hey, you boys want to come home with us?" A woman's voice rang out from the car. It was Clorita, the waitress at the restaurant along with her husband, Bill. "Gonna be kinda chilly out here tonight... sposed to freeze."

The next morning, Jerry helped scrape thick frost from Bill's car windows.

A local reporter met us at the marina. At first, he was skeptical and seemed to think we were three guys out for a joy ride. But, the more we talked, the more he understood.

"Our journey is for education," Tom said. "It's like going down a hallway lined with doors. You open one of those doorways of knowledge and there's another hallway of doors with many, many more things to learn and find out about. The journey has been self-expanding for us."

"We are vertical in the social caste system on this trip," I said. "We are greeted and treated equally well by the very wealthy, the educated and the poor."

"At the beginning, we tried to get sponsors; but, nobody believed us," Jerry said. "So all of the expenses are coming from money we've saved."

Chapter 10

The Last Locks

"He is richest who is content with the least, for content is the wealth of nature."

Socrates

The frequency of riverside stilt houses used during summer months increased as we drew nearer the St. Louis metropolitan area. Likewise, the occurrence of KEEP OUT and NO TRESPASSING signs on shoreline and islands grew in number.

The island we slept on wasn't posted.

"Even if it was, who would ever notice or care that we rested here for the night?" I thought.

It was such a different world anyway, as we sat there drinking hot chocolate waiting for the fog to burn off, that I could hardly imagine other people existed. Then, out of the river mist, a man pulled up in a johnboat. He had a scowl on his face and looked perturbed.

"What's goin' on here?" he growled.

"Just headin' down river," Jerry said.

"I own this island; use it for huntin'!" he barked back.

The motor started up again and our visitor disappeared as quickly as he had arrived.

The river sparkled in the sunshine after the fog lifted, revealing a sweeping river panorama. We passed the confluence of the Illinois (another navigable waterway linking Chicago and the Great Lakes with the Mississippi system) and watched a tow pushing its barges upstream. The craft must have been at least a mile and a half away. We couldn't hear the tow but could see every color and detail of its superstructure in the late afternoon light. Over the smooth water, the tow looked more like a toy ship on a millpond than a 20,000-ton colossus!

Nine bowls of oatmeal bubbled in the kettle on the tiny stove. It held the energy we would burn for the greater portion of the day. My parents would meet us in St. Louis for a short reunion—so would Tom's family. Lock Number 27, twenty-eight miles away, would be our rendezvous point.

Luck was with us; we didn't have to wait at the busy and oftentimes crowded Alton Locks.

Our Secchi Disk read one foot above the confluence of the Missouri with the Mississippi and less than six inches after the waters met. Two miles below the confluence, the navigation channel branched into the Chain of Rocks Canal. Shifting sandbars created by the silt-laden waters of the Missouri dumping into the Mississippi prompted the government to build the canal to shuttle commercial traffic around the troublesome downstream stretch of water.

The sign at the canal's mouth read: "All boats must use Chain of Rocks Canal." One could run the river below the turn off but there is the likelihood of running into a problem much larger than a sandbar. In order to maintain a nine-foot channel at the Alton Locks, the government built a rock dam across the bypassed river. Not knowing if the dam was one inch or ten feet under the surface, we paddled the eight miles of slack water to Lock Number 27. Once we arrived, the personnel bent some of the rules. They found a safe place for us to store equipment and offered shelter for the night in case the rendezvous was delayed.

For the next couple days, our travels by automobile to and from a motel took us along the Mississippi. The highway view contrasted sharply with the perspective offered by our kayaks. I did not like the view from the freeway, everything moved by too fast. On the river, we could study an object for several minutes or even hours. Here, objects flashed by in split seconds, allowing no time for comprehension, only impression. It was like rapidly paging through a book, as opposed to reading one.

Tiny portals atop the 630-foot, stainless steel, Jefferson Memorial Arch gave us an aerial view of the great river. How different it looked: muddy, its shores heavy with industry, compared to our perch at Effigy Mounds four hundred miles upstream.

Dad backed his pick-up truck to the door where our equipment was stored and we unloaded provisions. A cooperative effort by all three families brought us food: canned tuna, casserole mixes, canned meat, soups, powdered milk, processed cheese, twelve pounds of homemade granola, ice cream buckets full of cookies and more. We unloaded an assortment of needed gear including: a lantern battery, charts for the lower Mississippi, candles, camera film, patching vinyl, contact cement and money orders from our savings accounts.

Lights from the locks reflected in the growing puddles on the wet concrete and made surrealistic images in the river. It was 10:00 p.m. and our support was well on its way back to Minnesota. Before resting, we wrote letters in the lockhouse, heated up cans of spaghetti on the stove for supper and left behind a half loaf of banana bread for the night shift.

At five-thirty, one of the crewmen walked to the storage shed where we slept. As he opened the door, Jerry immediately sat up in his sleeping bag. The resulting reflex action changed the wake up call into a brief startled wail followed by a series of expletives.

We could have hauled our kayaks to the other side of the lock where construction equipment would have made launching hazardous. Or dragged them down the slope and over the riprap to the front of the lock. Instead, one by one, the kayaks were carried to a movable catwalk spanning the lock chamber. With our paddles resting on the railings, we crawled into the boats. Then, the catwalk was lowered. As it sank to the bottom of the lock chamber, we grabbed our paddles and floated off. They were the last set of locks on the Mississippi; a thousand miles of free flowing river lay ahead.

"Without the limiting factor of locks, towboat captains push as many barges as they can safely handle," I wrote. *"A towboat passed us today pushing twenty-seven barges up-*

stream! Its wheel wash churned the water into rolling waves for at least a mile below it."

We were told some of the tows on the Lower Mississippi could push sixty barges at a time! Such a monster would maneuver acres of "boxed up" barges, oftentimes seven wide and eight deep. We steered clear of the huge tows, knowing, if we came too close, our kayaks could be sucked into their props like chips of wood or easily swamped by their turbulent wakes.

Below St. Louis, industry flanked us for miles. We passed a carbon plant, a bleachery and dozens of chemical companies. By 5:00 p.m. the unusually fast current helped us cover better than fifty miles in six hours.

The force of a river gathering strength was evident near Chester, Illinois. Tom and I double tied our kayaks, forming a floating boathouse. Jerry weighed his paddle down using loose rocks, which in turn secured the kayak via a safety line connected to a crossframe.

On our return from town, the three of us stared at the vacant spot where Jerry's kayak had been. Visions of the *Mississippi Queen* drifting aimlessly into the destructive path of a towboat left a sick feeling in the pit of my stomach.

"There it is!" Jerry yelled.

The kayak had been swept a quarter mile downstream before the floating paddle lodged against rocks near another boathouse. The river had taken and given back— we were lucky.

The current coupled with wind created other problems.

"We had a beast today..." my logbook recorded. "Wind from the south builds huge standing chops on the river as the current piles up water against the wind's face. In some sections before the aerial pipeline, the wind was so strong that I could not feather my paddle blades against it. The kayak would bounce, groan and shake as it hit the chops. Gusts up to fifty

miles per hour hit us on open stretches. We passed a spoil area on our starboard side where the blowing sand was so furious I couldn't see the trees directly behind the spoil. The strong wind, waves and blowing sand made it difficult to watch for accustomed to hazards: towboats, pile dikes and buoys. The sky was overcast and there was a strong feeling someone would get hurt or killed if we didn't stop soon!"

Chapter 11

Wind at Grand Tower, Illinois

"In every walk with nature one receives far more than he seeks."

John Muir

We pulled ashore on a sand flat at Grand Tower, Illinois. Soaking wet from the breaking waves, we decided to wait awhile.

Grand Tower received its name from a great chunk of limestone, which lies midstream in the river. Grand Tower Rock was a site to behold. The tree-topped behemoth rose nearly sixty feet above the water's surface and covered nearly an acre in area. We didn't dare paddle over to it. Rumors said the rock was surrounded by huge whirlpools, especially near the downstream side.

An hour after landing, we found Grand Tower's restaurant. We liked the place and would be back again for supper. The people there were friendly, served food family style and related some of the local history and "attractions" to us.

"The bricks you fellas walked past were part of the iron ore smelting ovens," we were told. "Back on Fountain Bluff there are Indian petroglyphs. Indians around here believed Tower Rock was inhabited by a spirit. Back in the early 1800s a wedding party was supposedly swallowed up by the whirlpool there."

"You boys landed at what's called Devil's Backbone Park," they said. Presumably, the remark was in reference to the bluffs there. Other nearby geological features also bore demonic references: "Devil's Elbow;" "Devil's Tea Table;" and "Devil's Bake Oven." We even passed the "Devil's Die" on our way back to the kayaks. It was the only feature we could positively identify— the block of stone was neatly painted with the appropriate number of dots per side.

The revetment rocks from the adjacent ferry landing weren't as big as the Devil's Die, but they did hold down the tent guy lines in the south wind. A well-dressed man watched us lug fifty-pound boulders over to the site and throw them down with a loud, solid thud. We were stuffing gear into the tent when he walked over.

"I stopped by just to take a look at the river... didn't expect to see kayakers in this kind of weather," he said.

His name was Jerry and he was from Memphis, Tennessee.

"I'll be out of town after the first of December. If you get down there before then, call me at this number or my folks at their number. We'll be lookin' for you!"

"If we don't get down to Memphis before December first, we'll not be in very good shape." Tom said. "Must be three hundred miles to Memphis from here."

"Yeah, it's about that distance," the proprietor answered. "You boys are goin' down kinda late, but not as late as those canoeists from Saskatchewan. They got caught in the December ice flows here and I trucked them the three hundred miles to Memphis so they could finish their trip!"

"Caught in the ice flows?" I said.

"If you're lucky, you shouldn't have much of a problem," he said. "Though you should have been here about a month earlier when the gum and sassafras were in their glory—was real pretty."

He also told us about a group of canoeists re-enacting the Louis Joliet/Father Marquette Expedition of 1673 and pointed out several pictures of the "explorers" in period costume. The group had stayed at Grand Tower for several days and had captured the imagination of the proprietor. Later, much later in the journey, we would talk with the priest who played Marquette. From him, the reality of the journey would be revealed. This re-enactment more accurately captured the actual event than a glorified chapter in a book.

Something was very different when we left the restaurant. Darkness had fallen; the temperature had dropped; and the wind was blowing—but there was something else. We didn't realize what it was until we reached the open river flats where the wind hit us in full force.

"It's changed directions. Its changed one-hundred and eighty degrees!" Tom yelled.

Before, our tent had been partially sheltered by the river bend. Now, it bore the full brunt of a strong north wind! Only half of it was standing. The rocks were still in place but several guy lines had snapped like thread in the full gale. We tied the lines back together and dragged over more rocks—only to have the same or another line snap.

"We'd better pull her down before one of the seams rip!" Jerry yelled.

We could hardly hear each other through the roar. We spit blowing sand from our mouths and wiped it from our eyes. I rolled the tent into a huge ball and stuffed it into my kayak so it wouldn't blow away. During the process, none of us dared let go of our sleeping bags lest they fly away like balloons.

At the park, we found a picnic shelter, turned the tables on their sides to protect us from the onslaught and hoped the kayaks wouldn't blow away during the night.

"Old Scratch' must have forgot to stoke his bake oven last night," I mumbled.

It was twenty-four degrees when we crawled from our sleeping bags. The wind was gone and the kayaks were half buried in sand.

Chapter 12

Approaching Caruthersville

"Do not go where the path may lead you, instead where there is no path and leave a trail."

Ralph Waldo Emerson

The short, narrow race immediately below Tower Rock pulled us along at nearly eighteen miles per hour. Here the river once had been obstructed causing a backup of water for hundreds of miles. Evidence of the impoundment could be seen on hillsides in the broad valley where watermarks were still visible. The river was different then and it would be different in the future. In geologic time, the river had seen United States' history in an instant —the noble and the shameful. We stopped at Trail of Tears State Park to pay homage to the latter.

A quarter of the thirteen thousand Cherokee People— men, women and children—died on that terrible march from Tennessee to Oklahoma during the winter of 1838-1839. Princess Otahki was one of them. We found her grave amidst the beech, elm, tulip and dogwoods. Like so many other places, the setting was now too peaceful and the facilities too soft for anyone camping in the park to visualize the suffering of one hundred and thirty-six years ago.

Kids were sitting on top of the floodwall at Cape Girardeau.

"Hey, where're you goin' in those things?" one of them shouted.

Thinking New Orleans was too close, I yelled back: "Miami, Florida!"

"You're crazy!" was the reply followed by shrieks of laughter.

When we arrived at the Cape's public landing, Tom watched the kayaks while Jerry walked to the post office and I made a long distance call to Bloomfield, Missouri. Two hours later, a car driven by Mike, an army buddy, roared up to the landing in a cloud of dust.

For three nights we slept at a home situated in a small community on the northern edge of the fertile Mississippi Delta. Hospitality radiated from Mike and his folks, from their relatives, Bloomfield and the surrounding countryside. We talked and joked with Mike's uncle who was harvesting cotton and visited his grand dad at his usual spot—the chair swing on the screened porch.

During our first day, while the entire family was at work, we ate lunch at a Bloomfield cafe where coffee cream was served in tiny glass servers and a full course meal cost a dollar. The lady there gave us extra portions because in her words: "You boys look hungry!"

When it was over, the three of us paddled down a seemingly unfamiliar river with seemingly unfamiliar kayaks. The last days had been a complete change for us and it would be a few hours before we'd re-adjust to the river.

For us, something as simple as forgetting to scan the river behind us for closing tows could easily lead to disaster. We normally did it, but this time we forgot. We were thinking of Bloomfield and busy watching an approaching tow.

"Watch out for the tow on your upstream side!" the bullhorn warned.

That moment was the first time we were aware of the tow in our "blind spot." We thanked the captain for his courtesy, reprimanded ourselves for not observing a cardinal rule of river travel and quickly got out of the way.

. Mileage on the Upper Mississippi was rapidly winding down. We camped near Commerce, Missouri, just below a ferry landing at Mile Marker 38.1 and reached the confluence of the Ohio River six hours after we launched the next morning.

At the junction, the Mississippi tripled in size. Here the Lower Mississippi began winding its way through a broad alluvial valley, nine hundred and forty-four miles to Head of Passes jutting into the Gulf of Mexico. The river was BIG. Of course, some parts of the Upper Mississippi were broader than the two-mile width at Cairo, but that was in the pools and lakes where the river was held back by artificial or natural obstructions. Nothing could stop the river now!

Due to the river's tremendous size, it was harder for us to tell where the navigation channel ran. Daymarkers and king-size buoys were spaced much farther apart. Consequently, it would be harder for us to steer clear of commercial traffic inside the channel and the government pile dikes outside the channel.

"The Upper Mississippi prepared us up for this part of our journey." I was writing by campfire light twenty miles downstream from the great confluence. Our charts called the place Wolf Island. From upstream hearsay, the island once was invaded by a movie producer and cast which included a lion. We found no trace of the animal but would have gladly invited any aspiring cinematographer into our domain to film a new version of *The Birds*. They would have had a cast of thousands. Our feathered friends finally quieted down, allowing us a peaceful evening to absorb and reflect.

"The tent, cooking gear, trees, food, jug and river travelers are illuminated by the soft glow of our campfire. The rigs are asleep on shore. I sit back and look at the mighty Mississippi flowing by and say to myself: 'I paddled here under my own power. I knew the Mississippi when it was small and sparklin and I know it now when it is strong and brown. I am content to be here'."

The chirping, clattering, blackbird hoard near our camp left shortly after daybreak. The fanning of their wings sounded like a great wind blowing through the treetops. I wished we could have departed as conveniently. We had a quick breakfast, put our rain suits on just before a violent thunderstorm and huddled amongst the trees until the downpour ended.

A strong, southwest wind followed the rain and left us battling heavy seas in a three hour, ten mile run to Hickman, Kentucky. There, we'd never forget the brief respite on the other side of the floodwall where Miss Katie McNeil had tended her general store for fifty-two years. I bought supplies from her five years before and it seemed nothing had changed since then. "McNeil and Company" was river heritage frozen in time. When someone else took over, repainted the sign, fixed the door and blew the dust from the cereal boxes, we knew a unique link with the past would be lost forever.

The charts showed the hard packed sandbar, where we camped, to be in Kentucky even though we were on the west side of the river. It was evident the Mississippi had changed its course more than once since the land had been surveyed. The charts were a hodgepodge of states: Kentucky jumped around; boundaries were marked indefinite; Missouri was west of the Mississippi and sometimes east; sometimes Tennessee was west of the Mississippi and sometimes the other way around. There are old accounts of the river changing course overnight, leaving a town high and dry, or cutting a channel through Main Street! Periodically, farmers in the area plowed up steamboat wrecks miles from the Mississippi's present channel.

The river's natural tendency to redirect itself during spring floods or heavy rain was dramatically decreased by vast networks of revetment, which protected shoreline from the gnawing current. The Corps of Engineers, more or less, now predetermined shifting course. Cutting through oxbows, a common practice since 1929 had shortened the winding waterway by one hundred and fifty-two miles.

From our vantage point on the sandbar, we could see the sweeping lights from a tow about to negotiate the great New Madrid oxbow. The lights were shining from two miles away yet, before the tow would pass our camp, it would have to travel over twenty miles upstream. At one time, there had been speculation over digging a mile long cut-off through the oxbow, but it was suppressed for a number of reasons: it would leave the Port of New Madrid, Missouri, which is at the top of the oxbow, ten miles from the main channel; farmland which the river embraces would become an inaccessible island and probably the most important, the cut-off would double the river current making it almost impossible to safely maneuver commercial traffic through the "raceway."

I told Sis and Jeer in a letter to expect us about November 20th. However, when the morning of the twentieth rolled around, we were still fifty-seven miles from their home at Caruthersville.

Sis was a persistent person who never took "no" for an answer. I met her and Jeer in the summer of 1969 when I stopped at their hardware store intent on finding materials to repair a broken kayak crossframe. Before I left Caruthersville, I had become Sis' "adopted son." I expected things to be no different the second time around, but first we had to get there. It was easier said than done.

"If I know Sis, she's cooking supper for us right," I said. "If we don't arrive sometime today, she's going to be mighty sore!"

"When I think about today, I see the dark, coffee-brown walls of waves rearing up from different directions— chops smashing and banging onto the kayaks. I see Tom dropping three feet over the crest created by a pile dike— they stick out from shore in many places making it absolutely impossible to seek shelter from the wind. I see all of us soaking wet from splash and Jerry severely spraining his right wrist by catching air in a deep trough instead of water."

We rounded New Madrid bend in the wind, hugging the dike-free Missouri side for shelter. A northbound icebreaker passed us in mid-channel.

"I wonder what that might mean?" Jerry yelled. "Water up there might be getting pretty solid!"

Amidst the dancing water, "freeze-up" was next to impossible to comprehend. Similarly, an earthquake in this area was equally as absurd. Yet, nature had frozen the water many times on the Upper Mississippi and had rent open the earth at New Madrid. (One hundred and sixty-three years ago settlers watched the flat Delta land roll like a heavy sea. Great chasms opened up and people and livestock disappeared forever. The cataclysm made the

Mississippi flow backwards and created Reel Foot Lake on the Tennessee side of the river.)

The sky remained pink for a long time after the sun dipped below the thin horizon line. Then, as the wind died, darkness settled over the Delta. We were twelve miles from Caruthersville.

In the murky world of night, we could barely make out tree lines along the river banks, sand spoils, marker buoys or dikes. It was a tricky, dangerous business to be floating along. Suddenly, we stopped. Jerry pointed to a row of pile dikes on our starboard side. A sand spoil with high banks was on our immediate port side. We could see the lights of a tow downstream. We were stumped. The charts made no sense as to our location. The old charts we were using didn't show the new pile dikes or the sand spoil where we were.

We sat there for nearly an hour attempting to determine the best route through the darkness. We were tired, wet and hungry, but Caruthersville was so close. Finally, Jerry determined an open stretch of water and we continued our progress. Another row of pile dikes swept past our starboard side.

"Oh God, please don't let us hit one of them!" I prayed. My mind could feel my kayak running a dike and swamping in the current. My mind could feel, with a shudder, the cold, icy water of the river.

"The lights! The lights of the barge construction work!" I yelled. "I know where we are now; can't be more than three miles from Caruthersville!" The barge works, lit up with huge floodlights, made the Missouri side of the river glow. The lights brought us a sense of warmth. We were like the lost hunter running to the light in the forest.

The floodlights interfered with what night vision we did have. Blinded by the light, we couldn't tell there was anything around us besides the barge works. Anything could punch through the circle of light bringing disaster with it at any moment— a dike, a marker buoy, or a tow. And there it was— a big shadow. We had a near panic situation on our hands as our voices rang out to each other:

"Towboat over there!"

"Where? I don't see it yet. Yes I do!"

"Is that the bow or the side?"

"I don't know. I can't tell!"

"He's getting close!"

"We'd better make our move pretty soon or we'll be run down!"

"Hell, we might paddle right into his path!"

"Let's get out of here!"

"This way!"

A flashing light marked the Caruthersville boat landing. All of us were soaked. Jerry was the wettest.

"Remember those two waves that rolled by after the towboat passed?" he asked. "Both of them washed right over the top of my kayak and drenched me!"

Sis answered the phone.

"Your guests have arrived," I said.

There was a long pause.

"Where have you been? I've been cookin' for the last two days and I just about give up hope you boys were comin' at all."

Sis washed our clothes (three times) and spent the remaining time cooking for us. She demonstrated how she used to "chop" cotton and talked about the '27 flood like it happened yesterday. Small wonder, over five miles of levees were washed out in the flood and water swirled through an area the size of West Virginia.

Jere drove us down to the "levee line." From a fifteen-foot roadway on top of a thirty-foot earthen embankment, we could see fertile, delta farmland stretching to the west. Trees and thick brush obscured the Mississippi, a quarter mile to the east.

"The levee we're standin' on forms almost a continuous line from just below the Cape all the way to the Gulf of Mexico— about a thousand miles I reckon," Jere told us. "The east bank of the Mississippi is 'walled-in' the same way, except the levee occasionally alternates with high bluffs."

On my first visit to Caruthersville, a part-time fisherman and his family introduced me to the levee line. This time, no one was home when we stopped.

"Those folks, I think, you'd like to meet," I told Jerry and Tom. "They didn't have much, but they were happy. I'll never forgot what the Mrs. told me: 'We might be poor, but our bellies are always full... and there's always enough for one more!'"

Quite a large crowd had gathered at the ramp to watch us depart. Hattie, Sis' cleaning lady, was crying when we left and Sis was biting her lower lip to keep herself from becoming "too emotional." The words she said the night before kept echoing in my mind: "It's nice to have boys' shoes around the house."

River Stories

"My feet are in the earth today, my mind is in the dawn tomorrow, my right points to the north where I have been and my left points to the south where I will go."

James J. Bauer

Randy Bauer

"Old Man River" rolled along in the stretch immediately above Memphis. Some people said it was the fastest water on the Lower Mississippi. We covered fifty-one miles from our sand island camp to the Memphis Yacht Club at the mouth of the Wolf River in less than seven and a half hours.

Generally speaking, the Mississippi is flowing south. However, a casual observer would never see the collection of currents making up the collective flow. During the Memphis run, our kayaks were pulled downstream by swift south currents, turned sideways and directed upstream by huge eddy currents spinning off river banks and held motionless by giant pie-shaped pools of flat water. Subtle changes of current were obvious to us. We could tell when the water flowed over a drop-off, deep hole or obstruction. River water piled up at dikes and spilled a swift current over their outer edges. We were constantly aware of "bobbing buoys"— marker buoys periodically submerged by the swift current. None of us cared to think what would happen if we were careless enough to drive over the top of one as it surfaced.

The Memphis Yacht Club faced a long, cobblestone levee adjacent to downtown. Embedded iron rings spoke of a time when steamboats lined the waterfront and cotton bails clogged the area. Now, the levee was used for a city parking lot.

"Jerry told us about the river travelers he met at Grand Tower. "We'll be right down to pick you up." We couldn't believe our ears! The short wait gave us enough time to collect our baggage, secure the kayaks and buy up-to-date river charts at the Corps of Engineers district headquarters a few blocks uptown.

Five years earlier, it was hot and muggy when I pulled into Memphis. Back then I met a kid named Larry. He was waiting for a raft heading down to New Orleans and I laid still my paddles for a few days on the same road. Larry and I slept in the clubhouse—the air conditioning nearly froze. Now, the clubhouse was heated and we waited inside to stay warm.

"I remember Larry entering my name into the yacht club register," I said.

We found the entry, but Larry had written down "canoe" instead of "kayak" for type of craft.

"He probably didn't know how to spell 'kayak'," Tom said.

His statement may have been true. Up till now, we had seen the name spelled a half dozen ways: "kayak," "cayak," "kayka," "kayack," "kiack" and "kak."

We could have stayed with Jerry's folks in Memphis for as long as we liked. However, we figured two nights was long enough. Lyle and Ruby wanted us to stay through Thanksgiving. It was a tempting offer, but we declined and were driven back to the Yacht Club to parcel out the remainder of the day as we saw fit.

Our explorations took us by old cotton factories and linters buildings. Old shops on Beal Street sold all varieties of potions including "graveyard dust" and "command powder." We photographed the statue of W.C. Handy, father of the Blues, saw another statue dedicated to Jefferson Davis and read a plaque describing "Casey Jones' Last Ride."

It was getting late in the afternoon and the phrase "think we should leave today?" floated through our conversations. The indecision ended when a new roster of travelers at the Yacht Club pushed our departure into the morning of the next day.

A sixty-eight-foot yacht called *Big Moose* and a huge catamaran named *Rainbow* were docked side by side. Ironically, from what we heard, both boats broke records for being the longest and the widest at the Yacht Club, respectively.

"We can even sleep in these little boats!" Tom told one of the crewmembers of a thirty-five foot Bristol sailboat bound for Hawaii.

We also met and talked with the crew of two other southbound sailboats. One was a ferro-cement boat with two former university instructors aboard, heading south with no destination in particular. The other was a small, homemade sailboat with a single cabin. A fella named Dave and his dad were aboard her. They had come from Louisville and were Florida bound.

Tom and Micky's craft was being repaired due to a common occurrence on the Mississippi—a prop bent from hitting a submerged object.

Tom had retired early. They sold their Chicago home and were also heading to Florida. Tom was originally a native of Pensacola, but time had taken him far away from the sea. Now he was returning. There was a glow in his eyes as he talked about shrimping in the Gulf waters. His wife, Micky, agreed it was the best he had felt in years.

We talked and drank coffee till midnight aboard their yacht and were almost asleep when the three sailors from the Bristol returned from a night on the town. I could hear footsteps and voices as they staggered up the dock. They passed Tom's boat and one of them called out: "Hey! You sleeping in there?" Tom, who was sleeping on a lateral dock next to his kayak, answered: "I sure am!"

"You really can't be in there, can you?" the voice replied.

Tom saw him lift up the poncho from the cockpit just enough to peek inside.

"I don't believe it. They really do sleep in those things!"

Thanksgiving dinner was celebrated on a sand spoil thirty miles below Memphis. We had a commanding view of the river both up and downstream and watched the sunset and the full moon rise as we ate. There was no real darkness throughout the evening. The quality of the light merely changed from a warm golden-orange to a cool silver-blue.

The traditional turkey, cranberries and sweet potatoes were absent. Hamburger hash, graham rolls from Lyle and Ruby, bread and butter, beef jerky, butterscotch pudding, lemon drink and tea were more than enough. We did have a lot to be thankful for and hoped that this Thanksgiving Day found everyone as happy and whole as we felt.

We met up with Tom and Micky again at Helena, Arkansas, when we completed the day's forty-two mile run. It was clear when we launched, but cloudy when we arrived at the marina.

"Thought you boys would pull in here," they told us.

"Saw our second deer of the trip," I told them. "Some hunters were dragging it down the revetment to their boat. By the way, what's the weather forecast?"

Tom shook his head: "Bad... bad... 'spose to get high winds and possible snow."

It rained hard on and off all night. Tom and I slept in boathouses and Jerry underneath a canopy. By 7:00 a.m. the wind had shifted to the northwest and a cold draft blew through the boathouse entrance—it was time to go.

Below the interstate highway bridge, immediately downstream from Helena, we passed into a "twilight zone" of thick fog and towboats. The nightmarish run lasted for three miles and it was followed by periodic bombardments of sleet and snow. Somewhere, during the ordeal, Tom and Micky passed us in their yacht. We waved, they honked back and then were gone—or so we thought. As we approached a westward bend and got ready to charge into the teeth of the increasing northwest wind, Jerry spied the yacht tucked away in a slip on the Arkansas side of the river.

"We thought you boys would like some company. It's gonna be a bad one tonight," Tom said.

We beached our kayaks on the sandbar between the main channel and the slip while Tom maneuvered his boat so it faced bow-first into the bar. Sixty feet of anchor line ran off the stern and a hundred feet of line led from the bow to the anchor buried in the sandbar. To prevent wind from dragging the stern anchor and swinging the yacht parallel to the sandbar, we fastened a heavy line to the stern and buried a "dead man" in the sand to hold it fast.

For supper, Micky made meatloaf from our combined larders. Occasionally, we'd wipe steam from a window and shine out a flashlight to catch faint glints of swirling snowflakes. About the only thing Jerry could pick up on his radio was live action from a local all day hog-calling contest. Although, earlier he found a distant station reporting: "Northeast Missouri had a foot of snow last night!"

We buttoned a cover over the yacht's bridge for our sleeping quarters. All night the wind whistled through the canvas and waves lapped at the hull. Fortunately in the morning, even though the temperature was in the twenties, the ground was still bare.

Watching Tom and Micky leave depressed us, but I'm glad they were not around to witness what happened next.

The water at the edge of the sand spit was eight feet deep and we managed to slide the kayaks off the sand into the water without getting our feet wet. The trick now and usually every morning, was to step from shore to kayak and shove off. If you kept your rear end low, it worked well, but if you maintained a high center of gravity during the transition, the boat was very unstable.

Tom forgot about the low center of gravity. Functioning with a sleepy, "half frozen" mind, he put one foot in the boat, proceeded to shove off, did the splits and fell head first into the Mississippi!

It's the rudest awakening he ever had on the journey and it's the angriest Jerry and I ever saw him!

Tom pulled himself out and I dragged his water-filled kayak far up on shore.

"Why did it have to do that?" he screamed and kicked his kayak. "After eighty-five days on the Mississippi, why the hell did it have to do that?"

Jerry pulled out a dry sleeping bag and was setting up the tent -- fortunately it wasn't needed. We had acted fast enough to prevent severe chilling and hypothermia. I had emptied the kayak to prevent gear from becoming waterlogged and much was back to normal after a half hour.

In spite of what became known as the "poop side down adventure," we managed to cover twenty-four miles before camping along a heavily wooded Arkansas riverbank.

The wood was stacked five feet high on the campfire that night. It effectively dried out the wet gear.

The weather was crisp and clear the next day. Someone had shut off the wind machine upstairs and we were able to cover fifty miles before dark. In the process, the current swept us past the mouths of the Arkansas and White rivers. A yellow tide funneled into the river from the general direction of the swollen Arkansas.

"We can take a 'short' side trip to Tulsa, Oklahoma," I jokingly said. "At least that's as far as the navigation channel goes up the Arkansas."

The quietude of the sandbar camp was wonderful.

"It's such a dramatic change when the wind ceases to roar through one's ears," I wrote. "Delicate, obscured sounds became loud—cracking driftwood logs in the campfire sound like gunshots. Anything over a whisper is a shout. We can hear the soup boiling from ten feet away. And if we listen hard enough, we can almost make out the sound of frost as it forms on everything outside the campfire's circle of heat."

Three sailors passed our sandbar in the pre-dawn light. We may have resembled Neanderthals huddled together for warmth in a barren setting at the close of the last ice age, but they never noticed. One of them was topside at the time. If he did see us, his mind probably registered: "Just another pile of driftwood logs, stumps, roots, or branches."

The Lower Mississippi had a handful of marine facilities for small craft. Consequently, after paddling the five miles of Oxbow Lake leading from the Mississippi to the Greenville marina, we met three teachers on the ferro-cement boat and docked next to the Bristol. We slept aboard the sailboat and swapped river adventures. Larry, Jerry and Tom were their names, and the way it sounded, their journey from Cincinnati to the Gulf was mainly for relaxation.

"The real work will start once we get to New Orleans. We'll train on Lake Ponchartrain and graduate into the Gulf before I take the crew to Hawaii," Jerry said.

In the realm of sailing, Tom, Larry and Jerry knew what they were doing. Likewise, the sailors understood the three kayakers were nobody's fools. Our mutual respect for the river was born out in emotion filled conversation describing storms and equipment failures.

"A couple days ago, our motor stalled on us," Jerry said, "just upstream from a series of government dikes. We cranked her over and over again while the current pulled us closer and closer to the dikes. Finally, we threw out our anchor and held fast until we got her started."

Larry related an equally "hair raising" story: "You know when you guys were up at Grand Tower waiting out the big wind? Well, we were anchored in the middle of the Ohio River waiting out the same thing! Wind bouncing the boat; rain and snow and towboats goin' up and down. We maintained our radio and listened to ship-to-shore telephone conversations from a few miles upstream. We heard the voice of the first mate crackling over the air: 'I quit! I just can't move her any farther downriver, captain! I got the flu and the weather's horseshit; and I just quit!'

A voice answered: "Well, you get Buddy to pilot the tow."

"Buddy can't drive this damn thing, he doesn't know how; I got the flu and I'm quittin' right now!"

The argument passed back and forth for twenty minutes or so.

"We were shaking in our boots. Our ears were glued to the radio and our eyes were fixed on the portholes. We thought ol' Buddy's tow would run right over the top of us, but they must have stopped somewhere for the night," he concluded.

Chapter 14

Sighting the Delta Queen

"The care of the rivers is not a question of rivers, but of human heart."

Tonka Shoza

Greenville appeared clean and kept. Even the ship-yards and harbor facilities looked well groomed. Perhaps, Lake Ferguson had something to do with our perception of the surroundings. Compared to the Mississippi, Oxbow Lake was "clean." It had a three-foot Secchi Disk reading, compared to a generous one foot on the river.

The "Port City" was home for more than seventy-two towboats of various sizes. The three thousand horsepower one we toured near the marina, was small compared to some of nine thousand. However, matched to their loads, each would handle what it was capable of handling. Likewise, several days later, our own comparatively microscopic engines were handling maximum load as they once again strained against the elements.

We were twenty-seven miles from Vicksburg. The wind built heavier and heavier chops against the current as it increased its intensity. The rain, which had held off for quite some time, came down in buckets. Waves periodically washed over all three kayaks and the wind prevented any of us from keeping a poncho in place over the cockpit. Rainwater trickled down my back and pocketed at the elbows of my rain suit. All three of us were soaked halfway through the run, but the thought of food and shelter at Vicksburg kept us paddling.

A blinding flash of lightning turned everything around me a brilliant pink. At the same time, I yelled: "Paddle failure!" The brass sleeve where the paddle joined together was bent and cracked. I crammed the useless blade into the aft end of the cockpit and snapped a spare set together.

"Maybe the paddle was struck by lightning," Jerry said.

"I don't know what really happened. I'm open to suggestions. I'm just glad the spares were handy. How much water ya got in your boat?" I asked.

"About five gallons," Jerry answered. "And how about you, Tom? Is it gonna sink on you?"

"No I'll make it, but I'm sitting in water right now!" he replied.

At the mouth of the Yazoo River leading to Vicksburg, a towboat passed us. By now we were a mile from our goal and I tipped my hat at the skipper. Yes, we definitely were crazy to be out in such weather. The skipper knew it too and cut loose with a salute on his air horn.

The Vicksburg marina was made from a series of old barges. The lady running the place lived aboard a houseboat and told us we could use a heated shack on the dock to sleep in.

The Bristol sailboat was there when we arrived, but the steamer *Sprague*, the "Big Mama" of the river, was gone. The *Sprague*, we heard, had burned in April. The charred hulk now lie a few miles up the harbor. We never went to see it; we weren't sure we wanted to see it. "Big Mama" was in service from 1902 to 1948, the largest paddle wheel steamboat ever built. In 1907 she set an all time record for tows by moving nearly seventy thousand tons of coal on sixty barges from Louisville to New Orleans.

"I do believe the river was trying to kill today," I scratched into the log that evening. "When we got here, the only thing dry on all three of us were Jerry's feet and socks; he had wrapped them in plastic bread bags before we broke camp this morning."

The day was appropriate for a battlefield tour—the sky was overcast, the trees bare and a damp chill penetrated the air.

The siege of Vicksburg started May 19th, 1863 and lasted forty-seven days. When the "Gibraltar of the Confederacy" fell, the Mississippi River was in Union control. Confederate forces were starving before their surrender on July 4th. Consequently, townsfolk for nearly a century afterward never celebrated Independence Day.

We walked past monuments, tablets and markers. Some pointed out remnants of trenches and earthworks, others were dedicated to regiments and individuals serving in the campaign or defense of the city. General J.C. Pemberton, with 18,500 effective troops, held out as long as he could to General Grant with an army of 45,000.

We were told, after heavy rains, grapeshot and mini balls still washed down hillsides. One antebellum home, the McRaven House, stills bore numerous siege-inflicted shell marks in the hall and parlor walls.

Towboats moved up and down the narrow Yazoo River and I wondered about wakes damaging our kayaks tied alongside the converted barges. On our way back from the battlefield, I checked the kayaks and discovered one of them missing—Jerry's! Apparently, wheel wash from the passing tows and increased current in the Yazoo from yesterday's rain had torn the boat loose. Again, I thought the craft was gone forever, but there it was lodged between the barge hull and a moored runabout. While I watched Jerry pull his boat back to its proper place, I was convinced a guardian angel was protecting the *Mississippi Queen.*

"Those boys over there are traveling in 'coyotes'," the waitress at the restaurant told a regular customer.

By now, we too had become "regular" customers at the Vicksburg Hotel Restaurant. The waitresses gladly kept our coffee cups full while we digested our food, wrote letters and relaxed.

Vicksburg also meant looking up old friends. Vic was now bedridden and very ill with cancer. It was hard for me to see him that way compared to the way he was five years before. Vic smiled: "Great thing traveling... its grist for the mill!"

Lilian took us back to the Marina and thanked us for sharing lunch.

"You brought Vic a moment of cheer in a world that's pretty bleak for him right now," she said. Vic died two weeks later.

The water jugs were half frozen the morning we left our campsite located ten miles below Vicksburg. That evening, fifty-two more miles downriver I wrote:

"I'm sleeping with my insulated long johns on tonight. The fire didn't seem to keep us warm. Frost covers everything— it's probably 9:00 p.m. I can see my breath in the tent as I write by candlelight. I'm sleeping on my life jacket, as usual, for the ground is very cold."

There's a thirteen-mile straightaway before Natchez, Mississippi. Natchez itself is situated on high, clay bluffs on the east side of the river. We nearly passed the town and backtracked to an area cluttered with a rusty barge, floating docks and a dilapidated barrel raft marked "Port of Lilydale, Minnesota," now 1,500 miles upstream. A cluster of old buildings including a hotel, general store and house stood at the base of the road leading up the hill to the main part of town. All were abandoned, except the house. People also lived in shacks scattered along the flats below the bluff. In many places, tarpaper shanties peeked at us through the thick river brush.

"This place looks like it's right out of Tom Sawyer," Jerry said.

Maybe it was! After filling water jugs and buying candy bars, we spied a sign lying in the weeds—"Jackson's Landing," it said!

Until 1963, near the Louisiana and Mississippi state lines fifty-four miles below Natchez, the Mississippi could have cut a new channel to the Gulf of Mexico. There in 1831, Captain Henry Shreve cut through a Mississippi oxbow to shorten navigation. Eventually, the upper loop of the river silted shut while the lower loop, called the Old River, remained a link between the Mississippi and Atchafalaya/Red Rivers. The Old River flowed both directions, depending on the water levels in the adjacent Red River. Eventually it displayed only a westward flow into the Atchafalaya.

If the process were left to continue, the Atchafalaya would have become the Mississippi's new channel, leaving a three hundred mile saltwater estuary all the way to New Orleans. Ironically, to offset the impending disastrous impact of human meddling, the Corps of Engineers built controls at the sight. A low sill structure near Old River permitted medium and low flows of the Mississippi to pass into the Atchfalaya River—allowing sufficient water depth for barge traffic. An earthen dam and twelve hundred foot lock at Old River itself allowed the Atchafalaya to remain an important navigation artery. During flood periods, the Mississippi's water could be spilled into the Atchafalaya River via an "overbank" feature adjacent to the "low sill" structure.

A giant sign on the west riverbank warned us of its presence: "Old River Control Structure. Dangerous Currents When Light is Flashing."

Parades of tows moved past. At one point, I counted five of them on the river ahead and turned around to see three more. The tows were tireless, always moving somewhere, hardly ever stopping— except for staging. We were humans, though and we had to eat and rest. By dusk, the day weighed heavy on our shoulders. The light headwind we had worked against for hours had proven effective in draining our energy reserves. We dragged our boats onto a gently sloping Louisiana mud bank and crawled into the woods to make camp.

The fire was almost ready for cooking when we heard the sound. Jerry was the first to break the silence of the campfire ring: "Sounds like somethins' comin' down the river. It ain't no towboat though!" We ran from the woods to the water's edge.

"The Queen! It's the *Delta Queen!*" Jerry announced.

The black silhouette of the great paddle wheeler slowly moved by as our ears were filled with the hiss of steam and the throb of paddle blades striking the water. She was bound for New Orleans.

"Funny, I'm not tired anymore," I said.

Breakfast brought a revelation—we didn't have much to eat.

"We should save what's left of the stove fuel in case we can't build a fire for a supper meal," I reasoned. "We need the bread for lunch on the water and we finished up the sunrise cereal yesterday. So we got raw oatmeal and powdered milk... that's it."

Jerry and I filled our cups and began spooning down the oatmeal.

"It's not bad, ya kinda get used to it," I said.

An incident occurred while cutting through a narrow chute. Jerry was ahead of Tom and me when we were surprised by a towboat pushing at least seven barges toward us! The chute was no more that thirty feet wide and was not part of the navigation channel. Tom and I had more leeway in between the tow than Jerry. He was literally squeezed between the monstrous steel hull and the clay bank and took the full force of the wake. The violent turbulence broke over his boat and nearly swamped him. We were close enough to see the pilot looking at our boats but he never cut his power.

Water sloshed between the banks of the narrow passage long after the tow left. Again and again I thought of the story near Winona where a tow accidentally ran over a fishing boat. The captain never realized he hit the boat until it came bottom-up in the prop wash. The fisherman floated to the surface about a week later.

The chute opened into the main river where a pipeline crossing offered a suitable place to land. The morning was rough on us and the evening tough on Jerry. I relieved at least some of the tension by walking quietly into camp carrying an armload of firewood and wearing a Spanish moss wig. I didn't have to say anything—everyone roared with laughter for the next hour.

Chapter 15

Changing Tides

"Heaven is under our feet as well as over our heads."

Henry David Thoreau

"I heard beaver last night but I don't know if they could live in this stuff," I wrote. We had entered Baton Rouge's giant petrol-chemical complex sixteen miles downriver from our camp.

The water turned from brown to orange. An irritating haze hung over the river and my lungs burned after we passed under the first bridge. We were bombarded by an assortment of smells—ammonia, oil, burning garbage, rotten food, raw sewage, glue and sulfur.

At Baton Rouge, the Corps of Engineers maintained a forty-foot deep channel to the Gulf. Ocean-going vessels, two hundred and thirty miles from saltwater, were anchored here. Ships were loading at docks; others rested in midstream with their bows facing upriver.

The sailors' boat was tied at Red's Boat Store and we paddled in alongside. Huge wakes continually rocked the dock. It was a bad place to be moored, but the only feasible place for small craft—commercial docks were eight to forty feet high. We'd run into town, buy a few supplies and leave as quickly as possible—or so we thought.

Compared to the river and the surroundings, downtown Baton Rouge was appealing. Poinsettias bloomed in many places and Louisiana's Capitol Building, completed in 1932, looked much like a miniature Empire State Building. The white, granite structure rose 450 feet above the flat land and proved to be a "time trap." A smiling guard wearing a size forty-eight belt, neatly lined with stubby bullets, greeted us just before we were shuttled off to the governor's room in hopes of meeting the Head of State, interviewed by the local news and shown our past and future watercourse from the observation deck.

A small tow named the *Dixie Ranger* was taking on a thousand gallons of drinking water when we returned to Red's. We followed suite and brought our supply to full capacity—six gallons. The skipper and his one-man crew invited us aboard for a late afternoon—meat, cheese and tomato sandwiches.

"Hell, that's nothin," he said and opened a refrigerator full of pork chops, T-bone steaks, turkey and more. They were planning on having shrimp for supper—we had popcorn.

Throughout the night, I was recurrently aware of spotlights, diesel engines, shouts and related noise on the river just outside the tent door. We had camped three miles below the second Baton Rouge highway bridge and had fallen asleep without giving serious thought to why the brush covered revetment was marked with old numbers and mooring rings. Now, we knew—a tow with twelve barges was now sitting alongside last night's vacant shoreline. Apparently, the crewmen staging the tow had seen our kayaks on the revetment and had given us ten feet to safely launch our boats.

We paddled the full length of the tow and barges, traveling the five-foot space in between it and the shoreline. Even though the tow engines were idling and the captain watched us clear, passing so close made us nervous.

Similarly, while we closed a fifty-mile day, we came unpleasantly close to a towboat pushing thirty barges upstream. As we approached, it had stopped along our side of the river and was in the process of turning. To avoid it, we had the choice of running across the front barges—the captain's "blind spot"—or paddling in between the tow and the shore. Common sense told us to do the latter. Consequently, we were forced to run past the tow's stern. I held my breath as we did. If the captain decided to open the throttle, releasing only a portion of the towboat's eight thousand horsepower, we'd receive the full force of the prop wash and be like toothpicks caught in a washing machine. Fortunately, when the water finally boiled behind the tow, we were far downstream.

In the evening, I walked the riverbank an hour after Jerry and Tom turned in. I was not really tired. The air was warm enough to walk comfortably without a jacket;

my stomach was full of macaroni and cheese. My mind was not yet cluttered with the debris that would flood it during the next two days. I was happy to be soon leaving the river, but I also was sad. The refineries across the river pulsated with strange, hellish light while I recorded final thoughts for the night:

"We all need at least two weeks rest from the trials and tribulations of the water. This is not to say I do not love the Mississippi. I would like to take the river journey again. God grant me the health and time to do so. The river holds so many secrets!"

The next day, we passed a complex of riverside industries, as well as old plantation homes tucked away amongst the trees. Previously, we had seen what looked like plantations near the river. Normally, we could only make out the mansion roof and a few small buildings. However, there was one where the familiar white columns were plainly visible. We also paddled by sugar cane fields hidden behind the levees. The town of Reserve, where the ferry landing was situated, employed a large number of its people at a nearby sugar company.

It didn't seem possible Christmas was only nine days away. A Christmas program blaring over a TV set at a small Reserve diner seemed phony and out of place. We were glad to leave when our hamburgers—the only thing served—were eaten. While we were on the river, we were sufficiently buffered from yuletide commercialism. We had seen kids stacking wood in the shape of tepees and log cabins along the high levees, but we didn't pay any attention to it. Later we learned the woodpiles were burned at Christmas or New Years when traditional bonfires dotted the Mississippi's levees. It was quite a serious business—oftentimes groups kept guard over their wood to prevent pilfering.

Back at the dock, we conversed with the night watchman who in turn conversed with the sheriff after we crawled into our sleeping bags. Apparently, the two "night owls" wiled away the hours that way.

Just before I dozed off, I remember the sheriff shining a bright flashlight into my face. I don't know how well you can identify a person from their lips and nose, but he did it anyway. "Just curious," I thought.

Tom complained of not sleeping for over two hours during the night. Unfortunately, river fatigue had made him forget to put sufficient padding between his sleeping bag and the ice-cold, steel plated ferry dock. I thought that was the reason why he was so quiet while we walked to a doughnut shop for breakfast. However, there was something else on his mind.

I was taking an Eckman Dredge sample off the ferry dock when I heard words break from Tom's mouth: "You know, I just might not be goin' on with you and Randy once we reach New Orleans! I've been thinkin'...."

I didn't catch the rest, but had heard enough. I pretended not to overhear Tom's words with Jerry. I kept my face directed at the dredge sample and worked with fingers numbed by the cold water. When I was done, I looked up at Jerry. His eyes were misty and reflected the red dawn spreading across the river. It was true—what I had heard was true, but I would wait until Tom told me the same thing.

The staging yards at New Orleans inner harbor were immense. Barges five and six deep lined the shore in some places. Tows moved up and down the river along with ships and tugboats. No place on the water was safe for us. Small towboats darted every which way, transferring barges from one raft to another. The place was a beehive of activity and no place for kayaks. Workmen aboard a floating loading dock yelled down to us as we passed: "Come aboard for some coffee, ya look tired!"

"Hell, that sure sounds good," Jerry said and we took them up on their offer.

There was only one problem, our kayaks had about six inches of freeboard— the loading dock about ten feet. It was a long climb to the top and a long fall to the water if we slipped.

The crew had just finished transferring wheat from barges into the hold of a foreign ship and was fixing their equipment before moving on to the next job. We talked and drank bitter coffee.

"Do you think we've entered Cajun land?" I asked Jerry. " I'm sure that was chicory coffee we had."

"Yeah, I think so," he replied. "When those two guys started talkin' to each other, I couldn't understand a word they said."

The three of us switched over to the right bank in an effort to follow the inside curve of the river. There, we met people in something a little closer to our own size— a johnboat with an outboard motor. They were "stringin' lines for big cats" and had seen us coming for some distance. The fishermen laughed about our boats.

"At first we thought they was pirogues," one of them said. "But as you got closer we could see they was different —somethin' that's come from a long ways away."

We shut down at one-thirty, soon after leaving the fishermen. The area was brushy with a clay bank deeply carved by wave and current action. A set of containerized barges was moored immediately upstream and a high levy sloped in back of us.

We were well within the Inner Harbor. Our camp was as close as we wanted to be to New Orleans without risking the danger of being caught in the harbor after dark. The Port of New Orleans, lined with over three hundred high wharfs, lie a little over four miles away on the other side of the Huey Long Bridge. The foot of Canal Street was only fifteen miles from our camp!

Jerry went to check what lie on the other side of the levee. Tom, who had been quiet since morning, except for functional conversation, spoke now: "Did you hear I might be dropping from the trip?"

"Why?" was my one-word response.

"Well, you think about a lot of things out there on the river... about your future and stuff. I want to go back and finish my degree."

I tried to reason with him, but it was apparent his mind had been made up long before he released the news to us.

By now, Jerry was back and both he and Tom went back over the levee. They returned shortly with a bottle of wine to "celebrate" the arrival in New Orleans. Of course none of us were happy, but it seemed appropriate to at least go through the motions of celebration. We attached the bottle to a line and threw it into the river to cool.

When I awoke from a long nap, Tom and Jerry were gone again and low and behold, the sailors were tying their boat alongside the containerized barges.

Jerry and the skipper walked along the bank to the kayaks and me.

"Long time no see. I take it you're going to run the harbor in the morning too?" he asked.

"It's a little safer that way," I answered. "Wouldn't be caught dead out there after dark."

"Hey, you're doin' a little fishin'. Catch anything?" he asked.

I pulled in the wine bottle, looked at it and said: "Darn fish didn't take the bait. Well, I guess we'll just have to drink it."

Jerry laughed and added: "You and your buddies are invited for supper on board. Just as long as you share the bait."

The sailboat bounced and rocked to the turbulence of passing craft while we ate. We were almost finished when a spotlight glared through the port window.

"Gonna have to move the sailboat," came over the bullhorn.

Jerry, Tom and I evacuated the cabin and climbed the makeshift rope ladder to the top of a moored barge. We hopped from the new containerized barges down the crumbling hulks of the old ones covered with rotten boards and shingling.

The sailors dropped anchor ten yards offshore in front of our camp. Tom stayed, in case the sailors decided to join our campfire and Jerry and I took a long walk. The December night was crisp and clear. From the levee, we had a good view of waterfront activities. The ocean ships looked ridiculously out-of-place on the river.

"Like whales in a swimming pool," Jerry said.

They were so big compared to everything else. Their fast, quiet movement followed by a wide, rolling wake amidst a seemingly fragile harbor could be compared to a gentle giant in a glass house. We watched one of the giants "sneak up" behind an unsuspecting tugboat. The ship's deep horn bellowed a half dozen times before the tug finally made way.

We must have walked seven miles in search of another bottle of wine. We found none and came back with a large bottle of beer.

Our sleeping bags were frost covered when we woke. Tom had saved a can of fruit cocktail for the "last" morning— we spooned it down without ceremony. The kayaks were packed almost mechanically and before we knew it, all three of us were on the water.

The morning was sunny with a light northwest wind. The sunlight painted everything in bright colors making the harbor more fascinating than threatening to us. We found the staging area of the Inner Harbor to be more dangerous than the Port of New Orleans harbor itself. In the staging area, huge rafts of barges were unpredictable. Some barges were being moved, others were temporarily stationary. Oftentimes, rafts of barges were separated by passages thirty to forty feet wide with tows darting in and out of them. The trick for us was to "jump the gap" without being run down.

On the other hand, the port's wharfs were stationary objects, forming an unbroken line for us to follow. The ships moored alongside them were not as agile as the towboats and wouldn't be as likely to "leap out" unexpectedly.

Traffic was heavy a quarter-mile out in midstream but comparatively quiet along the ten miles of wharfs bordering the New Orleans side of the river. We passed ships from all parts of the World—Germany, Italy, Argentina and Japan. Some were loading, others unloading. We saw trucks, bulldozers, earthmoving equipment, chemicals, containers and fruit disappear into holds and vice-versa. We moved past Celeste, Market and Orange Street Wharfs and saw names—Creole, Westwind, East Star African and Helenic Lines—that spurred our imaginations.

A working dredge forced us into mid-channel at the New Orleans highway bridge. We were in with the "Big Boys" now! Tugs and tows passed on either side. An oceangoing freighter passed starboard, as did another tug displaying a barely recognizable American flag blackened with soot. Dead ahead, two tugs gently pushed a ship sideways into a wharf and, in the distance, the West Side Ferry crossed the river to Algiers.

Downtown buildings grew larger as we approached Canal Street. The International Trade Mart and the Hotel Marriott resembled huge, white citadels.

"I see... I see the *Delta Queen!*" Jerry yelled.

She was docked at the Toulouse Street wharf on the banks of the Viex Carre. Jackson Square lie just beyond the wharf and we could see the steeple of St. Louis Cathedral. We had the urge to jump out of the boats and tramp around the Old Square, but there would be time later. We were still a long way from the New Orleans Municipal Marina on Lake Ponchartrain.

Early in the morning, at Mile Marker 105, we were five miles southwest, as the crow flies, from the marina. Now, at Mile Marker 94.3, we still had more than ten miles to go. The journey would take us another mile down the Mississippi and into the Inner Harbor Navigation Canal. We'd paddle the four miles of canal to Lake Ponchartrain, make a left turn and follow the shore five miles to the marina.

Since river height varies dramatically—during high water, one can look over the levee and down at buildings—the Inner Harbor Canal is equipped with a lock. A flotilla of pleasure craft, including the *Bristol,* was waiting for lockage when we arrived.

"Good! They waited for us," we thought.

Then a bullhorn blared: "All pleasure craft enter the lock except the canoes!"

The canoes (meaning us) waited another hour before our turn. Apparently, it was a matter of safety. Regardless, we were agitated and filled out the survey forms accordingly: Home Port: Minneapolis and Destination: Minneapolis were true; but the weight, 2,000 tons was wrong—even though it felt like it at times. Two-thousand three-hundred miles of river travel had washed the "M" off my boat, so next to NAME I wrote: *'Olly B.*

When the lock gates opened, we entered a world of barnacles and rust. We were in saltwater and soon would be paddling a current as swift as the Mississippi, but in the "wrong" direction.

At first, we thought the current was created by an ebb tide pulling the water from the canal through an outlet branch of the Intracoastal Waterway. However, if we could have seen the waves on Lake Ponchartrain, we would have known better.

The lake—a twenty-mile wide saucer of water with an average depth of sixteen feet—had a strong northwest wind that day. The wind created a tidal effect boiling up water on the south side of the lake, forcing it through the canal.

We fought the tidal current till we thought our arms would fall off. Paddling at top speed, the kayaks crept along at a snail's pace. My abdomen, shoulders and chest burned from paddling, yet I couldn't stop for fear of being swept back ten or twenty feet. Jerry and Tom seemed to have it a little easier. Their kayak hulls were narrower with less drag. I kept thinking of all the patches on the bottom of my boat "holding me back" and "holding me up."

Paddling under the bascule bridges was tough where the channel constricted and the current increased in velocity. Jerry spearheaded one attempt and was thrown back, almost swamping in the process when his paddle jammed against a bridge beam.

"She's really moving through there," he said. "Let's rest a minute and tackle her again."

"My arms are ready to fall off now," I moaned. I was ready to cry from the pain of fatigue.

Jerry rammed the current again. This time, it viciously grabbed his boat throwing it against the pilings. To my amazement, he was still paddling.

"Give her hell!" I screamed.

The paddles were a blur as Jerry pulled away from the current's clutches.

"Try the other side and watch the whirlpool!" Jerry yelled back.

Tom made it through with a burst of effort. Then it was my turn. The current gripped my boat like a huge hand. I could see water rushing around and through the pilings.

"Harder! Harder!" I screamed at myself. "Still harder! God this is terrible... you bastard! You're not going to hold me!"

The current weakened.

"You're bustin' through... keep it up!" my mind screamed and laughed.

Lake Ponchartrain was a blessing after the canal. The waves were three feet but easy to handle. By the time we entered the municipal harbor mouth, it was nearly calm and almost dark.

The sailors beat us by many hours. We finally found their boat amidst several hundred masted vessels and were invited aboard for the night. We'd see them one more time. Our roads separated in New Orleans. They were bound for the Gulf and Hawaii, while we'd eventually head east to Florida.

We were going home for Christmas! Jerry's sister and cousin were in New Orleans, staying with friends of Tom's parents. We'd be driven home for the holidays and brought back to continue.

Bud and Borg's home became an equipment cache for us. The spare bedroom of the condominium suddenly became impassible with canisters, kettles, packs, food jugs, sleeping bags, tent, paddles, life jackets and more. The balcony harbored our kayaks, where they had to be hoisted up from the parking lot by ropes.

We brought back gifts to the snowbound country of Minnesota: Cajun cookbooks, chicory coffee, grits, shrimp, Dixie beer, pre-season Mardi Gras beads and records capturing the music of Preservation Hall. Most important, we brought our families and loved ones kayakers, who after one hundred and one days of water travel, were weathered and hairy, but healthy and whole.

Jerry, Tom and I were scattered over the holidays. For Jerry and me it was a time of recharging; for Tom, a time of decision. It was strange to see the northern Mississippi locked in ice and the countryside blanketed in deep snow.

Two days before our return to New Orleans, Tom finally gave Jerry and me a final answer— yes he would be returning with us, but only to pick up his kayak and gear.

Chapter 16

The Intracoastal Waterway

"The power of imagination makes this infinite."
John Muir

Jerry and I worked on equipment. The *Mississippi Queen* with brass, aluminum and stainless hardware was, for the most part, ready for saltwater. The *Molly B.* needed a few more adjustments. I replaced all of the steel gunwale and cockpit screws with brass ones and used brass brads to reinforce where the hull and deck were stretched and stapled over the top longeron. All accessible, wooden parts received a thorough coat of varnish and the kayaks were scrubbed inside and out.

Since the early days on the Mississippi, Jerry had collected a dozen decals from the eleven states we passed through. At New Orleans, he decorated his kayak's free-board with them and made plans to paint the deck with words describing the adventure. While at home, Dad repaired the paddle shaft I had broken at Vicksburg. He restored the bent brass sleeve with a thick copper one and replaced the aluminum paddle tips with brass.

There were other subtle changes, but basically, our equipment stayed the same. Mom replaced the metal zipper in my kayak's removable spray apron with a corrosion resistant nylon one. Jerry's mom made twelve more pounds of granola for us. An army buddy gave me a new foam life jacket to replace the torn and patched kapok preserver. We brought razors and shaving cream along to maintain a "clean shaven" appearance until we got to Lake Ontario and packed a few extra dress clothes. Jerry's wardrobe included a leisure jacket and a pair of leather boots. We also brought another cassette recorder and a thick set of marine navigation charts.

Redistributing the gear was easier than we had first anticipated. Tom's kayak actually carried very little of the shared equipment, except for some of the food. With the Eckman Dredge, Secchi Disk and other bits and pieces of experiment equipment vacant from the hold of my boat, the prospects of having enough room were excellent.

Bud and his son watched us pack at the municipal marina.

"How can you get all of this into those two tiny boats?" Bud said.

"Sometimes it angers us, but we manage," Jerry replied. "It's like packing a space capsule—everything has its place!"

We waited three days over our original departure date for Lake Ponchatrain to calm down. Three days before, the temperature was eighty degrees; the day we left the mercury peaked at forty-nine degrees—rising from a low of twenty-two!

"Supposed to freeze tomorrow morning too," I said. "Must be the effects of the big storm back home."

To us the blizzard "horror stories" seemed unreal and far away. We paddled back to the inner harbor canal and down to the branch channel heading east. Bud and Pete followed us until they ran out of roads. I almost expected to turn around and see Tom bringing up the rear, but he was gone too. How strange it was not to have him with us.

We camped for the night on a vast, flat delta after charging through fifty feet of tall reeds lining the canal.

"Tom should be with us," I told Jerry. "Do you think he'll try to rejoin the trip?"

"No, it would be too hard for him," Jerry said. "Hell, we've cooked too much macaroni and cheese. Guess it'll be awhile before we get used to just two!"

Jerry and I were paddling through an Intracoastal Waterway canal bordered by marsh and bayous, squeezed between Lake Borgne on the south and Ponchartrain on the north. Fishermen appeared and disappeared along the canal, darting in and out of the maze of interconnecting back channels and inlets. One bayou fisherman stopped— a big Cajun with no front teeth in a large wooden boat

"Everythin' gonin' all right?" he asked. "Where ya'll headed?"

I nodded and grinned: "Pensacola!"

"In them small boats?" was his reply. "Good luck to ya!"

Another boat passed with two guys in it. One said to the other: "I see it, but I don't believe it!"

Every once in awhile we'd see flashes of what was soon to come. There would be a break in the rushes and we'd look through an open pass to Lake Borgne and the Gulf beyond. We did encounter some tidal current in the canal, but it was weak and hardly noticeable.

The canal ended at Rigolets, a three-quarter mile wide pass to Lake Ponchartrain. We crossed it, skirted partway down the backside of a five mile long island and camped on the sandy, clam-filled, State of Mississippi, shore of the Pearl River.

"It's amazing how rapidly the vegetation has changed!" I wrote. Tonight, palm plants, vines and grass surrounds us and shrubs armed with spines that'll tear your hide off if you're not careful. Jumping bugs hide underneath logs—I guess they're sand fleas. Earlier today we saw what looked like a muskrat or mink—most likely it was a coypu (nutria). It is very quiet and spooky here. How precious our equipment is to us now because it offers us security in a strange, 'hostile' environment."

Chapter 17

Salt Water Begins

"And the world can not be discovered by journey of miles, no matter how long, but only by a spiritual journey, a journey of one inch, very arduous and humbling and joyful, but which we arrive at the ground at our feet and learn to be at home."

Wendell Berry

Ocean! Actually, we were in Mississippi Sound on the Gulf of Mexico. Nevertheless, it was salt and for two people who had lived almost their entire lives in the Midwest, it was a sight to behold. The sky was partly cloudy and the water was smooth as glass—what a change from "boxed in" waterways. "BIG"—to put it in one word. We had moved from the mountain valley to the plain.

Islands, some watery looking, formed the shallow sound's south boundary. To avoid the sound's numerous shoals and shell banks, waterway markers marched away from us as we continued to follow the shoreline.

Waveland looked like a good place to beach for a late lunch. We bought food from a store plainly visible from the water and ate amidst a low tide world of barnacle coated pilings, crab skeletons, wet sand dotted with tiny "blow holes" and the strong scent of rotting seaweed.

"I feel a lot better than I did yesterday—must have got dehydrated from the sun," I told Jerry.

"Did you get a hold of that, Brother?" Jerry said.

"Yeah, Brother Joseph. I told him we'd be at the seminary this evening—sounds like he didn't know what was going on."

Brother Joseph knew my great aunt Barbara Bauer from the letters and packages she had sent over the years to St. Augustine's Mission and Seminary. By the time we arrived at Bay St. Louis and found directions to the seminary, it was nearly dark. Brother Joseph walked down to the shore with me, where Jerry had sat in the dark for the past hour.

"We have sleeping bags, so like I said, we can sleep in the gym, hall or outside on the grounds. Believe me, we're used to it!"

Brother Joseph grinned: "I think yer deserve somethin' better than that! I'll get you a room."

Jerry and I slept in a two-room suite fit for the Pope. In return, we took Brother Joseph out for dinner and spent the following day and night amidst the clergy of St. Augustine's.

The church and brick buildings of the seminary were sheltered among magnolias, cabbage palms and moss covered live oaks. Coupled with the traditional dress of the clergy, it was easy for us to imagine we were nineteenth century travelers instead of the twentieth.

Brother Joseph ran a small shoe shop at the mission. He joked about being a missionary for footwear because his work called for "saving souls," "healing them" and "tending to the dyeing."

I found the statement humorous, but Jerry admitted later that he was uneasy. Coming from a non-Catholic background, Jerry felt out of place at St. Augustine's.

"I figured someone might try to 'save' me," he said.

They were thoughts coming from Jerry's struggle with his own spirituality—something the journey was just beginning to reveal to both of us.

We spent a noisy, restless night at Gulfport sleeping lengthwise on picnic table seats, our kayaks tied to the bulkhead of the marina. It was fifteen miles and a world away from the peace and quiet of St. Augustine's.

After we crossed St. Louis Bay, the coastline straightened and grew more congested. U.S. 90 bordered the beach and it was quite obvious there was no place to camp. A boatload of drunken servicemen on the outskirts of Gulfport's main harbor gave us a clue to the existence of small craft facilities amidst the banana boat docks. We followed their wake of beer cans to shelter.

The harbormaster was amiable: "Got one of these kind of boats myself. They'll go through anything! You'll like it around here. These folks in the live aboard sailboat over there stopped for two days—that was over a month ago. Yes sir, this is a nice place."

His comments, of course, were from his perspective. The harbormaster could go home at six o'clock and we didn't have live-aboard kayaks.

During our walk to a seafood restaurant, we were "introduced" to the Gulf. Huge signs advertised and exploited the attributes of the Gulf: CHARTER FISHING BOATS, LIVE PORPOISE, BAIT HERE.

"Notice how all the signs are facing north," Jerry said. "We're coming through the back door."

We paddled the next day with visibility ranging from one hundred to less than ten yards. Offshore pilings marked "danger deep water" ran parallel to the swimming beach from Gulfport to Biloxi and used them as "stepping stones." During the ten-mile run, we stopped at Beavoir. Rows of hot dog stands, miniature golf courses and souvenir shops depressed us.

"Before Camille, it was a lot different," the lady at the Jefferson Davis home remarked. "The hurricane destroyed most of the old homes lining the beach. We had water four feet deep on the first floor of the home. Lucky it stood at all!"

Five and a half years after the fact, the Biloxi-Gulfport coastline still hadn't fully recovered.

"Let's get going," I said. " This place really isn't meant for us; just look at that beach sign!"

NOTICE

Sand Beach Ordnance:

NO Littering

NO Tents

NO Glass, China, or Pottery

NO Motor Vehicles

NO Horses or Livestock

NO Firearms or Airguns

NO Fireworks without Permit

NO Fires without Permit

UP to $2OO.OO fine.

Inch by inch we grew closer to Biloxi and the safety of a marina. The fog was so thick the pilings were impossible to see at times.

"You're crazy to be out there in those things!" was the harbormaster's opening statement.

We reacted by asking him for a recent weather forecast, restaurant facilities and the best place to put the boats so they would be out of the way. By the time we were finished, we had the key to the shower room and were invited to stay in the harbormaster's "see all" office in case it rained.

During the night, a strong, cold front swept down from the north bringing with it high winds and temperatures in the forties. When Jerry and I woke up, the docks next to the sailboats and yachts looked higher than the evening before.

"The tide! The tide! I shouted and pointed.

Instead of the Gulf's normal one and one-half to two foot tide, the north wind made the total drop over four feet—Jerry's kayak was lined for the former. And there it was, two hundred and fifty pounds of gear and kayak suspended in mid air by the bow and stern lines! Such experiences build memory cells—it never happened again.

The tidal shift made me nervous.

"If it goes out like that with a north wind, then it could be just as bad, only in reverse," I thought. "The wind pushing back the water would sooner or later have to subside or shift. Would the water then come back in a flood tide covering the sand spoil we camped on?"

We'd take no chances and tied the rigs securely to deeply rooted shrubs on the burnt-over island. We were directly across from the Pascagoula shipyards and from our vantage point could see what looked like Navy destroyers being constructed.

The highway retreated from the coast at Biloxi and turned northeast at Pascagoula toward Mobile.

"The other day humans limited our campsites, now we got all swamp along the shoreline," I said.

We stopped for a map check and decided to aim for a "high" island marked Isle Aux Herbes.

"Look! Did you see it?" Jerry yelled. "Sharks? No, they're dolphins! Look at them! They're all over the bay!"

We gazed with amazement at our first big school of dolphins. The day before, Jerry nearly jumped out of his kayak when one came up for air right next to him.

"The dolphin was so close, I could have reached down and petted it."

Maps can be deceptive. Our three-mile long, mind's eye, sandbar proved to be a swamp island of equal dimensions. In midsection, where the island almost pinched in half, we found a shell mound big enough to set our tent. A mile and a half west lay the channel leading to Bayou la Batre. Now and then, while Jerry cooked soup on the stove, we could see running lights of passing shrimp boats bound for the fishing village.

The bay was big—thirty miles deep and ten miles at its shortest width—its mouth was guarded by an island on one side of a three-mile gap and a fifteen-mile finger of land on the other. We were already in the protection of twelve-mile long Dauphin Island and if weather conditions improved, we would make the three-mile jump before the day was over. From experience though, we knew schedules seldom held on water—it was raining by the time we reached the end of the island.

"Well, you can keep them here in the marina garage, if you want," Lonnie told us. "And Tom and Diane will drive you down to the campground."

"No, I think we'll paddle down there. Then we have everything together. Thanks anyway," I said.

The Dauphin Island Campground lie a mile east. It was situated near the tip of the island amidst a small fleet of shrimp boats, a Coast Guard installation, an oceanographic school and Fort Gaines. We pitched camp underneath the tall pines at the edge of the campground and made plans to "sit it out."

Everyone on the island was friendly and hospitable. Jerry came back from a six-mile hike to the store in thirty minutes! A passerby on the road, running the length of the Island, picked him up and another party offered him a ride back to our camp.

Rain was falling when we fell asleep and continued; along with forty naught winds, through the next day.

A lull in the late afternoon allowed us to walk to the Sea house Restaurant where we had eaten lunch the day before. The trip was an hour journey through paradise. The road lead through misty corridors of tall pine, live oak and rain-soaked palmettos.

"Hope you can make it to the fish fry tomorrow night," the folks at the restaurant said. "All ya can eat for two bucks!"

"Wish we could, but we'll be gone by then—I hope. You have a beautiful Island here," I said.

"Yeah, we like it; kind of slack now. It's the off season for the tourists; gets pretty busy later on."

We did more exploring when fog kept us on the Island for another day.

Most of the instructors and students at the Oceano-graphic Consortium were gone. Those that remained gave us pamphlets to identify gulf vegetation and a dormitory room for the night"

"There's a remarkable correlation between state boundaries and topography around here," one of the instructors said. "Almost as soon as you leave Alabama and cross into Florida, the beaches become whiter and the water cleaner and greener."

Fort Gaines was situated a stones throw from the school on the eastern most tip of Dauphin Island. Once it guarded the entrance to Mobile Harbor, along with Fort Morgan on Mobile Point, three miles away. Because of its strategic position, Dauphin Island had seen Spanish, French and British forts, depending on who occupied the territory. The original work on Fort Gaines was started by the United States in 1821. The fortifications were built in the 1850s with thousands of slave labor bricks. The entrance wall was four hundred feet long. The other four walls averaged two hundred sixteen feet long, twenty-two feet high and five feet thick.

The structure, its bastions armed with cannons, looked formidable in the fog. Inside, we met a woman named "Sweetpea." She worked part-time at the fort and lived in the trailer closest to our tent. Her husband was a commercial fisherman.

"Saw you boys come in to the campground two days ago. Didn't see much movement over there, but could see a light in your tent," she said.

We talked about the island and its people.

"They used to call the campground 'Billy Goat Hole.' Sixteen years ago—before the bridge—the island was self-sufficient. The older natives still shy away from strangers," she said.

The bridge brought the bitter with the sweet—increased tourist trade stimulated the fishing community's economy, as well as, increased the petty crime.

"Ever seen 'gators before?" Sweetpea asked. "Go take a look at them. They're in the pen just across the courtyard."

All of them were captured on the island or in nearby swamps.

"Boy, I wouldn't want to tangle with any of them 'specially the 'Big Daddy.' He must be twelve feet long!" Jerry said.

The tent was down and some of our valuables carried to the dormitory, when the vegetable man rolled into camp honking his horn. He was a happy-go-lucky Cajun who picked up produce along the New Orleans fruit docks.

"What'll I owe ya for half a dozen kumquats and four bananas," I said.

He looked into the paper bag, winked and said: "Oh, about a dime."

We finished our chores, waved as the truck roared off to more customers and walked up to the Seashore Restaurant again.

"Well, we're here for the fish fry," I said.

"Sorry boys, no fish tonight, only shrimp," was the reply.

Each of us laid down two dollars and walked into the barroom for a feast of beer, shrimp and grits. The first beer came with the meal, but it seemed every time a can "bottomed out" there was a fresh one handed to us. Surrounded by an ever-growing pile of shrimp shells and beer cans, we talked, joked and carried on well past midnight.

Chapter 18

A Reunion with Tom and Micky

"We shall not cease from exploration and the end of all of our exploring will be to arrive where we started and know the place for the first time."

T.S. Eliot

The weather was clearing and by 11:45, we were making the "jump." A west wind increased our cruising speed to four miles per hour. Our kayaks crossed the same opening Union Admiral David Farragut charged through on August 5th, 1864, yelling the now famous remark: "Damn the torpedoes, full speed ahead!"

We passed Fort Morgan close to where the Tecumseh sank during the Battle of Mobile Bay. According to what we heard, the boat still carried the bodies of union sailors along with several hundred pounds of explosives.

Gently rolling waves took us to the east end of Mobile Bay, where we eventually paddled into a saltwater pool called Oyster Bay. A large, solitary Australian pine offered us a dry and reasonably level area to sleep. The tree was our security from the swampy area surrounding it.

"We can even climb it if the rising tide gets too high," I said.

It felt as though the tree liked us being there. I looked at it and knew, if it could speak, its comments would be reassuring. Before dozing off, I thought of my own consciousness as a living organism.

"Before I am, I was dispersed," I thought. "The elements now in my body were a part of something else, even possibly a tree like the one towering above us."

Sunday morning greeted us with a soaking, misty fog. We could see the tiny beads of water suspended in the air while we packed up. A radio station in Mobile announced limited visibility warnings for the city's freeways—fog related traffic accidents belonged to another life style remote and far away. For us, visibility was good enough on the canal and Jerry quickly turned the "useless" report off.

A moderate tidal current flowed against us for two hours until we reached the series of bays and lagoons leading to Pensacola and points beyond.

"We're almost out of Alabama. When we step ashore again, we'll be in Florida!" I said. "Like the man told us... look how green and clear the water's gettin'."

Paddling continued until dusk. Our plans were to call Tom and Micky from the marina, but no one answered the phone.

"Let's get some coffee and call a little later," I said.

We walked down the road to a place called Rusty's Fish Camp. It was packed inside. We asked the waitress what everyone was eating.

"You've never tried mullet?" she said. "It's all you can eat."

When the coffee was gone, we decided to try another phone call before settling down to eat.

"Nope... still no one home," I mumbled.

Meanwhile, Jerry was conversing with a family coming in from fishing. While on the phone, I saw their five-year-old son carrying a big stringer of fish up the dock. Before long, we were at Buddy and Sue's house eating a dinner of Red Snapper and sharing experiences.

Buddy brought us to our rigs about midnight and we paddled in bright moonlight to a sand point a half-mile away. It was warm and calm. The interface of gin clears water and white beach was impossible to determine. Our shapes caste moon shadows over delicately contoured surroundings and footprints glowed eerie green in wet sand as we walked to a dryer area.

In the background, in the far reaches of stillness across the bay, we could hear the surf pounding on the Gulf side of Perdido Key. Somehow, the contrast reminded me of what Buddy said earlier in the evening: "Shawn was born the day man walked on the moon and I was walkin' in the paddies of Nam!"

I opened my eyes to blinding sunshine and sand. Jerry was standing next to my sleeping bag.

"Come with me! It has landed," he said in a deep voice.

I was led to a fleshy globe, a foot in diameter, washed up on the beach.

"Like something from outer space," I said. "Yep! That's exactly what it is. Says here in the book that it's a Moon Jellyfish."

Tom and Micky had been looking for us since they received our Christmas card.

We conversed amidst an apartment full of maritime nicknacks and memorabilia.

"We really felt bad about leavin' you on that cold morning on the river. It gives me shivers just to think about it," Tom said. "We could of just set those little boats topside on the yacht or towed them, but you said no."

Bits and pieces of Tom's early days on the Gulf included: "I've seen sharks come up and eat the sea grass from boat hulls. When they'd get into a feeding frenzy, we could throw them anything. I saw one eat a toaster once! That bay the other night, I've seen the open Gulf the same way—not a ripple—and I've seen it stand on end!"

His sightseeing tour of Pensacola took us through the main part of town. Amidst the parking lots, gas stations, densely packed buildings and pavement, Tom then pointed out something very unique.

"See that house right here on the corner lot— the one with the big garden? It belongs to my brother-in-law's dad. He refuses to sell and continues to cultivate his garden as he's done for the past sixty years. Things are changin' fast here— the past is being swallowed up by development."

Like Mobile Bay, two forts guarded the entrance to Pensacola Bay. We visited Fort Pickens on Santa Rosa Island. The sea claimed Fort McRee, a half mile to the west, years ago. Fort Pickens, along with a portion of Santa Rosa Island, was part of Gulf Islands National Seashore. We strolled along the gulf side of the island and watched the surf break onto the shore.

"Later in the year, the sand gets so bleached it looks like flour. Notice how it squeaks under your shoes," Tom said. "After big storms people comb these beaches."

Now under protection, the beach and dunes of this part of the "Miracle Mile," would remain natural. Its open spaces would not be cluttered with high rises or would its surface feel the bite of dune buggy wheels.

"Hey look! We're passing right over the top of Fort McRee!" Jerry yelled.

There, below us, was a wall of the fort.

Chapter 19

Florida Islands

"Earth laughs and flowers."
Ralph Waldo Emerson

Randy Bauer

We crossed the entrance to Pensacola Bay and landed on Santa Rosa Island, two miles east of Fort Pickens, to explore a nearby nature trail. The walk took us past Slash and Sand Pines, Blackjack and Live Oaks, Wax Myrtle, Sweetbay Magnolia, Inkberry Bushes and patches of Saw Palmettos.

We set up the tent at dusk in a grassy area protected by overgrown dunes. Sea oats grew in a few places. Here, for the most part, its job was done—other plants had established themselves. However, on the primary dunes, on the gulf side, sea oats grew in abundance where their elaborate root system helped anchor sand from the sudden erosive action of storms. Consequently, laws protected sea oats from the whims of all terrain vehicles and people interested in uprooting them for floral arrangements.

Darkness closed around camp. A squashed, orange moon rose over the dunes during supper and disappeared as a black line moved across it—we were socked in by thick fog.

The experience re-enforced the warnings Tom had given us: "Comes in quick!" he told us. "And leaves you blind!"

He related the time he and Micky were fishing in their boat off Coney Island. They day was clear as Tom bent down to grab some tackle. When he raised his head, he could see no more than five feet in front of him!

Santa Rosa Island was forty-five miles long and created a narrow sound bordered by Pensacola Bay on the west and Choctowhatchee Bay on the east. Waiting for the morning fog to lift gave us less than seven hours of daylight for paddling. We took one of the many "boat passes" under the Pensacola Beach Bridge to avoid being tangled in tackle from dozens of fishermen above us. Shortly afterward, we cruised by Naval Live Oaks on our port side. Just as naval stores of Long Leaf pine provided pine tar and pitch for caulking, these trees were placed under protective management to provide the Pensacola Naval Yard with timber for shipbuilding.

Jellyfish paraded by suspended in various depths. The clear water varied in color and made me thirsty.

"The limes, forest greens and yellows look like Kool-Aid to me. I almost wanted to dive right in and drink my fill," I told Jerry.

The end of the day found us camped underneath pines on the north side of the sound.

"This area reminds me so much of northern Minnesota in the summertime," I wrote in a letter home. "Yesterday, during a hike, we saw loons in their gray winter coats."

We paddled twenty miles the next day and spent two days on a small sand island directly across from Mary Esther, Florida—a suburb of Fort Walton Beach. Again, fog was the culprit. It settled in for the night and stayed for the next thirty-six hours. The island was security for us. The vapor sucked up sounds like a soundproof room and obliterated any shore lights. The noise and distractions of a crowded city a hundred yards away didn't exist in our world.

Morning came and the blanket still covered us. By ten o'clock, the mist showed indications of lifting.

"We can paddle in it. The only thing I'm worried about, Jerry, is getting run down by something."

My fears lasted an hour; they evaporated with the fog.

Large hotels lined the eastern side of Santa Rosa Island, directly across from Fort Walton Beach.

"I'm glad we're movin' along. It looks like this place is strictly for the 'Big Time'," I said. "What a contrast from the other side of the island"

The "narrows" opened into Chactowhatchee Bay. We steered clear of the inlet at Destin, heeding the warnings people had given about being "sucked out" with an ebb tide. Fortunately, the bay remained reasonably calm throughout the day. Its twenty-five by five mile spread, with the right wind direction, could easily become a "washing machine."

We covered better than half the bay and camped on the tip of Four mile Point. There was daylight to spare but not campsites. Our charts indicated the next dry land on our course lie six miles on the other side of Hogtown Bayou and marshy Live Oak Point.

"It is cool now," I wrote. "In the fifties. A north wind is blowing through the pines. Now and then drafts reach us as they rattle the palmettos. We are on the Intracoastal Waterway canal again. Actually, the canal is below us—we are camped on a levee. If I walked thirty feet, I'd fall off a twenty foot sand bank into the waterway. If I walked forty feet to the south and over the levee, I would fall into a swamp!"

A wilderness of swamp, marsh and forest surrounded us. Jerry commented: "This area is so different than I thought Florida would be. It's not heavily populated, 'cept for the wildlife."

From what we learned from a fellow we met on the levee before dark, wildlife in the area included: white tail deer, squirrels, raccoons, wild hogs, turkeys, water moccasins and alligators. He didn't, however, mention anything about the "creature" that lifted Jerry's kayak out of the water!

The incident occurred shortly after we had entered the canal. We were paddling along as usual when Jerry's kayak suddenly grounded on something and proceeded to rise, exposing the entire side of the kayak's hull. Then, the kayak was gently lowered back into the water. At least thirty seconds passed before Jerry blurted out: "Did you see that?"

"No I didn't, but I saw what it did! Whatever it was, it must have been awful big!"

Afterwards, we conjured up explanations as to the creature's identity: dolphin, manatee, manta ray, a log and our imagination, Nessie.

The "creature" may have been a giant sea turtle coming up for air. Turtle heads we had frequently seen bobbing to the surface were as large as a humans and we had heard they could weigh almost a ton with a carapace exceeding five feet! Regardless, the incident will forever remain shrouded in mystery.

The fellow we met on the levee told us he knew the Captain of the dredge and invited us to stop by for breakfast the next morning. We tied up alongside, climbed aboard and quickly learned Johnny did in fact know the Captain because he was the Captain!

The cooks made whatever we wanted—four eggs apiece, toast, sausage, grits and coffee. When breakfast was finished, we proceeded to shave and shower. By the time we were done, lunch was ready!

"Look at those guys eat," Jerry heard Ralph, the first mate, whisper to Johnny. "They must have been starving."

We were on the dredge for four hours. While we carried our "clean up gear" back to the kayaks, Ralph approached us: "You boys buy a good meal for yourselves on me." He shoved a ten-dollar bill into my pocket!

West Bay was fuming when we reached it. Common sense told us to hold up in a sheltered area at the mouth of the canal and cross the water in the morning.

From someone else's point of view, our nylon tent glowing green with light from the candle lantern must have looked strange.

"Hey! I just saw a light flash on the tent," Jerry said.

A few seconds later, we heard muffled voices and footsteps.

"What is it? What is it?" the voices kept saying.

"Come on over!" I yelled.

And Jerry and I popped from the tent.

"Don't shoot! Don't shoot!" the hunters yelled back.

They thought they had bumped into the game warden on a stake out.

"Wow! Think we just scared the hell out of all of us," Jerry said.

The four of us talked for a few minutes and then said good night just before it started to rain.

Ever since we arrived in saltwater, Jerry and I had heard of the "no-see-ems." We didn't pay any attention to them until the next morning. The warm, calm night brought the critters out by the millions and we had slept with the tent flaps open. The insects, no bigger than pepper specks, made sleeping in our tent living hell. They crawled up our noses, in our eyes, ears and mouths, biting and chewing anything exposed.

"My face feels like it's on fire from these bites," I told Jerry.

We tore the tent down and ran for the kayaks. There, the bugs feasted until we launched.

"That's enough to drive a person crazy," Jerry said.

We stopped at an isolated beach bordered with live oak draped with Spanish moss. The area was beautiful and clean. It was obvious people had been there but we couldn't find any trash. Jerry and I went our own ways exploring the trails connecting the campsites.

"In these surroundings, I should be wearing a white suit and sippin' a mint julep," I thought.

The atmosphere made me think of other things, like the fleet of junked warships we had paddled by when we left St. Andrew. They were cutting the ancient destroyers and two small submarines into scrap metal. I wished that was the way it was with all war materials, but I knew better—the ships had merely given way to more lethal arsenals.

The no-see-ems were small enough to fly right through the tent's mosquito netting. Determined to keep the hordes out, we zipped the flaps shut and plugged every nook and cranny with spare clothing and beach towels. The trick kept the bugs away, but not the "foragers."

"Last night it was the coon hunters... tonight it's the 'coons," I recorded in the log.

Rattling pots and pans shattered the stillness of our camp. Jerry's mess kit was found ten feet from the tent and an inverted cooking kettle had an obvious "tampered with" look.

"I'm glad it's not bears," I said. "These critters are more of a nuisance than anything else."

We watched telltale silhouettes of the "bandits" climb over our covered kayaks before they slipped into the shadows. They never bothered us the rest of the night.

Chapter 20

Dry Land— Overstreet and Apalachicola

"I am forever walking upon the shores, betwixt the sand and the foam. The high tide will erace my footprints and the wind will blow away the foam. But the sea and shore will remain forever."

Kahlil Gibran

The tiny borough of Overstreet lies Southeast of Panama. We reached the only dry place for miles around at dusk after paddling twenty-four miles of East Bay and three miles of canal.

Overstreet consisted of a combination general store, post office and gas station on one side of the canal; a swing-bridge made from an old barge floating on the canal, a control shack, outhouse and our tent on the west side of the canal.

Jerry and I spent a large part of the evening conversing with Conrad, the second shift bridge tender.

"Back durin' the Depression we used to make kayaks from wood frames too, 'cept we covered them with layers of newspaper and varnish," he said." Hull was as hard as nails—a twenty-two bullet would glance right off!"

"Wish I could say the same for my hull," I said.

In the morning, Jerry and I warmed up at the Overstreet store.

"Store was established in 1916," the folks said. "Shortly after the canal went through, not many roads cut through this part of the country, too much swamp—it's actually closer by water to Apalachicola than by road!"

Twelve miles from Overstreet we intersected the Port St. Joe Canal and shortly after passed under a small bridge marked "White City" on our charts. The surrounding land took on an eerie and abandoned feel. We paddled by the remnants of a logging trestle and entered a world that would have delighted any swamp witch. The water was fresh. Cypress covered with Spanish moss were everywhere—some living, others dead, contorted stumps stuck out of the water, as well as, thousand of cypress knees. The canal opened into Lake Wimico—a five-mile stretch of water set in the middle of a cypress jungle. From a distance, the shore looked solid enough, but it wasn't.

"Keep your eyes peeled for any high ground," I said. "We'd better find some in the next forty minutes, otherwise it'll be dark."

We scanned the shore with binoculars—nothing.

"Let's see if there's anything on the charts. There's a place called Huckleberry Landing about three and a half miles from here, Jerry."

It was dark when we reached the end of the lake.

"Looks like there's a fisherman down the river," I said. "Let's ask him about the landing."

The fisherman turned out to be a contorted cypress stump. We knew it would be extremely easy to miss the high land in the dark, so we timed our progress. At the end of thirty minutes, we stopped and scanned the shore with flashlights. The light revealed cypress and then picked up a concrete ramp. We were at Huckleberry Landing!

Apalachicola was our first mail pick-up in thirty-four days. At the most, we expected to spend one layover day at the town preparing for the three hundred mile "jump" to Tarpon Springs. Four days later, we were on our way. Even then, it was too early for us to depart. We simply fell in love with the community and its people.

Apalachicola was a seacoast town of about three thousand. We saw oyster boats and shrimpers everywhere. Tom, at the marina, said that over ninety percent of Florida's oysters were landed here. He also told Jerry about the "Great Master."

"You can blindfold Great Master, put him anywhere on Apalachicola Bay and he'd know where he was," Tom said.

We saw "Great Master" while we ate supper at a place called "The Grill." The weathered gentleman sat down at a table and soon was surrounded by other fishermen. It seemed that "Great Master" didn't say much, but when he talked, everyone listened. We wanted to meet "Great Master" and tap some of his wisdom about the miles ahead, but the occasion never came. When I looked toward his table, it was empty.

"I just saw him go out the back way," Jerry said. "Just as quietly as he came in."

We spent Sunday repairing, repacking, drying gear and washing clothes.

"By the maps, it looks like we'll be spending a few nights in the swamps, Randy. Tom says there's not much to camp on in the next hundred or so miles."

My biggest worry was my boat. If it sprung a leak in an area where I couldn't land, I'd be in a real mess. Therefore, I spent most of my time reinforcing patches with extra glue and sheet metal tape. Jerry spent time repacking food so it could be easily reached.

Near suppertime, a sailboat pulled into the marina to spend the night. On board was Barney, a vacationing Everglades Park Ranger, who had kayaked along the swampy coast of Apalachee Bay. By the time he was done poring over our charts, Barney had circled every fragment of dry land he knew in between Apalachicola and Tarpon Springs. True, some were farther apart than others and would require a bit of luck and long hours of paddling to reach, but now we knew they were there.

Apalachicola had a NOAA Station above the post office. Jerry and I stopped there in the morning to check weather conditions and left with three reporters from the local newspaper. Kerry, Charlie and Jay were intrigued by our adventure. While we posed for pictures on the dock, surprisingly, Dave, the fellow we had met in Memphis, walked up.

"Well, I see you guys made it this far," he said.

The reunion called for a celebration. We had it that night at Kerry and his wife's home.

Dave's brother, John, was now with him on the sailboat. They, like us, were preparing for the jump to Tarpon

Springs. We talked about the water and close calls and listened to Kerry give a rundown on local history.

Union gunboats oftentimes blockaded the Apalachicola River during the Civil War. Earlier in the day, Kerry showed us an abandoned mansion, about a mile upstream from the mouth, where a lady used to set a barrel on her roof to signal Confederate lumbermen that Union forces were near. If the barrel was visible, the loggers would turn their boats around and go back upstream.

"Most of the big cypress has been harvested in the area," Kerry told us. "Most of it was shipped to Europe. Liverpool, England was built from Apalachicola cypress. The harvest continued for years. Some lumber outfits hired men to pole the log rafts downriver to the Port. When almost to Apalachicola, someone hiding in the brush would shoot them as they passed by."

The surrounding swampland was big and held many secrets.

"The light in the next yard is the last one for miles and miles," Kerry said.

From his commentary and our experience in part of the vast quagmire, it didn't take much imagination for us to figure out why a portion of land just north of Apalachicola was called Tate's Hell Swamp.

Jerry and I stayed two nights at Kerry and Robyn's home. We were fogbound the morning we planned to leave and spent the day at the newspaper office watching Kerry, Charlie and Jay "in action." In between orange seed spitting contests, Thursday's paper began to take shape.

"If you guys stick around a few more days, you'll see the article about yourselves," Kerry said.

"No, we'll be gone," Jerry said. " We've gotta leave tomorrow or we might grow roots here. If the weather's good, we'll be gone."

Dave and Johnny left early in the morning bound for Daytona Beach. Barney and his dad left the day before. Jerry and I were gone by late afternoon.

Before our departure, we visited the town's museum. It was dedicated to an obscure inventor named Dr. John Gorrie. His discovery was made in 1844 when Apalachicola was a cotton port and malaria raged in the region. Thinking the disease was caused by "swamp vapors" and heat aggravated the situation, Dr. Gorrie cooled two hospital rooms with refrigeration equipment. When ice was found in the tubes of one machine, the surprised doctor went on to build an ice-making machine. No longer would ice have to be shipped from the Great Lakes.

"Who back then would have ever dreamed in a hundred years time Apalachicola's commerce would switch from cotton to shellfish? Who would have dreamed, including Dr. Gorrie, that refinements of his invention would play an integral part in preserving those shellfish?"

Those thoughts swept through my mind as we paddled past the dockside ice plant and stopped at the back door of the newspaper office. Kerry was there. He took a few more black and white shots and then threw down an empty collapsible developer container.

"I washed it out good... take it along, you'll need it in the Everglades."

Randy Bauer, on Bank, and Jerry Mimbach Put Kayak in Indian River at Jensen Beach
. . . the two young men are halfway through 7,000-mile journey they hope to complete this fall

Kayaking Down the River
No Sunday Afternoon Trip

By JANE SCHOLZ
Popular News Writer

They packed up their gear and shoved off in mid-September hoping to beat the cold weather as they paddled down the Mississippi River from its Minnesota headwaters, but winter caught up with them along the way.

Four times they paddled through snowstorms, and at night they huddled in their tent against temperatures that dipped to 16 degrees.

It sounds like an excerpt from the skins of animals but not naugahyde. They didn't have to worry about hunting and fishing for their meals, either—they bought supplies at grocery stores in river towns along the way.

Randy says it's the romance of kayaking that inspired him to make the trip. For Jerry, it was a desire to really see the country.

Another reason for along the trip was that the pair didn't really have much to do in Minnesota. He come down. Randy, a college graduate, couldn't get

Canal to Lake Ontario, cross Georgia Bay to Lake Superior and paddle across Lake Superior to Duluth, Minn. and Lake Itasca, their starting point. They hope to finish the trip in the fall.

"People ask us when we're going to be somewhere — what's our ETA (estimated time of arrival)," Randy laughed. "We have more of an "EAM" — Estimated Arrival Month — and even that may be a few weeks off."

The twosome started off as a threesome at Lake Itasca, but the third man gave up

Chapter 21

The Everglades

"I care only to entice people to look at nature's loveliness. My own special self is nothing. I want to be like a flake of grass to which light passes."
John Muir

It was four p.m. when we left. The wind was blowing from off shore and across East Bay when we launched.

"Don't get too close to the breakwater. The chops there are bad!" Jerry yelled.

The structure was actually a mile-long finger of fill forming the causeway crossing the bay. Once on the other side, the water was calm.

"Look at all the people! They're scoopin' up oysters from the bottom with rakes, Jerry."

There must have been a hundred twelve-foot boats in the shallows off East Point. We paddled through the flotilla in morning light following St. George Sound to Carrabelle.

Jerry and I envisioned a quiet half hour or so in the Isle O' St. James Restaurant at Carrabelle drinking a few cups of coffee before camping for the evening. What we didn't realize was Jay from the Apalachicola Times had dropped off a stack of newspapers a few hours before we arrived. The newspaper had given us a full-page story; we signed autographs and talked with a half dozen people, including the Marine Patrol.

"Did ja see anything unusual in the water this mornin'?" he asked us. "A twelve-foot boat capsized in chops under the East Bay Bridge. One fella made it to shore, the other two are missin'. Found the boat in the Bay seven miles from the Bridge!"

The officer was gone before we could thank him for the coffee. We were ready to depart when the owner said: "Why don't you stay for supper. It's on the house!"

Fred, his wife Lois and daughter Gail were bound for the Florida Keys. For them Carrabelle was a "spring-board" to Cedar Keys one hundred and fifteen miles across Apalachee Bay. His family and yacht would hit the Keys tonight. For Jerry and me, the run would take almost two weeks and more than twice the mileage.

Fred told us stories of Apalachee Bay that didn't sit too well with us. "It's one mean stretch of water," we learned. The bay is a nightmare for most navigators because of its reefs and choppy water that can grind and pound a boat to pieces. Deadman Bay and nicknames like "Suicide Alley" reflected the nature of the waters we were about to enter.

"Our day has been longer than Fred's and he's already in Cedar Keys," I moaned.

It was dark and we were still paddling. At dusk, Shell Point looked so close. Now, the lights seemed to grow no larger. The dip of the paddle blades was all I could hear in the quiet night. Our bodies ached from fatigue and we were hungry.

Finally, the shore was there. We were at Shell Point, but where was the channel to the marina? The darkness hid it. We paddled up and down the shore three times before Jerry spotted the way and once in the channel, I proceeded to smash directly into a barnacle covered piling. I couldn't see! I was so tired I couldn't focus my eyes! Fourteen hours of paddling had taken its toll.

The next day, growing weekend crowds from Tallahassee made us edgy.

"I wish I knew this 'tourist resort' when it was a fish camp or when they used to mine salt around here during the Civil War," I grumbled. "Let's get out of here!"

Barney had circled St. Marks' Lighthouse and Rock Island as our next two stepping-stones. St. Marks was seven and a half miles away and the "Rock," thirty-six! Our choice was obvious.

The 18 lighthouse, adjacent buildings, water, saltwater marsh and scattered highlands were an artist's paradise. The scene melted away our uneasiness. The place was wonderful until fading daylight-unleashed hordes of hungry mosquitoes. We took turns cooking supper and running back to the tent for shelter.

"Soup's almost done, Randy. Hell! How do you turn this thing off?" Jerry shouted.

The stove had blown its relief valve and a foot-long blowtorch flame shot from it. We ate half-boiled noodle soup in the tent and wondered what would break down next.

"I'm glad our shelter's still in one piece. If you listen, you can hear the mosquitoes pelting the outside surface," Jerry said.

The bugs made a sound not unlike rain. They literally covered the outside of the tent and bit through the wall if we leaned up against the nylon during the night.

"Somewhere through the mist there's land. Somewhere there's an ocean. Somewhere there's a world," I said to myself.

Chapter 22

Rock Island

"If you love it enough, anything will talk with you."

George Washington Carver

The fog came in unexpectedly soon after we launched from St. Marks. Jerry and I followed a compass heading to the Aucilla River eleven miles across Apalachee Bay. At New Orleans, Jerry had mounted a small automobile compass in the cockpit of his kayak. The dial floated in a plastic globe and didn't have to be held steady. Bearings from the maps, taken with a Pathfinder compass, were transferred to Jerry's compass and we pushed ahead through the cloud. Changing wave patterns, exposed, razor sharp oyster beds and crab trap floats reassured us we were actually making progress.

"The Bay in this area has been poisoned by paper mills. You can smell it in the air. Look how brown the water is," I said.

Suddenly our thoughts were diverted from the pollution to a shadow dead ahead. Land! We had reached the swampy banks of the Aucilla River—at least that's what the sign said nailed to the post.

We were halfway to Rock Island and celebrated our "navigation skills" by gobbling down several peanut butter and jelly sandwiches before pushing on. The fog lifted a bit. It was a relief to see the shoreline but aggravating to feel the wind pick up. Eventually, we could see our refuge far in the distance.

"I think It'll be dark by the time we get there unless we speed up," Jerry said.

The wind was working against us and the wind was wearing us out. In the growing darkness, I lost track of Jerry. He was somewhere between the island and me, but I couldn't see him. The chops were big enough now to capsize either one of us and I tried not to think of an accident alone on the water.

The time we were separated seemed like forever. I was worried and angry with Jerry for letting his excitement carry him away. The work and frustration of the past three days had been working on me and I felt like breaking my kayak paddle over his head.

A hundred yards off the island, I thought I saw the faint silhouette of the tent on shore. I yelled at the top of my voice but there was no answer. All I could here was the slapping and breaking of waves. I yelled again, still no answer.

"Here I am!" Jerry yelled back.

And even then I couldn't see him.

Again he yelled: "I'm right here!"

We exchanged "words of wisdom" for a few minutes. The discussion probably would have amused a listener if there were any around—or was there? If the dark square, silhouette wasn't the tent, then what was it? We paddled closer and shined a light on the object. It was a home-made houseboat anchored firmly to the rocky tidal flat of "our" island.

"Ahoy! Ahoy! Anyone aboard? Ahoy there!" I shouted.

Again, the only sound was the slapping of the waves. We would investigate the boat in the morning. Now, all that mattered was getting ashore, hauling the kayaks to a safe place above the marl flats, getting some nourishment into our bodies and sleeping.

Jerry and I woke to fog and a strong south wind.

"Looks like another layover day, Randy"

There was nothing we could do but wait. During breakfast, in a world so seemingly isolated and cutoff from anything and everything else, we were horrified to see two men walking along the rocky shore in thick rubber hip boots. They were commercial crabbers who used the island as a way station for their traps ten miles out in the Gulf. We talked with them while they waited to see if the winds would die down. They had come from somewhere up the Fenholloway River about four miles to the southeast.

"The old man leaves his boat here. We was just goin' over to it to make some coffee when we saw your boats," one of them said.

Like us, the crabbers complained about the sickening, sweet smell in the air.

"Comes from the mill up the Fenholloway," the older one said. "People 'round here have nicknamed the place 'stinkholloway'. Used to be lots of mullet in the river, but now there's nothin'!"

The wind increased, but the crabbers left to retrieve their catch anyway. The two disappeared into the mist with their tiny, open boat. They said there were eight-foot seas ten miles out yesterday and at least the same height today. Stone crabs were their bread and butter and the weather wasn't going to stop them.

"Ya get about a dollar a pincher. Ya keep the claw and throw the crab back. It grows 'nother one," they said.

On a twenty-minute circumnavigation of the island, I thought of a story they told about the stormy night their dad rode his boat over the top of the island—right over submerged palmettos, grass and poison ivy and right between the scattered live oak and small cabbage palms.

Jerry and I took separate "tours" of the "Rock." To me, the shoreline looked like decayed coral or very old, pockmarked sandstone. Amidst an area where everything else was either water or marsh, I wondered how it originated—possibly an old reef. Jerry on his jaunt wondered why the island's only noticeable inhabitant was a large Barred Owl. It never occurred the owl was the apex of the Rock Island Food Pyramid—until that night.

"We're surrounded by them. Must be hundreds of the little bastards!" I said.

We threw more wood on the fire and Jerry readied a club. We were being invaded by Rice Rats! Some ran right into our food supply. A few bold ones darted across our legs! By the time the evening closed, we had all of our food and smellables suspended between trees. The little devils didn't bother us after we hit the sack. Apparently, the rats were attracted by the campfire and food cooking and scared away by the three casualties from Jerry's club.

Chapter 23

Gales at Horseshoe Beach

"In the end, we will conserve only what we love, we will love only what we understand, we will understand only what we are taught."

Baba Dioum

It was foggy when we left the Rock and the wind had switched to the southeast. Under normal conditions we would have stayed another day, but we were low on fresh water and were afraid the rats would attack in full force come evening.

Our course took us to Dekle Beach, a one-time fish camp now owned by private individuals. We arrived soaking wet, felt miserable and were greeted by an older woman who said we would have to go out into the fog and wind and find another place to camp. Jerry and I told her it was too dangerous to return to sea, but "stone face" would not compromise.

So, we "left," paddled our kayaks two hundred feet down the channel, carried them to the top of the sandy bank and walked five miles to a grocery store. The woman there was good to us. We talked about the area and learned the abandoned buildings marked Jug Island on our charts, adjacent to Dekle Beach, were at one time a sponging camp.

"If you see a fisherman walking around with a bad limp, they probably stepped on a stingray— got a poison spine at the base of their tail sharp enough to puncture boots!" she warned. "They sit right on the bottom, so shuffle your feet ahead of you when you're wading around to scare them off."

We also asked her about the platforms we had seen in the area.

"Oh, those wooden platforms," she said. "They're bird racks. Years ago a fella built those things. Thought he was gonna get rich harvesting bird manure, you know, like bat guano! It never panned out for him. The last hurricane wrecked most of them."

We finished up our bologna sandwiches and left with a can of free mosquito repellent.

"Here! Take this," she said. "You'll need it sooner or later!"

By mid morning, the crabby lady found us camped on the other side of her canal. She was screaming, cursing and yelling at us threatening to call the sheriff if we didn't leave immediately. It would have been interesting to stay, but the fog was lifting and we didn't think much of her hospitality.

A northwest wind pushed us from our musty camp at Hagen's Cove sixteen miles to Steinhatchee. The town was built along a river with the same name. Like so many others, Steinhatchee was an old fishing village. We paddled by scores of crab boats and other commercial craft and came to rest at a marina catering to sport fishermen. The folks there were friendly to us. Jerry and I slept on the floating docks that night and paddled out of town with the dried salt spray washed from our bodies and three post cards in hand with the following instructions: "We get all kinds of people stopping here at the marina, but we never here or seen them again. I'd appreciate if you'd send one at Miami, the other at New York City and the last one when you get home."

Big raindrops made strange sounds as they hit the water three hours out from Steinhatchee.

"Look there's bubbles on the water. It's going to stop soon, Jerry."

Four hours later it was raining harder than ever and we were soaked to the bone. Handling the wet paddle shafts had rubbed our hands raw and I didn't believe in bubbles on the water anymore. Both of us sat silently in our kayaks for nearly an hour while the tin roof of the Horseshoe Beach Marina resounded like a tight drumhead.

We discovered the mayor of Horseshoe Beach in the grocery store-cafe on the other side of the canal. He didn't look like he owned most of the cottages and land in the village, but that's what the folks said. The mayor wanted to rent us a cottage for the night, but we convinced him a sheltered boat garage would suffice. A few hours later, we had our tent pitched in a vacant stall and were sound asleep.

Horseshoe Beach looked abandoned when we arrived—it wasn't now. Nearly everyone stopped to examine the "curiosities" at the boat shelter where equipment drying in the sun was strewn all over the place.

"We usually have oatmeal on days like this," Jerry said to one visitor.

"How about a change of pace?" was his reply.

Soon he returned with a dozen eggs and a steaming kettle of grits.

"Here, try this on for size. It'll stick to your ribs."

Our equipment looked safe, so we left for a while and returned to a camp full of bird dirt and shredded wrappers.

"Those gulls had a ball with your bread," rattled a voice from a boat next to my kayak.

It was our first encounter with "Bob" the "old sea captain" of Horseshoe Beach. Two years ago, he stopped to repair the "Eight Horse"—his wooden single cabin boat. He was a diehard character with a weather beaten face, scruffy beard and clear blue eyes that sparkled when he talked. He wore an ancient, black captain's hat and chain-smoked cigars. Bob had charisma and a gift for gab. During our first night at Horseshoe Beach, Bob was on the Gulf with a shrimper.

"It was beautiful out there. We were right beside several company ships. Their wings out made them look like great big birds on the water. If I'd known you were here, you coulda come along," he said.

The weather turned bad and we were given a small cabin to stay while the gale blew itself out. Bob was with us most of the time. I remember crawling into the bunk one night while Bob was talking with Jerry and waking up at 4:00 a.m. to discover Jerry fast asleep and Bob still sitting at the table. Conversations ranged far and wide.

We winnowed out topics such as: The astronauts traveled at the speed of light when they went to the moon, but kept others: Streaks in the sky this evening, winds gonna blow all night and probably tomorrow and if the tops of the trees are moving just like that, waves in the gulf are too big to go out.

The gale was at its height the third night. High tide was at midnight and the wind had added several more feet, pushing water well above the docks. Bob, Jerry and I spent most of the night helping Woody, the marina caretaker, re-tie boats and pull others out of the water. In spite of the effort, one line ripped off a rising yacht's cleat and another, across the canal, was fast aground the seawall.

"It's a good thing you guys stayed here," Bob said. "If you would have been on any of the low islands around here, you'd been washed off. Lots of fishermen have drowned that way."

His warning reminded us of Rock Island and how lucky we were not to be there during the storm—he had lost two sons to the sea.

Bob was asleep when we left Horseshoe Beach. I knocked on the Eight Horse's hull, but no one answered.

"You gotta learn patience, boys. It will keep you from getting' hurt or killed," were words of wisdom he left us.

Chapter 24

The Crow's Nest
and Gooney Bird Marina

"People who successfully maintained a low material standard of living and successfully cultivate a deep, intense inner life are much better able to consistently maintain a deep ecological view and act on behalf of it. And I sit down and breathe deeply and just feel where I am."

Arne Naess

We were caught in darkness six miles from the Keys but managed to pick our way through the shallows into the harbor. Low tide grounded Jerry's boat, but mine, with a shallower draft, allowed me to find deeper water.

"If you can pull your rig off the bank, ya got deeper water up here!" I yelled.

We found the channel and soon were in the marina.

After the boats were carried to shore, we decided to sleep in them. Jerry called the experience a "living nightmare." "I was wedged in my kayak all night long and woke up with a stiff back. My legs were toward the stern and my head was through the widest crossframe. I couldn't change my body position and could only move my right arm just enough to open and close my sleeping bag zipper." The experiment was never repeated.

A road connected the main portion of Cedar Keys to the mainland. We explored the village before the tourists woke and tried to imagine what the place was like before it "was found out." Still, the Keys retained some magic of yesterday. We walked past white, wooden buildings with second story porches and ate breakfast at an old drugstore. A lady working at the community library said the Keys were an important railroad head and principal shipping port in the Eighteen Hundreds. At one time, there were active salt mines and, as the name implied, large stands of cedar trees.

By noon the increasing activity and heat of the day had evaporated the early morning mystique. It was time for us to leave. We launched from the boat basin and headed across the flat water of Waccasassa Bay. Our navigational aid was a five hundred foot marker twenty miles away—the twin stacks of the Crystal River Power Plant.

The dead calm and eighty-three degree temperature cooked us in the bay.

"We're startin' to get into some of that Florida heat," Jerry said. "We've rounded the Panhandle and daily progress will bring us further and further south; things will warm up real fast!"

That night the temperature never dipped below seventy while we slept out of our sleeping bags for the first time on the trip. The tent was pitched on Marl Spoil Island a mile from the incomplete Trans-Florida Barge Canal. As I lie on my sleeping bag, I wondered what would happen if the canal, stopped by executive order, was completed? Would the mixing of Gulf and Atlantic waters invite an invasion of life from the Atlantic devastating the Gulf? After all, an introduced tree, the Australian pine, grew on the very sand spoil we slept. Could something deadlier creep through an open water corridor?

I slept fitfully during the night and woke at 3:00 a.m. to discover water lapping at our tent pegs! Before dark, the water line was fifty feet from the tent. Now, it looked as though we'd be awash. The kayaks were next to the tent, lined securely to rocks and a smashed crab trap but we didn't have to board. The tide tables were accurate and sleep came again after the water retreated.

The jetties for the Crystal River Power Plant ran nearly six miles into the Gulf. The trick was to find one of two main openings in the spoil wall and we ended up backtracking seven miles before we crossed the jetty. Soon we were in a region marked Suncoast Keys. Even though yellow on our charts indicated high ground, there was none to be seen.

"I think we've finally entered mangrove country," Jerry. "All of the islands and keys we passed were covered with a jungle-like growth of leaves, branches and roots. It'd be impossible for us to camp on any of these islands unless we had a machete to chop through the maze. Even then, I don't think we could. Barney's got a place here circled at the mouth of the Homosassa River. Let's try it!"

The decision to put up at the Homosassa River mouth instead of Bayport, a town fifteen more miles down the coast, was a good one. A fancy building appeared from behind the mangroves and we paddled to it to investigate.

"Some type of resort house," I said. "Out in the middle of nowhere."

The building called the "Crow's Nest" was part of a recreational facility with its main complex five miles up the Homosassa River.

"People from the hotel come here by water taxi," John, the manager at the Crow's Nest said.

We ate a late lunch there and filled our water jugs before camping on the shell island across the channel from the building.

"Fresh water's a premium here. It has to be hauled in by barge," John said. "Hey, if you don't mind, I'll try to drum up some publicity for you. I'll let you know tomorrow morning. You're invited for breakfast!"

John and his wife opened the door to newspaper reporters, a hotel room at the complex and a change from our normal campfire meals.

The complex included an area called the "Attraction"—a zoo, in a forest of live oak, Magnolias and palms, stocked with peacocks, alligators, herons, monkeys and geese. In spite of its natural setting, the "Attraction" felt like a prison to us. The tour saddened more than intrigued us. The wildness and freedom we shared with our brothers "out there" was not present here. The most depressing thing we saw was a chimpanzee. The chimp had been raised and loved by human parents until it grew too strong and unruly to handle. As a result, the chimp was caged and now part of the "Attraction." He'd throw rocks and feces at anyone approaching too close. From what we heard, he'd go berserk whenever a former member of his human family "visited."

We met many people during our "public relations" stay. One person was planning to backpack to California by eating only high protein brownie bars made from his own recipe. While talking with him, we arrived at common ground describing traveling as a personal search for the "truth."

With the "Attraction" firmly branded in our minds, a field naturalist with four PhDs, talked with us about semi-domesticated animals. John related a story about an alligator that was innocently fed marshmallows. People came from all around to see the alligator eat. Then one day the alligator grabbed hold of something besides a marshmallow—the leg of an unsuspecting bather.

"The father couldn't save the girl—'gator just pulled her right down!"

In my notes that night, I summarized an important pearl of wisdom John gave us: "Have a general knowledge of things in your field. Many people become so specialized, they are unable to communicate with others."

Back at the Crow's Nest, we received careful directions on how to thread our way through the Chassahowitzka National Wildlife Refuge. From atop the lookout tower, we could see the maze of mangrove islands three and a half miles away.

"Just take the shortcut through the pass," went the information. Jerry and I kept whispering it over and over again—until we were lost.

Around and around the maze we went. Through one channel till it dead-ended and then back down another.

"This is insane!" I shouted.

At last, we found a marked swamp buggy trail and followed it to open water.

"I hope no one at the Crow's Nest saw us, Jerry. They'd be laughing their heads off. How embarrassing!"

We were glad to be on open water again. However, west winds increased steadily through the afternoon and forced us to retreat behind the lee side of a mangrove island for protection.

"Pine Island is marked "high ground," has a road into it, but it's about three miles away," Jerry said. "And we can't stay behind this island all night."

We decided to charge ahead and rode small breakers into the narrow beach on Pine Island. Both of us got soaked, but were now safe from the wind. While unpacking, Jerry called something to my attention: "I don't know how hard the wind is blowing, but look at this!" His wet boat cushion was pinned by the wind four feet up the trunk of a palm tree!

The wind switched to the northwest during the night and the Gulf flattened considerably. The water was clear and shallow. We had to paddle a mile from shore in most places. Even then, we often dragged bottom. "As a general rule of thumb, water drops about a foot for every mile out in this area," I remembered John saying back at the Crow's Nest. Rocks were everywhere in the emerald green and lemon yellow water. They resembled aged barnacle clusters—very craggy, jagged, pitted and dark brown in color. Boulders strewn along the sandy bottom in one area had been given the name Devils Rock Yard.

Jerry was at least a hundred yards ahead when I crossed the channel marker leading to Port Richey. Both of us had been paddling for the last couple hours in what we called a "mind set" or trance to relieve ourselves from the late afternoon paddling doldrums.

"Hold up!" I yelled.

On the third try, I shattered the spell and got Jerry's attention.

"This is the place!"

Gordy, the owner of the Gooney Bird Marina, didn't know what to think when we pulled in—we didn't either.

"I thought you guys were just practicing for the canoe races on the river. We have a big doins coming up," he said.

"Can we sleep here for the night?

"Hell no! You can sleep over there in the building where it's warm and dry."

Gordy left us to ourselves. We walked up town and found an all night restaurant where we ate and pulled together the happenings of the day.

That night both of us began to see through the myth—we were not taking the journey— the journey was taking us! We were now operating on "function time," instead of "clock time—something we had slowly been moving toward from the onset six months earlier. Since New Orleans, Jerry and I had learned to work effectively together and the "waves" produced by Tom's quitting were merely ripples now. The holes ripped in the fabric of the journey were healing.

"You know the dried salt burns my skin, Jerry and I itch all over! I'm tired and sunburned, but happy!"

"So am I," Jerry replied.

At dawn the Gooney Bird Marina was quiet, but when we returned from breakfast, Gordy asked: "Where have you guys been? The phone's been ringing off the hook for you all morning! There's been a television crew out from Tampa and all sorts of other people!" Before it ended, we had talked with a half dozen reporters on the telephone or face-to-face, had been taken out to dinner by a retired couple and had spent an hour on a local radio program answering call-in questions. The day was rewarding, but it drained us. We found refuge back at the all night restaurant and talked about it.

"This wears me out more than paddling," Jerry said.

"We made a lot of people smile today, Jerry. Especially on that talk program. Most of those retired folks were able to identify with us or relive an adventure they had years ago."

The day had been a sharing experience and warmed our hearts. Amidst the confusion, we did manage to retrieve mail at Crystal Beach. Included in the supplies and messages from loves ones were two long sleeve shirts Jerry's Sister made us. Each one was light blue chambray with the name "Trilogy Crew" embroidered across the back.

Crowds gathered at the Gooney Bird to witness our departure. Rich drove the forklift into the boat shed and came out with our two kayaks. Jerry and I climbed into the rigs and the lift lowered us into the water like a giant, loving hand. Amidst the fanfare, someone tossed a can of insect repellent into Jerry's boat. That evening he found it and remarked: "I think someone was thinkin' about us!"

Three hundred miles of open Gulf lie behind us. Anclote Key five miles below Port Richey marked the beginning of generally sheltered waters all the way to Fort Myers. It also marked the start of crowds and congestion. We saw it during our mail pick up where Jerry remarked: "I think we could have paddled to Crystal Beach faster than crawling through all this traffic!"

Tarpon Springs was now on our port side. Years ago, the major industry of the town was sponging. The town still had an annual tourist oriented "spongeorama." We paddled by the harbor mouth just as a tour boat passed. The guide's voice on board sounded mechanical and hollow! I seriously wondered if any of the people on board would actually feel the spirit of their surroundings. In the distance, we could see high rises and condominiums and wondered where we would camp for the night.

We hoped the question would be answered at Dunedin when I called relatives of a friend back home. Bill and Irene knew we were coming, but they never expected to put us up for two nights. Later, Bill confessed he was unfamiliar with the rigors of water travel.

"At first I was reluctant to help you fellas out, but I'm sure glad I did. I really can't imagine what you've been going through on this trip," he said.

Bill and Irene lived in a retirement village similar to the hundreds that had been built in the "Sunshine State" over the past few years. Needless to say, our kayaks sitting side by side in the guest-parking stall in front of their home drew a lot of attention.

A reporter from the Clearwater Sun was out to interview us the next morning. He titled his story: "Just Two Friends Out for a Ride" and emphasized that the biggest problem on the trip so far was making people believe us.

The Crystal Beach mail pick up revealed John Winkler and his wife were visiting relatives in Belleair only a few miles away. Bill arranged for us to meet John at a nearby restaurant. Afterwards, John invited us to the house for a few drinks.

"I swear, I didn't recognize you at first without your beards, John said. "'Stella and I can't believe you paddled all this way. When I saw you leave Hannibal that cold day last November I just shuddered."

The time went too fast. We visited for an hour in Belleair before Bill and Irene were back to pick us up. It really didn't matter. John and 'Stella would be back at their winter home in Naples by the time we paddled down there anyway.

The channel and borderland made us feel ill at ease. People, boats and buildings were everywhere. Speedboats sped up and down the channel, sometimes recklessly. In a place called the "Narrows," a jet boat full of kids tried to swamp us. They roared by on their first pass and then came by again close enough to clip Jerry's paddle blade. It was an awful, helpless feeling. Fortunately, the idiots must have found another diversion for they never returned.

We spent the night on a rare sand spoil in the midst of civilization. I concluded the day by entering:

"Compared to the noise and confusion of today's run, the sounds of birds, frogs and crickets on the island is certainly music to our ears."

Tampa Bay lie before us now. Our plan of attack led us across the bay by following the Sunshine Skyway Bridge—four miles of causeway, five miles of concrete "legs," steel span and one and one-half more miles of causeway to a sand island and safety. The colossal size of the structure with the vast Gulf on one side and giant Tampa Bay on the other made me feel like I was paddling a tiny two by four instead of a kayak. Jerry and I bobbed up and down five-foot swells with the main bridge span one hundred and fifty feet over our heads. I wondered how many people above us were looking out over the bay at that instant. From their perch, inside speeding, air conditioned canisters, the bay may have looked sedate. To us, it was alive and filled us with apprehension. Not until we were camped, did the bay resemble a thing of beauty. From the edge of the beach, we looked over a fallen tree and past the sea grape to the distant superstructure of the "toy" bridge. The scene was tranquil now and spoke of nothing we had experienced earlier.

"You know, Jerry, it's hard to believe we were in that painting a few hours ago. I'm glad it's over."

Before we left Apalachicola, Kerry had given us directions to the home of a Sarasota newspaper editor.

"You can paddle your boats right up to his back door," he said.

We were bound and determined to do just that. With Kerry's directions in hand, we knew nothing could go wrong. The approach to Sarasota was breathtaking. We paddled on smooth crystal clear water, investigating the shallows as we moved along. Zebra fish, barracudas and puff fish darted by. The underwater sand patterns changed constantly. Down the twelve-mile expanse of water lie a city, but we couldn't see it—yet. Then a dot appeared on the horizon and then another—distant buildings. The shimmering phantoms grew solid and other objects appeared beside them. The City of Sarasota was being born before our eyes! The skyline enraptured Jerry and me. Someplace in that complex was the home we sought. We paddled underneath the first bascule bridge, the second and the third. We passed condominiums, high rises, marinas and then homes and more homes. We were on Oyster Bay now, a tiny pool of saltwater between the mainland and Siesta Key; and we were stumped.

"His home's got to be around here someplace, Jerry. Let's find out directions back at the house where those people were."

"According to the telephone number, the house you want is two to three miles back," Mr. Carter said.

Unknowingly, we had followed Kerry's directions right past the editor's home!

We never saw the editor of the Sarasota Times—although we did make front-page news: "Coon Rapids to Oyster Bay At Three Miles Per Hour." After one of the Carters' daughters came out and later, a visiting girlfriend of hers, we really didn't care to see the editor's home at all.

Originally, we were invited to stay with the Carters overnight, but ended up staying four nights. They treated us like members of their family and Jerry and I found it nice to be around Theresa and Virginia. We toured the city and its environs and tasted the life style of "rich kids." The incident occurred when we were invited to Theresa's twentieth birthday. Everyone there, except the kayakers, of course, was involved in professional English riding competition. People were bragging about their horses, cars, homes and whatever other things they had. Jerry and I could not relate to the conversations and thought they were ludicrous. Likewise, the people there really could not relate to us. A lot of the questions asked us ended in "why?" or knitted brows. We did our share of laughing and dancing, but the prickling sense of "these people are from a different world than ours haunted us all the way back to the house.

During our stay, we also scraped barnacles from Mr. Carter's boat. The prolific crustaceans were a third of an inch long when the boat was raised from the water.

"They grow fast down here in the warm water. You don't have to scrape if you don't want to," he said, but we insisted.

Armed with putty knives, a brush and garden hose, Jerry and I attacked the prop and drive shaft while Mr. Carter scraped the hull. The rock barnacles stuck fast to any and all below-water surfaces. We worked and worked and seemed to get nowhere. After three hours he said: "That's all for today, time to rest." Our faces and arms were splattered with barnacle shells. Our knuckles and fingers were cut by their sharp edges and we had barnacle-frosted hair.

Our stay never saw us asleep before 2:OO a.m. Conversations went on for hours in the comfortable atmosphere of an un-air-conditioned, well ventilated home. It was hard to leave.

The day we left, the headwinds had an extra bight bite and the tidal current in the channel outside of Venice, seemed especially merciless. Nightfall found us sleeping atop the canal's high banks within eyesight of the Ringling Brothers winter circus grounds. We didn't talk much that evening. Our thoughts were back at Sarasota with Theresa and Virginia.

Jerry and I didn't remember much about paddling through Lemon Bay, except it was crowded and it rained on and off. Other things that stuck in my mind included: Heavy machinery plowing out natural vegetation to make way for new developments and an old timer complaining how dredging had ruined fishing in the area.

By evening we were set up on an on-land sand spoil. Jerry's radio picked up the feeble music from our favorite Sarasota FM station. The music didn't brighten our dispositions, but the campfire did. It was the first fire in nearly a month and its flames and coals reassured us of better days ahead.

Lemon Bay opened into Gasparilla Sound and Charlotte Harbor.

"The Ides of March—the thermometer in my kayak registered a hundred degrees today," I wrote.

We took one break on our twenty-three mile run at the island town of Boca Grande. Jerry reassured me the trees I was looking at were coconut palms. The town had the old mixed with the new. It was connected to the mainland by railroad and highway umbilical cords. The center of town spoke of bygone days when people arrived by train. The depot looked abandoned and in dire need of repair and the fringe of new homes surrounding the older core seemed incompatible.

"Boco Grande may have looked picturesque at one time, Jerry, but I think its growing pains have taken away some of the town's shine."

Our day was filled with wealth from nature's treasure chest. A flock of Roseate Spoonbills flew low over the waterway in the early morning light. Ospreys dove for fish and carried them away in their sharp talons. Stingrays skittered to the side as our kayaks made their way through the shallows of Pine Island Sound. Cone, Whelk, Conch and Cowry shells lie scattered over the beach of North Captiva Island.

The strip of sand where we landed was no more than a hundred yards wide. The placid waters of the Sound contrasted sharply with that of the Gulf. We watched in silence as the sun set through the breaker haze.

Near the mangrove portion of Sanibel Island named "J.N.'Ding' Darling National Wildlife Refuge," Jerry watched a manatee surface.

"It was about a hundred feet away— sort of hairy looking with a big snout," he said.

Until now, manatees or sea cows were something we had only heard about and it felt good to be in their company. A small, crescent-shaped island dotted with sea oats and Australian pine became our oasis for the night. Its cove provided an ideal landing place away from the chops we had fought all day. From it, we could see Point Ybel on the tip of Sanibel Island and its 1884 lighthouse.

Fort Myers was only a few miles up the Caloosahatchee River. If we wanted, we could have cut across Florida to Stuart on the East side via canals and Lake Okeechobee. Most transient boaters did just that, but the Everglades lure was stronger than ever now and we had friends to see in Naples.

When I opened the tent flap in the morning, a large Ghost Crab greeted me. Jerry's sleep was short-lived. When I tried to scare the crab away, it raised up and scooted its five-inch carapace into the tent. By the time it ran out and buried itself in the sand, both of us were out of the tent and wide awake.

We left with a remote feeling we could possibly be at John and Stella's home in Naples shortly after dark. After twenty-three miles and eleven miles to go, we decided it would be wise to meet the Winklers during daylight hours while we were reasonably refreshed and knew where we were. The day had been tough on us. We meandered through Estero Bay and then into the mangrove choked reaches of smaller and smaller pools and passages. We had lunch with seagulls on a sand spit no bigger than a picnic table. We watched a brown pelican attempt to swallow a three pound mullet and spotted a bald eagle sitting atop a mangrove while we were lost in a back channel. The tidal current eventually led us to Wiggins Pass and the Gulf where it felt as if someone left us out of a hot, stuffy, airtight box.

Paddling eleven miles in wind and rough seas is comparable to thirty miles in sheltered water. The Gulf was flat when we started but soon turned nasty. We fought a strong south headwind with chops and rolling waves. Crawling along at a snails pace, we watched converted warplanes spray insecticides on the mainland to keep "pests" under control. When we drew alongside Naples proper and looked at the solid wall of hotels and condominiums where beach access was completely blocked, I wondered what action, if any, was being taken to control the mushrooming oceanside realty industry. Fortunately, only a part of the shoreline was "walled." Eventually, the chain broke and public beach stretched ahead of us. We landed in gentle surf next to the municipal pier.

Jerry stayed with the boats while I walked to the Winkler's address and announced our arrival. John and Stella were both home when I walked in with arms and chest caked with dried salt spray.

"Stay as long as you want," Stella said. "You deserve the rest!"

We were in Naples a full week but it seemed like only a day. Like the Carter's home, John and Stella's place was not air-conditioned. It was an older home that took advantage of shade trees and cross ventilation.

"I couldn't stand to be boxed in by air-conditioning," Stella said.

The Winkler's home was open to the tang of salt air and the perfume of blooming flowers. They were in harmony with their Florida surroundings. John, in his seventies, walked to the beach and swam a mile in the Gulf every morning. Stella loved exploring the natural world and her enthusiasm fired our imaginations as to what lie ahead in the Everglades.

We stocked up on food—rice, jelly, processed cheese, margarine and peanut butter—and made sure we could carry sufficient freshwater to get us through the 'glades. I replaced my shredded tennis shoes with a new pair and Jerry finally found the time to paint the deck of his kayak. Using fabric paint, he lettered TRILOGY on the port side of the deck and MISSISSIPPI QUEEN on the starboard.

"Remember we're a lot closer to the equator than the folks in Missouri or Minnesota. Long twilights are common up there, but here they're practically non-existent." After witnessing our last Naples' sunset followed by an unusual phenomenon called the "green flash," John gave a sigh and continued: "So far, we've kept this area free from high rises, but they're always trying to re-zone so they can get their way." As John spoke, I could see the wall of buildings in my mind's eye and the sign: "Sunsets and sand for the privileged few. All other keep out!"

Chapter 25

Everglades National Park

"Life is a part of the earth, a biochemical clay; the earth, a dynamic mold altered through time, will in turn be the changing mold which shapes life."

Eric Phair

Our week with the Winkler's detached us from the daily routine of paddling. To make up for the void, our subconscious minds worked overtime. The night before we launched, I dreamt I was propelling my boat down a strange watercourse. I didn't know where I was. Jerry also had a dream and vividly recalled the location. "I was paddling my kayak around Africa just before I woke up." In both dreams, we were alone; now together, we were back in reality bound for the Everglades.

We slept on a brushy shore near Goodland and reached Indian Key Campground, just inside the National Park, the next day. The island was sandy, covered with yucca, prickly pear cactus, buttonwood, cabbage palms and mangroves. Three other campers were on the island when we arrived. They had just canoed from Flamingo, on the south tip of the park, to Everglades City, five miles away from the island—a total distance of almost a hundred miles.

Jocelyn, Ken and Nancy were part of a college group from Connecticut, spending time down in southern Florida on a credit-based learning experience. They told us what lie ahead in simple terms—"beautiful mangrove wilderness loaded with insects. Out here in the Ten Thousand Island Area, the breeze is keeping the sand gnats and mosquitoes away, but in the interior, where it's quiet, they're fierce," they warned.

We shared supper with the canoeists, as well as a small bottle of cognac we had picked up in Naples to celebrate the two-hundredth day of the adventure. Jerry and I proposed a toast to the Everglades— that they may be Ever Glad!

"Everlasting," Jocelyn added.

Their Everglades' journey was almost over. Ken's thirty-five millimeter camera was now at the bottom of one of the bays; Jocelyn's poisonwood rash on her arm and Nancy's undecipherable, waterlogged notes written in felt tip pen attested to the trial and tribulations of the trail.

All three were asleep when Jerry and I—excited about what lie ahead—decided to hike around the perimeter of the island. Our hour-long night walk was the medicine we needed to unwind. Daylight had revealed sea cucumbers, horseshoe and fiddler crabs, oysters and scallops on another island beach where we had stopped for lunch. Now, in moonlight shadows, we used our ears more than our eyes. We could hear the surf far out in the Gulf, the chirping of crickets and then the scolding cries of an osprey as it flew over its nest on the Key's south tip.

At Everglades City, we obtained a back country use permit and ten gallons of fresh water, dispersed in six bleach bottles, the three gallon collapsible container Kerry had given us and an empty food jug. The precious commodity would need to last a week, or until we reached Flamingo. There would be no fresh water through the area we'd be paddling.

Everglades National Park consisted of many natural communities. The mangrove portion we would traverse was only a segment of the total Everglades. Farther inside, the park opened to communities of bald cypress, pinelands and vast areas of saw grass dotted with hammocks.

Our maps showed canoe route campsites. Some were located on old shell mounds, others were situated on sparse high ground and a few were platform shelters called chickees.

We spent our first night at Lopez River Camp. The site bore the remains of an old foundation nearly hidden by wild tamarind and was equipped with a self-contained latrine, picnic table and fire grate. Ironically, we were in a wilderness area using facilities that were usually absent in our primitive camps in non-wilderness areas.

The mosquitoes chased us into the tent to finish supper and chased us out of camp in the morning. Noontime found us investigating the Darwin homesite—what little there was to see.

"Wish the old man was still here, Jerry?"

From what we heard, Darwin had moved to the Everglades some thirty years before to "get away from it all." Now, poor health forced him to live at the island community of Chokoloskee just outside Everglades City. The homesite was in shambles. Vandals had burned the house and the area was littered with trash and beer cans. That prodded us to leave soon after we landed.

Surprisingly enough, the canoe route markers led us past two active homesites and signs reading "5 mph" in the narrow passageways connecting the bays. By late afternoon, we were at Onion Key. Both of us wore rain suits to protect ourselves from the clouds of no-se-ems and mosquitoes. I kept wondering how Indian people and Darwin coped with the creatures.

"Either, they had some kind of very effective repellent, or they lived in perpetual smoke," I grumbled to Jerry." And if this is the dry season, what's this area like in the summer?"

In spite of the pests, we still were able to absorb the beauty of the water and mangrove. There was a special lure here—a spirit, a mystery. I could understand why people like Darwin had chosen to live in this part of the world.

We were told about a strange creature that made its home in the park. People called it the "skunk ape" in honor of its hairiness and terrible stench. Jerry and I never saw the beast, but we did see the results of its handiwork.

"There's a giant hole in the deck of my kayak, Jerry!"

Of course, it would have been logical to conclude the muddy raccoon tracks across the deck were somehow connected to the cavern, but the "skunk ape" story sounded better.

I hurriedly covered the hole with a sticky, bugs-mixed-with-glue, eight-inch patch while Jerry fanned the hungry hoards away from my face and hands. We frantically reloaded the boats and launched into an insect free environment.

"Wow, I'm glad that's done," I sighed.

In my haste however, I neglected to check the hull. After two minutes of paddling, an electric shock ran through me when I felt my legs and backside getting wet. Water was pouring in from an unknown source! Our kayaks did an immediate about face while I fought a sickening fear of sinking before reaching Onion Key Camp—the only high, dry place for miles around.

Jerry and I watched in disbelief as thirty gallons of bilge water poured from a hole eaten in the hull of my kayak below the waterline. Two thousand bug bites later, with the situation under control, I stomped angrily back into the water, barefoot to relaunch the boat and jammed my toes into an oyster bed. The sharp edges of the shells cut my toes like razors and the reflex action made me fall into the bed, cutting the base of my thumb.

"What the hell can happen next?" I screamed.

What an understatement. We fought wind in the open bays and tidal currents in the channels for most of the day and were glad when the sign for Broad River Campground appeared on the shoreline. It was a beautiful campsite, set amidst mangroves and a few cabbage palms, but when Jerry jumped out of his kayak to investigate, he landed in knee-deep mud. It took him several minutes to climb to the top of the bank. I could barely see him in the dusk as he flailed his arms.

"The bugs are so bad here I can hardly breath!" Jerry yelled. "Let's head for the Gulf, Randy. We'll never get the kayaks on shore here. We'll never get ourselves on shore."

We had heard of Indian people moving to the coast during the summer to avoid insects and on this windless night in March, we were too!

Darkness came by the time we broke free into the glassy vastness. The relief didn't last long. The water we were paddling in was shallow and the tide was still going out. We paddled up the coast and soon found ourselves stranded on a mucky tidal flat a hundred yards from shore. I grabbed the flashlight and trudged off to the mainland. My first try was in vain—I couldn't find solid footing to get to shore. The second probe though, brought me to a suitable campsite surrounded by Australian pines and coconut palms. Two hours later, after a seemingly endless parade of hauling equipment and kayaks to shore, we were inside the tent eating peanut butter and jelly sandwiches and drinking warm water. The radio droned a barely audible Motown tune. Our bodies were covered with dried silt and caked salt. We were too exhausted to talk.

The night left us refreshed and to celebrate Easter Sunday, Jerry cracked open a coconut with a screwdriver and jackknife. The half-day of relaxation was going fine until the knife slipped from the coconut shell I was peeling, plunging the blade deep into my left palm. I let out a scream and held pressure on the wound for a long time before it stopped bleeding.

"I think I can still paddle if I bandage it up," I said. "Let's get out of here. This place is jinxed!"

We were ready by early afternoon. The tide brought the water within a few feet of the boats and chops were working the shore. Our destination was a campsite marked on our chart with a black tepee. It was situated six miles to the south, on the north side of Ponce de Leon Bay. We didn't know "P.A." to the right of the tepee meant "Position Approximate." We had our own definitions for the letters: PA = "Public Access," or PA = "Possibly Abandoned." When the camp didn't appear, we were edging on the latter.

Finally it appeared, tucked into a sandy area where a stream ran into the bay.

"It's called Graveyard Creek Campground," I said. "I wonder what that's supposed to mean?"

After the sun went down, we figured the name derived itself from the ultimate fate of those unwary boaters who stayed the night without bug protection. In less than five minutes, our tropical paradise turned into something that could have come out of Dante's Inferno. The mosquitoes stayed out of the tent, but JAWS, our new name for the no-see-ems, sifted through every conceivable opening. We abandoned the shelter for five minutes while Jerry fumigated it and returned with bandannas over our faces to avoid breathing the strong vapors. Things were fine—for a while. During the early morning hours, Jerry's shirt, which had plugged the back window flap, either fell down or was pulled down by hungry JAWS, eager to get at our hides. They came in by the thousands and chewed on us until we left.

The route led us from Pounce de Leon into Whitewater Bay. Suddenly, a powerboat passing far to starboard altered its course and headed toward us.

"He must have got the message we left in Everglades City," Jerry said.

The patrol boat glided up and there stood Barney with a typical grin on his face.

"Well guys, I see ya made it," he said in his low expressionless voice.

Barney was headed to a distressed houseboat when he spotted our paddle flashes. We were planning on camping at Wedge Point, but the conversation changed our plans: "You can stay at the walk-in campground at

Flamingo for two dollars a night, or camp out behind my quarters for nothin' and shower up."

Jerry and I pulled into the ranger's section of the Flamingo complex around 9:00 p.m. The last three miles of Wilderness Waterway was canal and an incoming tide forced us to "burn daylight."

The Rangers at Flamingo were a tight knit group. During our first night behind Barney's second-story, hurricane-proof, "super economy" apartment —a bedroom-kitchen combo with a bathroom—we were approached by another ranger who was very leery of our credentials.

"What are you doing here?" he said.

We told him and it was obvious he was a non-believer. Barney overheard the conversation from his bed and bellowed out: "They're my guests. They've paddled all the way...."

"Okay, Barney," the Ranger said." I know... just checkin'... good night."

We wanted to absorb as much information as we could about the park through nature walks, evening programs and conversations with rangers. Those who had worked in the park for any length of time were very pessimistic over its future. "The Everglades may be the first National Park to be destroyed," the naturalist said. Ground water in the area had been lowered over sixty inches since 1900s, causing more and more saltwater encroachment. A few rangers said they could taste salt in Flamingo's freshwater supply, which came from wells seventeen miles inland.

"The surrounding area keeps growing," Barney said. "More homes, more bathtubs, more showers, more water demand—we're losing the battle! The 'Glades lifeblood is being sucked out of it by wells and canals."

What was happening made us sad and depressed. I couldn't sleep and stood looking across Florida Bay. In the distance, I could see the faint glow of lights from the

Keys and now and then the phosphorescent sparkle of plankton. I waited until 2:OO a.m.—late enough for the Southern Cross to rise a few degrees above the horizon. In the presence of the constellation, I wished for eternal preservation of an ecosystem unique to southern Florida and the world.

Green coconuts appeared in our kayaks. Evidently, it was the work of the phantom that also left coconuts at Barney's doorstep.

"Coconuts are illegal to pick in the park—so we do a lot of confiscating. "As you can see, we have a disposal problem," Barney muttered. "By the way, you are invited to our end-of-the-season party tonight over in the activity building."

The following week, most of the seasonal staff would leave as the park entered its skeleton crew "summer season." During the wet season from May to November, we heard stories of the remaining park staff coating themselves with insect repellent before going from one building to another. Patrol boats, moving along mangrove lined waterways, drove fast enough to avoid being swarmed.

We were fortunate not to encounter poisonous snakes in the Everglades until a park ranger, during a demonstration, displayed several snakes common to the area.

"All the major groups of poisonous snakes found in the United States are found in the Everglades," he commented. "Found this guy just the other day about a mile from here."

He pulled a harmless water snake from a glass case and the curious crowd immediately took two steps back.

Alligators and crocodiles were also absent in our observations, but they were around. Saltwater loving crocodiles were rare in the Everglades and the American alligator preferred brackish or freshwater to live.

We did, however, see a myriad of bird life. "George," the common egret, which hung around the shore near the rangers' quarters, reminded us of the Rookeries we had seen in the interior. The one at Whitewater Bay had egrets and ibises nesting together by the hundreds. We also saw turkey vultures, anhingas, brown pelicans, wood storks, ospreys, cormorants and herons. In perspective, our limited observations of individual species were but a tiny fraction of the total in the park.

"The Everglades, throughout the year, contain over sixty per cent of all the bird species found in the Eastern United States," a ranger told us. "And what is here now isn't anything compared to the numbers and species that were here before the onset of outside development and the invasion of this area by plume hunters in the early nineteen hundreds."

Florida Bay, a broad reach of very shallow water, bordered by the Keys and the Florida mainland, was before us now. The boundary of the 1.25 million acre park extended into its waters. We heard it was one of the most fertile fish nurseries in the world and accounted in part for the Everglades abundant and diverse flora and fauna.

"The bay can be compared to your Boundary Water Canoe Area in Minnesota," Barney told us. "The keys and banks would be comparable to the forested areas and the deeper water to you lakes."

"It," we were told, was for the birds—literally. Landing a watercraft on any high ground, except those few designated areas, was strictly forbidden and violators would be fined. A nesting pair of bald eagles used a small mangrove island just out from Barney's apartment and three flamingoes waded in inch deep water on one of the grassy banks we paddled by,

Nest Keys, a designated campground, lie twenty-seven winding miles east of Flamingo. We told Barney (with our fingers crossed) we'd be there before nightfall and we made it with time to spare.

Past Whaleback Key, through Buttonwood, Blackwater and Barnes Sounds, we paddled. We were on the Intracoastal Waterway again following the west side of Key Largo bound for Miami. A small, clean island in Card Sound, studded with Australian pine, became our camp for the night. Barney had pointed it out as "being high enough for camping" while we were at Flamingo.

The "mythical" City of Miami was close to becoming a reality. Since New Orleans, Miami had been in our minds as a goal and now it was within reach. Somewhere to the northeast of our camp, was the city. Although we couldn't see it, radio stations reassured us of its presence. Between short bursts of music, we were informed of an impending water shortage for residents of Dade County and a seventy-four degree surf temperature.

"Somewhere below that horizon are an awful lot of people, Jerry."

The "deluge" came sooner than we expected. The next day, our kayaks drifted into a public access area at Black Point. Lunch at a nearly deserted picnic ground, in the shadow of the Turkey Point Power Plant, warned us of the impending population crunch. A hyperactive guard drove up and down the road constantly checking to make sure "all was well." The lunchtime "people watcher" made us nervous. Now the presence of people also made us nervous. We just weren't used to seeing so many at one time. "People were everywhere," I wrote in my logbook. "There were at least a thousand scattered along the channels. People coming out of the trees!" Coming out of the Everglades into the city would take some adjusting on our part.

Looking for a place to land took us up Gould's Canal to a dead end. Our intent was to ask if we could camp on the edge of the canal for the night, but before we knew it, we were offered shelter from Lou and Dot and another fellow named Dave. The warmness made me ashamed of the way I had felt coming into the canal. The crowds then were just crowds—people without faces. They made me feel threatened because I was hungry, tired and needed a place to sleep. Now those people had faces names, feelings and hopes. Lou and Dot lived only a few blocks away. In 1963, Lou had taken a twelve-foot powerboat from the Carolinas to Florida.

"Back then, it was just Lou and his dog on the trip," Dot said. "He hasn't talked about the trip for years."

Lou disappeared for a few minutes and returned with a set of well-used charts.

"I'd give these to you, but they kinda got sentimental value to me," he said.

Dot added: "He's still has the boat sitting in the front yard, ain't much good now. I guess it'll be there forever."

Dave decided our choice of where we'd stay for the night. When he found out we were from the same state he was, he practically picked up the kayaks himself and put them in the back of his pickup.

Two days later, we left. Dave was working, so a neighbor drove us back to the canal. Reporters from the Homestead newspaper interviewed us while we packed. We told them we'd be in Miami or Key Biscayne before nightfall. They never asked us where we'd be staying for the night— and if they did, we wouldn't have known anyway.

"Why don't you sleep on the beach like the hippies do?" the guard at Key Biscayne told us. Then he added: "If you go way down the beach, you might not get arrested."

The conversation was leading nowhere. We had put on eighteen miles, it was dark, the people apathetic and we wanted no hassles. Earlier, I told the guard what we were doing.

"Bound for New York City," I said.

"New York?" he answered. "Oh, that's easy to get to —just follow the coat and you get to New York."

Sadly, he was serious about his answer. It was obvious the Key Biscayne marina was no place for kayakers on a budget. We found refuge fifty yards away on a tiny shrub-covered sand spoil with hardly open space for our tent and kayaks.

"The city roars around us," I wrote. "I guess no one knows we're out here, especially the cops. Please don't bother us—just let us live—in peace."

The "conversation" with the guard ended with him refusing to answer any more questions. The statements he did make were added to our ever-growing "pearls of wisdom" catalog. We joked about them, taking turns imitating the voices that had carried the messages: "March winds are coming. You boys better paddle up the Suwannee River for a month or so till they die down." "It's too dangerous to go around the tip of Florida. The current's too fierce. The skippers even avoid it. You'll have to take the Caloosahatchee Canal." "It is impossible to go beyond Apalachicola cuz the channel stops; it's all swamp! You'll have to end there, I'm afraid." "Water's too shallow in Florida Bay; you'll have to go on the outside of the Keys." "How you gonna paddle in the ocean at Miami? I've lived here all my life and there is no Intracoastal Waterway north of the city."

The last and most recent addition topped the list of erroneous statements; even the Florida highway map showed the waterway extending north through the city.

Our "Miami myth" quickly eroded once we were there. The city irritated us and we wanted to paddle through it as soon as possible. Early in the afternoon, we stopped on an island in Dumfoundling Bay. The canal started on the other side of the bay and the prospect of vacant places to camp looked bleak. The island was riddled with survey flags and soon it would look just like the landscape surrounding it—highrises, condominiums, hotels, concrete, houses and confusion. Our free, open-air life style clashed with what we imagined were the lifestyles of those living in the high rise communities. We called them "people warehouses." They depressed us, so did the dead osprey lying on the shore near our tent.

"I wonder how it died, Jerry? Poisoned, shot, or natural causes?"

I also wondered if the lack of our bug "friends" had anything to do with the state of the environment here.

The kayaks pushed northward into even more crowded areas. The Intracoastal Canal was narrow and teaming with pleasure craft. We cut through the "Gold Coast" area of Florida and stood aghast at the materialism before our eyes.

"This area must be worth millions, probably billions!" Jerry said. "Definitely, it's a place for the 'big shots'."

Forty-foot yachts were everywhere—nestled in expensive marinas or moored at private docks. Fancy facilities, operating-room clean, beckoned with the silent words: "You can stay here, if you got the bucks, Buddy!" We passed a marina charging dockage fees five times the going rates we had seen earlier. On shore, manicured lawns were the rule. One monstrous home had a yard adorned with what appeared to be imported statues.

A tour boat rolled by with a woman singing "Sweet Gypsy Rose." We supposed the people on board were having fun, but most of them looked tired and bored—hardly any of them waved to us.

The waterway was full of chops from passing craft. The waves ricocheted off the concrete canal walls and continually bounced our kayaks. Maneuvering kept us so busy we nearly missed a roving Ft. Lauderdale reporter who flagged us in with a six-pack of local Minnesota beer.

"Tried to catch you guys at the last two bascule bridges, but you just were moving too fast," he said.

Jerry climbed atop the breakwall, while I stayed aboard my craft to steady it in the dancing water. When the interview was over and the six pack empty, we were invited to the reporter's house in event we couldn't find a place to stay in the crowded area. However, after five more miles of paddling and a telephone call, our plans worked out and we were with Ed, Tilly and their family.

Ed described our entrance perfectly: "They walked into the house covered with salt and marched directly into the shower."

He could identify with us. Back in his younger days, Ed led an adventurous life.

"I'd leave home for weeks at a time," he said. "My folks, most of the time, never knew where I was or where I had been. I used to ride a Harley and I still borrow my son's, once in awhile, when I get the "bug."

Tilly still had some Geauga County maple syrup from the area where my family used to live seventeen years before. The syrup, poured from a mason jar onto hot pancakes, brought back a flood of childhood memories from Ohio. I was glad I had spent part of my life on an Ohio farm. I remembered going to Ed and Tilly's with my brother and dad for our first dog. Carrying him to the car was quite an effort—Jim picked up one end and I the other. I remembered emptying sap buckets and mom boiling maple syrup. I remembered my first pet chicken; Elvis, the albino rabbit; building hay forts; weeding the garden; picking cherries; going over to Mrs. Jones' for eggs and the day Jim and I cried because "Sam" and "Cleo," our pet pigs, were sent to market. I remembered going to Pennsylvania in Ed's dump truck to get coal, hauling firewood from the wood lot and my brother and I standing on top of the hot air register while Dad got the fire going in the monstrous farmhouse furnace.

More pancakes and syrup reminded me of Dad running up and down the road, trying to round up "Bob" and "Bell," the two workhorses; the fifteen cats in the house and barn and hitting mom's baseball—the one signed by Mickey Mantle—only to lose it in the apple orchard. I remembered helping to carry the Christmas tree back home from the Balsam stand and my first bicycle—one that Dad rebuilt. It was painted brilliant fire engine red. It didn't have a seat, had balloon tires and I loved it.

"Well, that's all the dough," Ed said. "You ate twelve pancakes apiece!"

Before leaving, we autographed copies of the Ft. Lauderdale paper carrying a story titled: "See the U.S.A. the Kayak Way" and overheard a neighbor commenting: "This is the most exciting thing that's ever happened on the block. Most of the time it's just waterway funeral processions!" A hundred paddle strokes later, we were out in the main channel again.

"How do you like the Sunday traffic? You can just about walk across the channel on the boat decks, Jerry."

Lake Worth was a welcome sight. Halfway through the narrow twenty mile long stretch of water, we paddled off the strip chart we had picked up at Port Everglades. An inset of West Palm Beach, on our Florida road map, helped direct us to Peanut Island near Lake Worth Inlet and a feasible place for camping.

We were "running blind" the next day. In our case, the charts were critical for indicating possible campsites and giving us tide timetables. With the tables, we would attempt to run with the current in narrow stretches of the waterway. As far as pointing out the direction of the waterway, we would merely look for markers and follow them, oftentimes in a hypnotic trance, one right after the other. Such was the case, when the Intracoastal Waterway made a ninety-degree bend to our starboard side, near Jupiter Inlet. We were paddling down the Loxahatchee River headed west instead of north. We would have likely paddled the wrong direction for several hours, if it hadn't have been for an approaching squall line crackling with lightning.

"Let's get back to the marina we just passed, this thing looks bad," Jerry said.

During the retreat, my boat took a different path than Jerry's through the bridge pilings and rammed an oyster bar. I ignored the damage and caught up just as the storm broke. The rain came in sheets, occasionally obliterating the marina dock we were tied to. Twenty minutes and an inch of water later, it was over and the sun was out again.

"Kayak, okay?" Jerry asked.

"No she's leakin' but I can hold the water out till we reach a campsite," I said. "By the way, the guy in the shop says the waterway turns up here. We were going the wrong way."

The next marina on the waterway sold strip charts. Jerry made sure we were well stocked before leaving the place.

"I got them all the way to the Florida-Georgia border now. So we won't have to worry about getting off course for a while."

The morning went well while in sheltered waters bordering Jupiter Island. However, once at St. Lucie Inlet—the confluence of the St. Lucie and Indian Rivers—easy times were over. The Indian River ran between barrier islands and the Florida mainland from Stuart on the south, to Titusville on the north. It's width varied, but on the average it was two miles. It was frustrating to be rewarded with such little progress as we clawed our way up the frothing stretch of water. The roar of the wind kept us from communicating and non-verbalized thoughts bounced around in my head.

"If we have continual wind like this, It'll be a month before we finish this hundred mile river," I kept thinking.

We rested at a causeway bridge cutting across the water and squeezed through a narrow inlet on its west side to avoid some of the wind's sweep. Our efforts were to bring us close enough to Jensen Beach so we could call relatives of my dad's friend.

As luck would have it, the family we were supposed to contact didn't know who we were! Plus, the marina we had pulled into for shelter was "cold and clammy" toward wind burnt, salted kayakers paddling into their high-class place.

"Tyin' your boats up kind of secure," was the welcome we got from the dockmaster.

By now it was dark and we'd be charged to moor our boats for the night. So, we climbed back aboard, untied the lines and headed to any vacant shoreline we could find.

Our rigs were out of range of the marina lights, when we heard a voice echo over the water: "Hey, come back! Come back!" The people hailing us were a couple from Battle Creek, Michigan. "Some folks around here are kinda stuffy, but you can stay with us. You'll be our guests," they said.

Dean and Ruth helped us park our kayaks in front of their camper. They fed us a meal of freshly caught Kingfish aboard their boat and let us sleep in the back of their pickup truck. It was the beginning of a plan, which would keep us at Jensen Beach another four days as special guests of the Florida Institute of Technology.

The woman working at the Chamber of Commerce called the Jensen Beach Branch of the Institute. By evening, we were in an air-conditioned dormitory room and our kayaks were locked inside the racing shell shed.

We learned F.I.T. Jensen Beach was a school that stressed practical application of knowledge in the marine sciences and environmental technology. Dr Gross, head of the science department, gave us a tour of the grounds. We saw ongoing experiments with the growth rates of lobsters in one of the oceanographic labs and stepped into a classroom where marine navigation was being taught.

The following morning, questions asked by four reporters during a press conference elicited responses from Jerry including: "Before I started the trip, I had all kinds of thoughts running through my mind—could I do it, or couldn't I do it? In that way, the journey was a personal challenge for me." Shortly, afterward his comment was re-enforced by an instructor who said: "If you get a chance to do something, for God's sake, do it!"

A couple hours later, Jerry and I were asked if we wanted to go down to Key West on a weekend snorkeling trip. In lieu of what we just heard, our answer was obvious.

The traffic and crowds on our two-day trip bothered us. We encountered traffic jams on many of the bridges spanning the Keys and were alarmed at what commercialism and rapid development were doing to a once pristine area. We were also concerned over what we couldn't see. We were told development related dredging and consequent situation was killing many of the area's coral reefs and soon they would be gone. We stopped at the National Key Deer Refuge, where we sampled coco plums growing on a nearby tree, spotted a camouflaged tree snail on a Gumbo-limbo and looked at vacant pens where sick and injured deer were kept. Over hunting, poaching, destruction of habitat almost eradicated the tiny Key deer. Before the refuge was established in 1947, biologists estimated the population to be under fifty animals, now it was sixty—at least it was a small victory, even though the total picture for the Keys seemed to us like holding back a moving sand dune with a picket fence.

We toured the congested community of Key West on foot. If we wanted, we could have bought a truckload of Key West souvenirs, ranging from scrimshaw to seashells. We tried to look through the varnish of tourism to find things lying closer to the heart of the community. Many Cubans lived in Key West and one didn't have to be reminded why they fled their island home sixty miles to the south. Many of the refugees landed on the Keys in boats smaller than our kayaks—the thirst for freedom is universal!

Jerry and I walked down residential streets, past John J. Audubon's house and Ernest Hemingway's home. We passed a window advertising "Bail Bonds" in giant red letters and saw a church being "tented" for termites. While we were waiting for our companions back at the car, a guy on a bicycle spotted the Connecticut license plates and asked: "What part of Connecticut ya from?" Jerry answered: "Minnesota" and the biker rode away laughing hysterically.

We spent half a day snorkeling the warm, clear shallows of a small bay surrounded, surprisingly enough, by vacant shoreline. When it came time to leave, I was so relaxed I could hardly support my body weight on shore.

"Don't step on the Portuguese Man O' War!" one of the students said. "I've seen people screaming in agony after becoming wrapped up in their stinging tentacles."

My right foot bypassed the jellyfish and landed in a warm, sticky, oozing mass of tar—I was no longer mesmerized. The sludge apparently came from the tanks or bilge of an oil tanker.

"They're not supposed to do it, but lots of them still flush out at sea," I was told.

It took awhile to wipe the black vomit from my toes. Afterwards, my foot was stained brown. I shuddered to think what a large spill would do to the already stressed, fragile environment of this area.

The Jensen Beach Campus contacted the Main Campus at Melbourne and mentioned two kayakers would be paying them a visit in four days. Starting at Fort Pierce, we utilized sand spoil islands alternating on each side of the Intracoastal Waterway. The high, dry land made ideal campsites, as well as, wind breaks while paddling.

During the sixty-seven miles, we wandered into a pizza place at Vero Beach for coffee. "It's all you can eat," were the only words we needed to eat three pizzas apiece and six bowels of salad!

Seven miles from Melbourne on an Australian pine covered spoil, the windless evening was a welcomed relief. In the overwhelming silence, we heard the lap of ripples against the shore punctuated by dolphins coming up for air twenty feet from our tent door.

Our stay at F.I.T.'s Main Campus allowed us to visit Disney World and Kennedy Space Flight Center. Visions of those experiences danced though our heads during our last night while we settled down to eat bologna sandwiches and drink a few beers in the confines of an air-conditioned dorm.

The advances in technology and the products of humankind's creativity displayed in the things we saw, contrasted with what we had heard on the radio. The announcer mentioned gasoline prices would go up if consumption this year is greater than last year. Since the commentary alluded to economic discrimination and freedom of mobility, we felt threatened. We couldn't understand if technology could send people to the moon and make a Hall of Presidents at Disney World, why did it seem impossible to produce a marketable, high mileage automobile?

Listening and conversing with people had become an integral part of the journey. Therefore, it also bothered us to encounter people with closed minds and not enough time for human interaction—this time it was a college student. We saw him as we carried out our gear from the room.

"Must be going camping," he said.

"Yeah, almost eight months now," I said.

But he didn't hear me. The door to his room had already slammed shut. What made the encounter more alarming was the student could have been me five years before—a frenetic college student with an open mind only to test questions and answers. I was glad I had grown and hoped the person behind the door would, too.

Chapter 26

Last Days in Florida

"When we show our respect for other living things, they respond with respect for us."

Arapaho Proverb

A few miles north of Melbourne, the Florida coastline begins to bulge into the Atlantic. Merritt Island divides the Indian River to the east from another body of saltwater, the Banana River. In turn, Cape Canaveral forms the east shore of the Banana River. Many people call it the "Space Coast," for obvious reasons.

"Down here, we can see rockets from the Cape blast off," I remembered someone saying at Jensen Beach—almost a hundred miles away!

From our spoil, Jerry and I could see the watery image of a distant rocket gantry and the huge, vehicle assembly building rising 525 feet from the otherwise monotonous horizon of shoreline vegetation. From what we heard, the world's largest scientific building was so big central air-conditioning had to be installed to prevent artificial rain showers. We studied both objects with binoculars and concluded there was a rocket standing on the launcher next to the red gantry.

"Must be the Canadian communications satellite they're going to launch in a week," Jerry said.

Until a few days before, we never realized the Space Center rented its facilities and rockets to other countries for peaceful endeavors. I dreamt of the rocket blasting off in the middle of the night, flooding our camp with brilliant light, but it was still there in the morning waiting for its appointed time.

The waterway made a right turn shortly after we passed Titusville and we paddled through a narrow canal linking the northern end of the Indian River with Mosquito Lagoon. A spotted eagle ray jumped from the water during the transition, startling both of us. When things returned to normal and we were again gliding down the smooth water of the lagoon, my kayak suddenly grounded to a halt. Before I had time to think, the water boiled to a froth and the kayak shuddered. After a few seconds, the water returned to normal with quiet ripples spreading out from the epicenter, just under the seat of my boat.

"What the...?" I yelled.

"I thought you turned over!" Jerry said. "What was it?"

"Don't know, Jerry, maybe a Manta Ray. I suspect it was at least ten feet across from the turbulence it made."

At camp I pulled out our fish book.

"It says here, although not dangerous, the Manta Ray often leaps from the water to terrorize fishermen in small boats."

Before darkness sealed the lagoon from our sight, Jerry did see "our friend" leap from the water—all six hundred pounds of it! Mindful, I refrained from my now customary saltwater rinse—to replace caked on salt with the lesser irritation of a thin salt film—out of respect for the "harmless" denizen of the deep.

"The ocean has made us strong and brown," I recorded. "It also makes us very lethargic especially when the mercury hits ninety degrees and above." Both of us could feel the effects as we lie in the stuffy tent, scratching away in our logbooks. We hoped the thunderheads hanging like a mural in the west would refresh us, but rain never came, nor the slightest breeze. I wrote and sweated.

"We're encountering marked oyster beds again and flounder fishermen. At night, the flounder rise to the surface. For the past two evenings small fishing boats equipped with underwater lights for spearing have plied the water near our camp..."

I looked up from writing and found Jerry fast asleep, pen still in hand, his logbook entry trailing off into a mass of scribbles. We were both more tired than we thought.

For the next two days, the temperature again broke ninety. The waterway, for the most part was canal again, save for the Halifax River at Daytona Beach.

"Home of the World's Most Famous Beaches," the sign said. "Who cares," I grumbled. "We're looking for a place to eat."

Easter break was over long ago and the sunburned college students had come and gone. We tried nine different places before we found an open restaurant and concluded we were experiencing Daytona's "slack season."

Dolphins occasionally inspected our boats as we paddled along. Consequently, we thought dolphins were what we saw along a stretch of canal strewn with weathered limestone rock.

"Those ain't Dolphins," Jerry concluded. "They're sea cows!"

We reversed our course and tried to catch up with the bobbing mammals swimming south.

"Looks like two adults and a calf, from what I can see, Randy."

The sighting made the day for us. By nightfall, we were on an island watching rice water bubbling over a campfire directly across from Marineland. It was quiet and a southbound tug just passed though the channel pulling four tandem barges. In anticipation of what we'd see in the morning, Jerry recalled the story John told us while we were at Homosassa Springs:

"It happened when I was at Marineland having a good time. Come Sunday morning, I was pretty 'pie-eyed' and walked through the unlocked gates. I strolled the empty walkways to the porpoise pool and took a look over the edge. Then, WHAM! A volleyball hit me smack-dab in the middle of the face! There in the water was a porpoise giving me the eye."

We saw the show at Marineland, the "porpoise school," the trained whale and the marine life in the oceanarium. We also learned things about the facility besides porpoises jumping through hoops or a dog being pulled around on a surfboard to the delight of spectators.

"Marineland is a research center, too," the curator told us. "Neurological studies going on with nurse sharks may someday pave the way for paraplegics to walk again or may allow humans to carry on conversations with other creatures inhabiting the planet."

The curator took us to a holding tank.

"This is Kogia, a baby Sperm whale," he said.

Dolphin-size, Kogia was found stranded on a beach not far from Marineland. He was so cut up form thrashing around on oyster beds that the scientists at the facility didn't expect him to live. "I think he's okay now," the curator told us, while he gently stroked the whale's head.

The Intracoastal Canal was now part of the Matanzas River leading to St. Augustine. During a short diversion, we followed a back channel winding through the marsh grass within a hundred feet of Fort Matanzas. The fortress was built in 1742 from native coquina rock to provide the Spanish, fifteen miles away at St. Augustine, a southern defense line. A few tourists clamored up and down the stone works. They were oblivious to our kayaks floating in the nearby reeds. I wondered if such would be the case if the hands of time were turned back. Suddenly, to me, the tourists were helmeted Spanish guards and we were British subjects. My imagination breathed a sigh of relief when our kayaks slipped back into the waterway—undetected.

Our entry into St. Augustine came the day after we slept on an immense mud flat just east of Butler Beach. We hoped to be at the city earlier, but launching through low tide mud, reeds and razor sharp oyster beds was tedious and time consuming. En route, a third party joined our flotilla of two. For several minutes, which seemed like hours, we nervously paddled the waterway watching the dorsal fin of a ten-foot sand shark. During the episode, my mind wrestled with itself. The "whatever happens, don't panic" philosophy butted heads with a then popular movie about a great white shark. The paddle slaps seemed to attract the shark's attention because he circled both kayaks three times before swimming off.

"Just curious," I said.

"Must be full," Jerry added.

He had long hair, a beard, dark brown eyes and dressed in a loose fitting, white robe when we met him. Stan appeared to be in his thirties, but as our lunchtime conversation progressed, we concluded fifty was a closer approximation. His wife and three year old child, also shared "sustenance," as Stan put it, with us—fresh pineapple, goat's milk, cheese, peanut butter, unsweetened oatmeal cookies and apple juice. We sat on the floor and ate while our conversation probed the realms of a beautiful, radically different, life style.

Stan didn't own a car. "To get around, we use the bike, a seventeen foot canoe, or our feet. Many people in this part of the world are possessed by the automobile," Sam said. "Sometimes, I feel like sawing the top off the big cross standing on the shore and putting a car on top of it. That's what a lot of people worship."

Stan's wristwatch lies somewhere in a palmetto patch along Highway A1A. "I had a flash and realized I didn't need the stupid thing... time is relative... eternity is now!"

The same thing with the TV set. Stan and his wife got rid of it nine years before. "It's sad how some people are not mature enough to just sit and talk. Either the television must be on, or they must be playing some kind of silly game," he said.

Stan replaced television with reading and meditation. "The human mind is like a lake— the calmer the water, the deeper one can see into it."

Stan and Dolores left us with a package of dried fruit to help maintain us physically and promised they'd meditate for the successful completion of our journey. "God bless you, brothers," were Stan's last words to us.

The tidewater crept in and flooded the grassy area around the tent. St. Augustine had a four foot mean tide range and by the time we reached Brunswick, Georgia, less than a hundred miles away, we'd be experiencing seven to nine foot tides. Such vast displacements of water, especially in constricted areas, such as canals and inlets, can create problems. For the first time, our nautical charts displayed Tidal Current Data at strategic locations along the waterway.

"Look at this, Randy. It says here the Pablo Creek bascule bridge has a flood tide current of 3.4 knots and an ebb current of 5.2 knots."

Since our kayaks could only do two and one-half knots on the average, it was logical to conclude we'd better learn to work with the tidal currents as soon as possible.

It was hard to believe we'd soon be out of Florida. The higher tides, occurrence of wood ticks, disappearance of Australian pine and mangrove and the thinning of palm trees all indicated our northern progress.

We spent two nights on an island within eyesight of the St. Johns River, listening to evening taps from the Mayport Naval Station and watching ships make their way in and out of the Jacksonville harbor. It was a situation where the weather prevented us from moving—rain settled in after a foggy morning and forced us to re-set camp.

The wait allowed us to draw up long-range plans to get us to Charleston, South Carolina. The charts indicated we were about to enter a fairly desolate area with high tides, strong currents, lots of saltwater marsh and few towns. Our main concern was maintaining a supply of fresh water, so we made note of every possible water stop en route.

Our first stop occurred the next morning, after we crossed the St. Johns River and tied up at Dandy Dan's Fish Camp. Sure enough, everything was "dandy," except the water. The well pumped out what appeared to be sulfur water. The smell was revolting, but we filled one jug anyway. That evening, though, the smell was nearly gone and by morning our jug of "bad" water had lost any trace of foulness.

The same day we picked up the sulfur water, I rammed both feet into oyster shells and sliced both middle toes to the bone. Our camp that evening was in a remote place marked Crane Island. I elected to rest and doctor up my feet while Jerry departed to keep a promise. Jerry left camp at 8:OO and returned at 2:OO in the morning.

"I had to walk over twelve miles! The dry swamp was full of water when I returned, so I had to wade through it—I almost got lost! Had to wait two hours before I could get through!"

So ended Mother's Day for us.

We paddled and drifted on an ebb tide to Fernandina Beach, bought groceries and waited for the flood before we crossed Cumberland Sound into Georgia.

The tide pushed us with lightning speed. I turned to look behind and could see the walls of Fort Clinch, at the entrance to the Sound, glowing in the afternoon light. When I looked again, the fort was gone and so was Florida. We raced with the sun and beat darkness to a high spot of land called Cabin Bluff. There, we pitched our tent at one end of a grassy landing strip and shared the field with five deer that came to feed.

Chapter 27

Fort Frederica and the Georgia Storm

"If a man does not keep pace with his companions, perhaps it is because he hears a different drummer. Let me step to the music which he hears, however measured or far away."

Henry David Thoreau

Generally, we'd be running behind barrier islands and crossing huge sounds all the way to Charleston. To avoid negotiating St. Andrew Sound during ebb tide, we followed a series of creeks, cuts and back channels effectively leading us to Jekyll Sound and the southern end of Jekyll Island. Depending on the way the sea drained from the labyrinth of waterways, we either found ourselves fighting or flowing with the tidal current. Mud flats were visible everywhere on Jekyll Creek. Floating docks and some boats at the island's marina, sat directly on exposed ooze. Seagulls and willets, clamored about picking up tiny crustaceans and fish left behind by the retreating water. The fresh smell rotting seaweed was everywhere.

Jerry and I walked up a steep stairway to the top of the fixed dock.

"Where are we?" I asked some folks returning to their sailboat.

"Don't you know? This is Jekyll Island, at one time the most affluent summer resort in the Nation."

Our brief history lesson told us that the island, before World War II, belonged to millionaires who formed the exclusive Jekyll Island Club. The mansions, or "cottages," found throughout the park-like setting, were originally used from mid-January through Easter. In 1947, Georgia purchased the island for a state park and, as far as we could see, had done an effective job in preserving the area's elegance.

The sailboat couple also revealed another point of interest to us—Fort Frederica.

"It's an old fort, used to protect Britain's southern territory from the Spanish. The National Park Service maintains it now—you'd be there by dark if you hurry."

We took their advice and left. The channels would be flooding again within the hour; we'd be across St. Simons Sound by then. If our timing were right, we'd be effectively pushed to the fort site by the current.

In making the run, we passed a stranded sailboat, heeling precariously on its port side; its keel was stuck fast in the shallows of Jekyll Creek. The crew was waiting patiently for the water to rise again. The sight reminded me of stories we had heard about Georgia tidewater: One mariner woke up to find his boat high and dry in a field. Another crew was thrown from their bunks when their grounded sailboat, set adrift by rising water, caught its mast in the crotch of a tree.

At least tonight, our fate wouldn't be the same as some of those before us. With the current in our favor, we meandered swiftly along the Frederica River and slept high and dry at the site of the old fort on St. Simons Island.

The grounds keeper was running a fog machine through the Frederica town site when I looked through the window. I wished he would have come around the night before, when heavy air brought mosquitoes and sand gnats. With such practice, Jerry and I doubted whether a modern day tourist driving to the fort could understand the full meaning of an historic sign at the information center:

"On the 18th, the flies began to plague the horses so as to make them almost unserviceable," Francis Moore, April 18th, 1736. "At one this morning, the sand flies forced me to rise and smoke them out of the hut. The whole town was employed in the same manner." Charles Wesley, 1736.

At one time, fortified Frederica contained a population of fifteen hundred. Now, "talking boxes" told us of a fort and town that were gone, save for a few foundations and depressions in the Georgia soil. The recorded messages let us hear the ring of a blacksmith's hammer, the bickering of two Frederica town housewives, soldiers on parade and the snapping, "Halt! Who goes there?" This was the sound of an alert guard "checking" all those who passed through the tourist gate. Two hundred year old live oaks, laden with Spanish moss and loblolly pine enhanced the setting and coaxed us to stay another night.

When our kayaks finally touched water again, a two-man crew who had their sailboat anchored directly in front of the fort delayed our departure. Joe and James were their names. Joe had bought the used sailboat a few weeks before and he was "warming up" for his "big break" from St. Simons Island—his home. Both were characters. Joe wore a red bandanna around his head and sported a long handlebar mustache. James was a big guy, with a huge red beard, blue eyes and a sun burned face. He was slightly overweight and wore underwear elastic for a headband. They shared cream corn mixed with boiled red beans and they saw us launch just before the strong ebb tide pulled their boat into the reeds.

The current was sucking our boats out to sea. En route we spied what appeared to be two logs bobbing in the water.

"They're not logs—they're 'gators!" Jerry said in a loud whisper.

All that stuck above the water were the tip of their noses and the eye ridges. We drifted by and they dunked out of site.

In our excitement, we failed to notice storm clouds building to the southwest and that the current was increasing in velocity. By the time we reached Altamaha Sound, we were caught in a raceway to the open sea with a storm fast approaching. Halfway down the sound, we were surprised to see a Georgia marine patrol closing in on us. He verified what we saw.

"Big storm coming! Better get off the water!" he said—and then roared off—apparently to warn others.

His advice was easier said than done. We reached Wolf Island and paddled as best we could against the hungry fingers of the sea. The current tugged at us and it looked for a moment as though the storm would hit before we could safely disembark. One hundred yards, fifty yards, twenty yards, ten—land!

"Get out quick! Here! Grab this! Here it comes!"

Jerry's boat was out—mine caught several storm waves broadside and shipped several gallons of water. We didn't say much. Both of us knew if the storm would have hit a few minutes sooner, or land was farther away, we probably would have drowned. Our refuge from the short-lived storm was, ironically, Wolf Island National Wildlife Refuge. Come high tide, though, the area we stood on would be submerged and the boats would be our only refuge. Therefore, we left at the beginning of flood tide and found a high shell mound, just past some fishing shacks near Doboy Sound.

Our tent was pitched underneath a few scraggly pines and sheltered from anything that might blow in during the night. Through the trees, we could see buildings we had passed. I wondered how the folks liked their way of life—no roads, no cars, just boats, the water and the vast saltwater marsh—stretching in some places as the eye could see. Out in the sound, individual shrimp boats moved silently across our field of view.

"This is Georgia lowland country at its best," I said. "What a change from this afternoon."

"You not trespassin' if ya camp below the high tide mark," the marine patrolman said, in answer to our question: "Is it okay to camp here on St. Catherine's Island?"

All three of us knew he was upholding the letter of the law and all three of us knew, as soon as the patrolman left, we'd have equipment and tent set well above any high tide mark. The officer told us the island was used by the University of Georgia and was stocked with a variety of exotic animals including Cape buffalo and imported deer.

"The only animals we're concerned about are JAWS," Jerry said.

The officer dug around in the back of his speedboat for a few minutes.

"Somewhere in this mess, I have jus what ya need! Ah, here it is! It's a lady's bath oil, but it works like a charm."

Just as the patrolman was pulling away, he added another bit of information to our lengthy conversation: "Forgot to tell you; there's 'sposed to be a gorilla on the island too!"

"The thunderstorm, probably kept the gorilla away," we joked. "There wouldn't have been enough beans, applesauce and grits for three anyway."

During a lull in the storm, I left the tent. In the blackness, I imagined a re-enactment of King Kong and wasn't outside for more than a minute. Shortly after, Jerry was called and returned with: "Hey! All the shrimp boats are parked in our front yard!" Sure enough, a traffic jam had formed on Walburg Creek. Our sheltered spot gave no hint of the wind and high waves on St. Catherine's Sound from where the shrimpers had just retreated.

Another barrier island we passed was more blatant in notifying mariners of a hidden threat: "Warning, Health Experiment, National Health Department, Danger, Keep Off!" Our minds filled the paddling time with plausible answers to the riddle—Anthrax, germ warfare, maybe something akin to the "Andromeda Strain"? —But we never found out what lie beyond the posted shore.

The waterway continued to meander through a maze of river systems and sounds. Almost any landmass we paddled by was isolated by water in some way.

At a place called Long Island on the Skidaway River, Jerry returned a "runaway" boat to its proper owner after it had floated off the boat trailer. In the process of towing, Jerry pulled against the tide and split his paddle shaft in half. He held the shaft together with his hand until he reached the shore and saved the runabout from being smashed against a bridge abutment. I saw the owner wave a few greenbacks at Jerry and heard him say: "Here, take this!" But, Jerry shook his head and laughed. "Be more careful next time So long, we gotta make it to Savanna before dark."

Savannah, Georgia, lay a few miles off the Intra-coastal Waterway. We never set foot in Savannah proper, but we did spend time in nearby Isle of Hope. At one time, the area thrived with active plantations. We walked past the entrance of one in our hunger-driven search for a restaurant.

"I guess Savannah supposed to be the oldest town in Georgia, from what they say at the marina," I said.

Old, southern mansions didn't interest us that day, but the letters on a mailbox did. "Take a look at the first and last names—notice anything?" Before Jerry could answer, I replied: "N's are backwards!" I found the irregularity to be a refreshing change from the spit and polish of the community in general and the fancy marina boats with their letters in precise regimentation.

The pilot of one such boat apparently considered himself "Ruler of the Waterway." The forty-foot yacht powered up to us and blasted over its bullhorn: "This is the Intracoastal Waterway! You are gambling with your life!" I gave the pilot some descriptive sign language and wished my craft were equipped with torpedoes. Such flares of arrogance were rare on the waterway and a few hours later, a houseboat full of happy-go-lucky week-enders greeted us. We accepted, as they put it, to attend a "genuine Georgia barbecue," but declined the ride to Daufuskie Landing.

"No thanks, we'll camp at Elba Island tonight on the Savannah River," Jerry said.

"But Elba Island is full of rattlesnakes," one of them replied.

It probably was in our best interests that the steep, clay banks on Elba modified our plans. We landed at a bridge construction sight with a reasonable approach and solid ground—all else was sticky Savannah mud. Apparently, the night watchman realized our situation. His truck headlights inspected our camp and kayaks a couple times but he never bothered us.

We waited for a fast moving tanker and made our jump across the Savannah River into our fourteenth state. Names like Thunderbolt and Sandfly, Georgia, were behind us now. Calibogue Sound and Hilton Head Island lay just "up the road."

Chapter 28

The Carolinas

*"What lies behind you and what lies in front of you
pales in compares to what lives inside you."*
Ralph Waldo Emerson

The tide tricked us on Calibogue Sound. We were certain we'd reach the slack water stage where the sound constricted and divided into Mackay and Skull Creeks. Then, we'd feel the draw of Port Royal Sound a few miles to the north—but it didn't happen. Jerry and I huffed and puffed against a strong ebb tide flowing south and finally pulled in near the sight of an abandoned ferry crossing to make camp.

The spreading darkness helped to rinse the frustrating tidal current from our minds. "What secrets do this part of Hilton Head Island hold?" I wrote. Earlier, at a plush marina at Harbour Town, we had learned the fifteen-mile long island, like most of the others, had been plantation land—long-staple cotton had been grown until the Civil War. More recently, the island had given into a residential and recreational community.

The next day, two sets of horse trails ran along the sand beach where we ate lunch before the jump across five miles of Port Royal Sound to the Beaufort River.

"If our camp last night would have been on this beautiful spot we may have seen riders," I thought. At that moment, I wanted to be on one of those imagined horses and not worry about the tidewater of the sound.

Before we left the beach, three shrimp boats passed close to us pulling their nets behind them. Later, we heard sometime during the same day, a shrimper fell overboard and drowned in Port Royal.

"His big rubber boots just pulled him right down," the man said matter- of-factly. "It happened so quick there was nothin' nobody could do."

The news was given to us at Gallop's Marina across the river from Beaufort.

"I'm just glad we made it across okay," Jerry said.

Both of us had picked up an ill feeling about the sound and a death of a fisherman only compounded it.

"Maybe we picked up on bad vibes coming from Parris Island," I said.

The Marine Corps Recruiting Depot echoed with the pop of mortar and rifle fire, as the waterway lead us past its shores a few hours earlier.

"Remember what Stan said about people being like radio antennas, Jerry? If we picked up any broadcast from those boots on Parris Island, it certainly wouldn't have been one of peace and tranquility."

Another transient at the marina overheard our conversation and that night gave us a gift.

"I want you boys to have this," he said. "It's a lucky bean and it's supposed to protect mariners. I've carried it around for years. You can see how shiny and worn its gotten from bein' in my pocket. I figured you'd need it more than me. Good Luck!"

The crimson sun peeked over the adjacent marshland. It was a sticky, hazy dawn. Jerry and I had slept on the deck of the *Cross Rip*. Tied directly across from her, was the *Joni Ray*. Its two-man crew was bound for Chicago to pick up the president of the McDonald's Corporation. On this part of the inside passage, two unlikely boats, out of mutual need, were traveling together on their journey north. The *Cross Rip*, a day tour passenger boat, was being motored from warm winter waters to start the tourist season at Cape Cod. It was sixty feet long, made of steel and looked as though it could have been used as an icebreaker. In contrast, the *Joni Ray* was a custom made aluminum yacht, eighty feet long, with four bedrooms, including a large master bedroom with "his and her" telephones, chandeliers, a full bar, organ, washer and dryer, color television and two radar units. Its engine room was surgically clean—needless to say, the crusty two-man crew of the *Cross Rip* went hysterical when they saw it.

Six miles from Beaufort, we ran into a heavy flood tide on the Coosaw River. We looked for eddy currents along the swampy shore but couldn't find any. The current pushed us sideways, put a strangle hold on our progress and finally forced a retreat two miles to high ground across from Brickyard Point. The decision, even though frustrating, was a wise one—the next dry ground was fifteen miles away! There would be an advantage waiting till morning for compatible "tide timing." And it worked! The boats moved with the current effortlessly. We covered thirty miles in the same amount of time we did ten miles the day before. Our spirits glowed with the accomplishment in the fading twilight.

"Yeah, this hammock's okay," Jerry said.

The dry ground was a half-mile from the waterway on an oxbow of the Dawho River and held firewood to celebrate a special occasion. The masterpiece was baked in a large kettle over the coals, smothered in a cocoa mix/sugar frosting and topped with a plumber's candle.

"It's still a birthday cake, Randy, even though it sorta tastes like a pancake."

Before we could launch in the morning, the tide rolled out exposing acres of sticky, black mud, oyster shells and logs. Ten hours later with some wading through the muck, reeds and sticks, we pushed into the rising water and were gone. We fought current for two and a half miles until we reached the North Edesto River. There, the kayaks joined the flow and turned up the Wadmalaw River like they were shot out of a cannon.

Nightfall brought us to Yonges Island and to the doorstep of a Charleston area family. Actually, Billy brought us to the doorstep of the house. He was working at his cottage when I asked him if we could camp on the flats bordering his property. Billy didn't recommend it.

"That place is loaded with mocs!" he said. One thing led to another. I followed Billy to the top of the hill overlooking the waterway.

"I always go this way 'cause of the snakes," he said.

We ducked under a fence rail, where the sound of ripping cloth echoed the fate of Billy's new shirt and walked into the house. There, I found myself standing with three weeks of beard growth, bare chest and barefoot amidst seven smiling faces. For an instant, I felt so out of place, dancing a little jig, taking a bow and doing a quick about-face seemed better than explaining what Jerry and I were doing. But the words came out and a conversation ensued.

"Before we spotted the high land here, we were thinking about sleeping in the rusty landing craft moored to the old wharf a ways back. There's just not a lot of camp able ground along the waterway. It's either too low, or the banks too high to pull up on."

"Bring your kayaks up here and pitch your tent in the yard to catch the breeze," the folks said.

By the time Memorial Day weekend was over, we had helped repair the family's back porch, netted blue crabs in the tidewater and enjoyed the hospitality of a southern style, friends and relatives, picnic.

Under way again, we were taken by the flood tide to the tidal shift at Church Flats and the ebb tide through the Stono River, Wapoo Creek and into the Ashley at Charleston. The kayaks covered the twenty-mile distance in less than five hours!

The city, situated on a peninsula, jutted into Charleston Harbor. We were interested in the pre-Civil War city with its mansions, horse drawn buggies, manicured shrubbery and found the heritage preserved in the beautiful homes of "Old Charleston."

"Drop a person down into almost any modern shopping center in the nation and they'd be hard pressed to tell where they are, "Jerry and I heard a tour guide say. "The roots of many cities have died through neglect and unrestricted land use."

Charleston newspaper headlines though, showed another side of the city—a side of violence, unfairness, unrest and deep underlying socio-economic problems. Like many large cities we had visited, Charleston had a strong mixture of bitter with the sweet.

While in Charleston, we also were interested in contacting a company that sold kayaks. Jerry's boat was one of their pre-fab kits and it seemed logical they would be interested in our journey—well, yes and no. After we called, the company gave us the equipment we asked for, but they used the "Santa Claus" approach to our request.

"Someone stopped by here awhile ago and left equipment in your kayak," a woman on board a sailboat from Toronto told us.

I pulled back the poncho from the cockpit and there it was—a pint of contact cement to replenish our dried up supply, drip rings to replace the cracked and decayed ones on my paddle shaft, more fabric for patching and a new paddle for Jerry.

I was packing the badly needed gear, when Jerry received an unusual request from another transient on board a big yacht: "You wouldn't have a vacuum cleaner, by any chance?"

"Just a second, I'll check," Jerry said.

Bouncing back to his rig, he took a look inside.

"Nope. Guess not; do ya wanna sponge?"

As expected, we were the only travelers at the crowded marina who chose to sleep on the dock instead of our boats. The choice brought some interesting results about 1:OO a.m. when two night watchmen came down to the end of the dock where we were. I could hear their footsteps echo on the wooden planking until the probing beam of their flashlight froze to my kayak and then drifted over to my sleeping bag.

"Sir? Where is your boat?"

I answered: "I'm in a kayak; the other boat is over there," I said and pointed.

The two mumbled something like "Jess doin' their own thing" and then shuffled off into the darkness.

"Doin' our own thing" and yes, how beautiful it was, I thought. Earlier in the evening while I sat on the dock, my logbook recorded some deep feelings: "The journey has been good for both of us. Jerry has slowed down and is letting life soak into his being. He has also stopped smoking—a habit he once said would be impossible for him to break. We are nearing nine months on this adventure and my beliefs are changing. I am coming very, very close to a deep inner peace now. I am happy; happier than I have been before in my entire life. I think I may be opening the door to "what life is all about."

Historically, the Civil War started in Charleston Harbor with the bombardment of Fort Sumter on April 12, 1861. Jerry and I landed on a sandbar adjacent to the fort and explored the national monument with others who had arrived by tour boat.

It took over seventy million bricks to make the five-sided fortress. Its walls were five feet thick and reminded us more of a tomb than anything else. We were the last to leave the fort that day. The staff's launch roared away as soon as the final tour boat departed. We followed an hour and a half later, taking the flood tide across the harbor and into the narrow waterway bordering Isle of Palms. Tonight, we'd be the guests of the Darby family who invited us to their home while we were at Yonges Island.

Another family who let us keep our kayaks in their garage heralded our arrival at the rendezvous point—an X marked on the chart—. From that day on, whenever I looked at the largest patch on the hull of my boat, I was always reminded of the Isle of Palms.

Jerry had already disembarked when I accidentally ran over a hidden, razor sharp oyster bed, twenty feet from shore. The encounter resulted in a foot-long slice amidships along the port side. Water gushed in and the boat nearly half submerged before I thudded to shore.

"Now I know why we got this glue and fabric in Charleston," I said.

The Darby's home was on the Atlantic side of the island. After we cleaned up, Jerry and I sat with Mr. Darby on the screened porch. In the dark we talked and listened to the surf while a moist sea breeze poured over us.

"This is why I like this place," Mr. Darby commented.

Those were the only words spoken for many minutes. We all realized a person's need to relax, to absorb part of a greater wholeness in order to put things into proper perspective. There was no need for conversation.

"This is my parents' place," Mrs. Darby said as the car curved down the long drive lined with azaleas and arching cathedral oaks. The mansion loomed ahead of us. Its stately white columns reminded me of "Tara" in *Gone With the Wind*. King Charles II of England could date the eight hundred acre estate, like other areas between the 31st and 36th parallels, to the original Carolinas land grant in 1663. Originally, it was a rice plantation run by slave labor. We drove down to the old landing. Mrs. Darby motioned with her arms, while she described the place. Her description reminded me of the Charleston slave market area. I wondered if an entire way of life based on over consumption and the wasteful use of limited resources would someday seem as immoral as a life style based on forced servitude. And our tour continued.

"Back then a mammy raised the master's kids. One of the things she'd use was a jostlin' board, like the one here. It was sorta like a rockin' chair, except you would bounce instead of rock"

The contrast of rich and poor occurred immediately after we left the estate. Ben and Lela's home was a short distance, where we stopped to pick cucumbers and yellow squash. Compared to the material wealth we had just been exposed to, Ben and Lela had very little. Yet, they radiated a special warmth stemming from a much simpler life style. They spoke Gullah, a hybrid language originating from the colonizers—slaves from the West Indies and the English. Both of them wished us luck and laughed when Jerry told them about our trip. They also refused to accept any money for the vegetables.

Along the highway, we stopped to look at the wares displayed by an older black lady weaving grass baskets. What treasures she had: Large and small baskets— some covered, some not— flower and napkin holders, place settings and mats. Her dress was from a bygone era. The empty beer can Jerry saw her toss into the bushes as we drove away—was not. In that moment, the romanticized image of the "black basket weaver" shattered for us. We were looking at a real person and both of us felt good about that.

Our stay at the Darby's home found us swimming and sailing in the ocean. We rolled and tumbled in the saltwater surf and balanced a Hoby Cat on one pontoon, as it skipped like a stone in the blue beyond the breakers.

The waterway was much different than the great sea. It had changed from a course following barrier island passageways to one resembling and called, "The Big Ditch." For the most part, we'd now be on it, except for a handful of sound and river crossings, until Norfolk, four hundred and sixty miles away.

The sleepy town of McClellanville, South Carolina, bordered the "Big Ditch." Francis Marion National Forest surrounding it and the adjacent Cape Romaine National Wildlife Refuge offered the town's residents a natural buffer from the commotion of the outside world. Here, Ed, a cinematographer settled for "spiritual exploration" and inspiration.

We had just finished mooring our kayaks amidst shrimp boats when Ed, out of a strange calling, came down to greet us.

"I knew someone would be down here," he said. "I just had the feeling."

Before long, our rigs were loaded atop a well used '61 station wagon and we were moved a few blocks to a shaded, tin roofed, rustic in town home with a big garden. We met the rest of the "family"—Randy, his wife Claudia and James, another friend. Randy made casting nets and guitars. The sum of our conversations took place sitting in the sheltered limbs of "Deer Head" oak, situated on a boulevard near the house.

"I've lived in crowded West Coast cities; here the trees even look like they're happy; they just love to grow. Hey, I'm alive! Hey, I'm a tree!" Ed said.

"In a city, a person has a tendency to rely on outside stimulation; out here it must come from within," James added.

Later, I wrote: "I watched the rain fall. The cat slept. Water dripped from the steep tin roof, from the sawbuck, off the branches and shrubs. It soaked the firewood logs and the ground. It was a happy, warm, misty day— another one spent at McClellanville." The karma held us for three nights and two and a half days.

The following evening, we shared a campfire near the waterway with two canoeists. They were paddling from Norfolk to Orlando and had their camp set up when we passed by. Butch's original partner had quit, so Gentry replaced him. His bushy beard and badly sun burned, hairless head, along with the fact he had broken a canoe paddle in half while trying to unsuccessfully collect a few mullet for dinner, amused us. Butch was the more serious of the two and had a philosophical approach to traveling. Jerry and I listened to Butch amidst croaking bullfrogs and Gentry's snoring.

"I love the life I'm leading now. This simple life style, the lack of material things, has cleansed my mind. What was important then, is just trivial and meaningless to me now."

Butch told us what lie ahead and we told him what was in store farther south. The evening conversation was so interesting; I made the mistake of sitting on the bare ground. I should have known better and used a boat cushion. We were in chigger country and the next day my backside was loaded with itching welts. On nature calls, it looked like I had contracted measles.

The marker buoys crossed Winyah Bay and up the Waccamaw River before the canal branched again. Cypress and Tupelo bordered the river and the water tasted fresh for the first time in months. It was incredibly beautiful, though it offered no high ground to camp until we reached the Wacca Wache marina and met Harris. Even then, the tent stayed in Jerry's boat after Harris made arrangements with his wife, Janet, to expect a couple of guests.

That night and the next morning, we were given red-carpet treatment. Harris worked with a man named Jim, who gave us a helicopter ride over the Myrtle Beach area. What a different perspective from water to air. Jim flew over the beach. Pinpoints of light stretched as far as we could see. Shadowy breakers rolled in below us and beyond them the infinite blackness of the Atlantic.

In the morning, we found ourselves roaring through the former rice and indigo bottomlands with Harris piloting an airboat. I didn't know how fast we were going, but when I looked at Jerry, the wind had pushed back his hair giving him a "Bride of Frankenstein" appearance.

Harris let us off and roared away with the intention of cutting a new path for airboat rides. For fifteen minutes the airplane engine mounted on pontoons droned like a bee—then silence. Ten minutes later, we caught the sputtering, coughing sounds of Harris' prize tour boat, as the machine came limping around the bend. We barely recognized the bent frame covered with mud and reeds. Harris had one hand covering a nasty looking knot on his head. As the crowd gathered, the only thing he could say was: "Hit a stump?"

Two days later, I had my turn. It happened as we crossed the border into North Carolina. The yacht *East of the Sun* (We talked with the crew the day before) roared up from behind, partially shut down, plowed water and produced a huge wake. I watched the roller break at the channel drop-off. Then, everything seemed to go into slow motion, as my rig broached the wall of white water and flipped upside down. Yellow—my eyes were open wide under water and that's all I could remember seeing. I rolled out of the kayak, as it turned over and popped to the surface. My visor hat and sunglasses were the only things missing. I grabbed a stray water jug, the 35mm camera bobbing around in its triple wrapper of bread bags and tossed them into the cockpit which was now even with the waterline. I looked around; Jerry looked bewildered. His boat had taken a few gallons of water in the process of riding over the breaker. *East of the Sun* was now completely shut down and idling sideways in the narrow channel.

"Oh my God! Are you all right?" they screamed.

"I don't know yet!" I yelled.

"Is there anything we can do?"

And they threw Jerry down a couple of dry towels.

"You better go before you get stuck," Jerry said. "We'll manage."

I didn't notice the blood until we got to shore. Somehow, my left hand tangled with an oyster bed and was sliced from the top of the little finger to halfway down the palm. At the moment, I didn't care about the wound and proceeded to pass equipment to shore and began bailing. However, that night, amidst the closely packed pine saplings, vines and poison ivy, sharks entered my mind.

"You're lucky there were none around," I thought. "This little mishap could have turned into something much worse."

"Sunday insanity on the waterway!" I wrote in my journal. "Boats everywhere! People darting every which way in a mad, frenzy! It seems they are here for some kind of 'quick fix, an adrenalin rush! It more than disturbs us ... it scares us!"

The water skiers especially worried us. A skier-kayaker collision, or a rope snapping across one of our necks would be disastrous. The boiling cauldron simmered down at dusk, as weekenders packed up to leave. Both of us remember "Mr. Out-a-sight-out-a-mind." He backed his camper down the dead end road near our pine-studded campsite, got out, looked around and then commenced to dump the contents of his holding tank into the Intracoastal Canal!

It seemed as though Lester and his family had been waiting for us. We apologized for leaving our kayaks in their vacant boat slip, but Lester didn't care. He was an easy-going person from Charlotte who listened intently to our story. I told him about the dunking two days before and Lester responded by taking off his sunglasses and handing them to me.

"Take these; you'll need them more than me."

We talked some more. As we did, two alligators surfaced a half paddle length from the kayaks. The reaction of kids aboard Lester's boat was immediate. Their eyes became saucer-size as they were sure the 'gators would "eat the little kayaks for lunch!"

Big water worried us more that alligators and the Cape Fear River entrance wasn't very far away. We assured the kids that if indeed the 'gators were following us, we'd lose them as soon as we left the channel.

The Cape Fear River was remarkably calm. The Frying Pan Shoal lightship was moored at Southport near the river entrance. It was one of many such ships rapidly being replaced along the Atlantic Coast by more sophisticated, self-sustaining, navigational aids. Farther up the line, a few miles before Snows Cut, the strong smell of gardenias wafted across the two-mile wide river.

We camped at on the west end of Snows Cut, directly across the channel from the six hundred foot Loran towers. The red lights winked to us from the tops of the masts. Even though Jerry and I had no way of deciphering the radio signals, we still felt comforted in knowing someone at sea was relying on the Loran beam to find their way.

The night was peaceful. My mom and dad were planning to meet us at Surf City, North Carolina, in two days.

"Thirty-seven miles in two days—easy," we told ourselves. "We'll make it, no sweat." We should have known better—the statement was not tempered with a qualifier.

Low clouds hid the towers at launch time. It would rain for a while and stop, each time recycling with growing intensity. We crept along the east side of the waterway through Myrtle Grove Sound, bucking tides and high winds. Both of us were deaf to waterway traffic approaching astern. It became an irritating, but necessary nuisance, to periodically crank our heads and check conditions behind us.

We were also deaf to each other. Our rain hoods and the roar of colliding water droplets, made talking or shouting next to impossible. Plus, I couldn't open my mouth—the cords tightening the hood over my head were held between my teeth because they were too short to tie around my chin. During a respite between sheets of driving rain, I gestured to Jerry and we headed into shore.

The folks at the Masonboro Marina suggested using their facilities to cover the *Molly B* with a fiberglass hull, but I declined. Long before their suggestion, I had become attached to the boat in spite of her frailties and with fingers crossed, I said: "If she made it this far, she'll go the rest of the way too!"

I hitchhiked to Surf City the next day to keep the rendezvous. By the time we got back, Jerry had been extended the offer of part ownership in a sailboat—if he could come up with three grand. Mom and Dad were also offered the cabin of another sailboat, but cordially declined in favor of a motel.

The reunion brought us up to date on things back home and replenished bits and pieces of worn out equipment and clothing. It also acted as a measuring stick, revealing change in Jerry and me. We were flowing with the journey and our speech and mannerisms reflected it. My parents couldn't get over how relaxed we were—especially Jerry. The last time they saw him, he was very impatient and hyperactive. It was different now, so different. I hoped my parents had absorbed some of the good karma we had acquired over the months before they drove north.

The Intracoastal Waterway ran through Camp LeJeune's gunnery range. As we floated there, I felt like telling the marines in the safety boat: "Why don't you pick on somebody your own size?" However, as we watched everyone else roar through, it was obvious that a johnboat equipped with a twenty horse Johnson could only stop kayaks. Although, they did tell us about a belligerent sailor who was surprised when a short shell trimmed his mast.

We couldn't hear anything. Apparently, the howitzers were back in the interior of the camp; the targets were somewhere out in the Atlantic; and we were in the middle. Three hours passed. "Okay, you can go now." While they sped off to the barracks, we sat in our boats wondering where they expected us to go?

"Hell, it's almost dark," I said. "We can't be on the waterway at night and we can't sleep in this place, or can we?"

We paddled as far as impending darkness allowed and put up a hundred feet from a range tower directly across from a "WARNING DUD AREA, NO TRESPASSING and U.S. MILITARY RESERVATION" sign.

"If they want us, they can come and get us," Jerry grumbled.

Fortunately, the only serenade that night was made by spring peepers.

The waterway led us to Boque Sound and Spooner Creek Marina. The wooden sailboat we had met during the morning was there and they invited us on board for fresh, baked clams. While disembarking, we met a family who recently had traded their home for a live-aboard sailboat. Sally, Sandy and their daughter, Parker, were settling into their new life style of "nomadism."

"Used to be I had to trim the shrubbery and cut the grass," Sandy said. "Now, I have other chores like polishing the brass and rubbing down the teak."

They drove us to a popular seafood restaurant in Moorehead City, where we ate soft-shell crab. "The crab is taken during the molting stage, when the shell is still soft," we were told. What a change from eating blue crabs, cracked open with the back of a table knife. For eating the stone crab claws, a pair of pliers was added to our tableware.

Jerry and I were plagued by storms, chores and general laziness at Spooner's Creek. The three-night stay and the hydrogen peroxide Sally had given me helped heal the "sun poison" on the backs of my hands. It seemed every time I'd reach into the forward part of my kayak, I'd scrap my hands on the edges of a conduit crossframe. The resulting, painful scrapes never totally healed in the sun and I was afraid I'd develop skin cancer. Earlier, I had shown my hands to a fisherman at Sneed's Ferry. He, in turn, showed me the backs of his hands, scarred with brown and white blotches.

"Don't know what it is', he said. "Jess gets that way from the weather."

The kids at the marina would have liked our camp-site alongside a narrow cut leading to Adams Creek and the Neuse River. Jerry and I figured with recycled aluminum selling for fifteen cents a pound, they would have cleaned our camp in no time. After gathering as many cans as we could and burning a considerable amount of paper and refuse, the area reflected a bit of its original beauty. The tranquility of the water, the nearly full moon and the pines produced a magical effect. A whippoorwill called from the deep woods and suddenly I was part of the old way.

"I am an ancient one tonight, sitting before the campfire," I wrote. "Listening and absorbing the sounds of my world. The forest primeval. For an instant, I am primitive again."

Come morning, the feeling was still there, captured in the cool, stillness of the glassy waterway and glowing forest corridor. As we absorbed the scene, two chalk-white shrimp boats entered and departed, rippling the water with surface harmonics. "Time to go," Jerry said in a low voice.

The eight o'clock start was supposed to give us enough time to cross the Neuse, but en route, a houseboat at the mouth of Adams Creek caught our attention.

"Where're ya goin'?" one of the men yelled.

"Minnesota!"

"Where're ya comin' from?"

"Minnesota!"

"Put it this way— where have you been?"

In one long breath, I yelled back a geography book of names and locations.

"Wanna beer?" was the reply.

Without further words, we joined the five-man crew.

"According to our wives," one of them said, "we're supposed to be on a fishing trip, but as you can determine for yourself, we have very little to show for our efforts."

The teeth of a strong northeast wind caught us as we rounded Winthrop Point. In the growing swells and whitecaps, both of us simultaneously agreed the six-mile crossing should be delayed till early morning and crowded the point until we found a suitable place to land. The sandy beach was scattered with half buried drift and bald cypress. A marsh bordered the back of it.

The wind died as late afternoon found us lounging on the beach absorbed in writing, planning and wondering. I held in my hand pottery shards our houseboat buddies had given us. Again, we were in an area where human footsteps had been felt for centuries.

Looking up, I saw another houseboat chugging toward "our" beach. This time, two men and two women, drawn by curiosity, parked while we carried on a dangling conversation.

"We've been out for nine and a half months now," Jerry said.

The dumfounded group was silent. Then the blond-haired women knitted her brow, looked at her cohort and said: "Some couples don't even stay married that long!"

We waved goodbye to the foursome, knowing they were leaving with more questions than when they arrived. The women's reply, probably said in jest, was actually quite profound. Jerry and I didn't know the answer either. We could only speculate on the bond between us. With all the difficulties we had gone through, why hadn't we given up? Why hadn't we had a serious fight? Why hadn't we, as the houseboat group couldn't figure out, killed each other by now? Perhaps, being in separate kayaks helped. Or, the fact we were able to compromise on major issues.

Whatever it was, it was working, oftentimes to our own amazement.

The evening ended with a final logbook entry: "We sleep on the beach tonight, under the stars, to insure us an early start. I'm writing by fading firelight. The red coals grow dim and I turn to write by the blue glow of the full moon. "

Jerry and I shook a dozen or so translucent sand fleas from our sleeping bags before we crawled from our cocoons in the predawn light. It was a cool morning; now and then a waft of warm air would wash over us as we paddled.

The journey across the Neuse River and back into a narrow canal leading to the giant Pamlico and Pungo Rivers was a bypass route for us. To the east lies Pamlico Sound—eighty miles long and from fifteen to thirty miles wide. The famous Outer Banks, part of Cape Hatteras National Seashore, bordered its eastern edge. Jerry and I debated the Outer Banks run while we were at Moorehead City and decided to stay in the "not so scenic," but more protected, waterway.

A lady running the general store at Hobucken warned us about the rattlesnakes usually found along the canal.

"A boy just got bit last week," she said. "Was playin' with the snake and it bit him on the finger."

We promised her we'd be extra careful in the swampy areas we were paddling through. The warning also made us think about the possibility of a rattler crawling inside one of our boats and revealing itself once we were underway. Consequently, I thought the worst when Jerry stopped paddling and stared with disbelief into his kayak.

"What the Hell?" Hey Randy, there's voices coming out of my boat!"

Jerry said they sounded like muffled radio messages. The mysterious transmission lasted for thirty seconds and then was gone. Blackbeard's Ghost? Maybe! He met his fate in 1718 outside of Ocracoke, about twenty miles from where we camped that night.

Luck was with us the morning we crossed seventeen miles of open water to Belhaven, North Carolina. The logbook captures the image that saturated our senses for six hours:

"The approach to Belhaven was unbelievable, the water was flat—slick. It gave us the impression we could climb out of our kayaks and walk across the water into town. Puffy clouds over the Outer Banks, fifty miles away, hung in the shapes of animals and people against a blue sky."

Jerry and I had been tipped off about Belhaven's famous smorgasbord restaurant. If the cooks knew we were coming, they would have locked the doors. For two hours we stoked up on enough energy to last us from noon till lunch the next day.

The quiet community held another remarkable spot called Eyi's Little Store—a one-time gas station, converted into an arts and crafts shop. The ceramics, carvings, painting and other displays of talent made a deep impression on us. The days of paddling and the harshness of our life style allowed us to appreciate the shop's fragile and delicate creations more fully than if we were traveling an easier way.

When we returned to our rigs, mid afternoon winds had whipped the Pungo River into a mass of whitecaps. Obligingly, we stayed.

The food, rest and fair weather the next morning were the ingredients for a thirty-seven and a half mile day, our best ever for flat-water paddling. Maybe the land had something to do with it, too. There was no place to camp in the cypress swamp surrounding our water highway. The Alligator-Pungo Canal led into the Alligator River and left us nothing to beach on except a lumpy, waterlogged spoil area at the river's southern end. The deer flies and mosquitoes were horrendous. We lifted the kayaks through a maze of sharp stumps and tied them fast. Our tent was a few feet higher, on a mound covered with thick weeds. As far as we could tell, it was the only place to camp and a dangerous place to camp. We were at an elbow of the Alligator River, which reached some forty miles north into Albemarle Sound. Although the area we were in had no cyclic tide to speak of, any storms coming in from the north would have all too easily washed our tent, kayaks and bodies into the bowels of the swamp.

At first light, we paddled thirty miles straight north to Haulover Point across from Durant Island. The warm, wine colored freshwater of East Lake leading into Albemarle Sound, along with beach sand that squeaked under our feet, established it as the favorite swimming hole of the entire journey.

The trick in crossing Albemarle Sound involved an eastern circumnavigation of the big water. A series of jumps took us from Haulover Point to Fort Raleigh on Roanoke Island (ten miles), Roanoke to Kill Devil Hills (seven miles) and from there to the mouth of the North river (seventeen miles). The whole thing looked simple.

"Should take us no more than two days, Jerry."

In reality, it took seven. Again, the determining factor was weather. Our anticipated, brief stay at Roanoke Island ended up being a five-day educational seminar induced by rain and high winds.

One of the caretakers, much to his surprise, found us the first morning sleeping underneath the nurse's station near the waterside open-air theater. However, before we left the island, we were staying at the performer's living quarters, a few blocks away.

Historically, Roanoke Island was the first attempt at establishing an English colony in North America by Sir Walter Raleigh. The first settlers came in 1585, followed by a group of over a hundred men, women and children in 1587. England's troubles with Spain caused the colony to go three years in the North American wilderness without outside aid. When supply ships returned, in 1590, the colony had disappeared.

The "Lost Colony" play, based on fact and conjecture, gave Jerry and me an idea of what could have went on in the hearts and minds of those left behind. We saw the drama twice—on the third and fourth nights of our stay. By then, the heavy rains had stopped, but the wind was still strong. On Monday night, it was gusting to fifty knots. I don't think many members of the audience noticed the sails were not unfurled on the "ship." If they were, the prop would have been airborne along with the stagehands who—while standing in waste deep water—held fast to guy lines attached to the masts.

It was that night, tropical storm Amy, lying some two hundred miles off the Outer Banks, filled Jerry and me with uneasiness. The storm was building and could either move toward land or out to sea. Thoughts of the devastation at Biloxi left by Hurricane Camille raced through my mind. Again, I saw the plaque in a Biloxi park dedicated to those who had perished during that awful night in 1969.

"Could the same thing happen here?" I thought, "Maybe."

Earlier, when it was light, open areas of Albemarle Sound were a mass of frothing, whitecaps. The impending disaster prompted Jerry and me to move our rigs from a safe to a safer location. In the darkness, we lugged them from the base of the sand dune, near the nurse's quarters, to the edge of the woods on top of the dune. During the tedious relocation, the wind and sand were blowing so hard we could hardly stand up! The screaming, wind-blown particles choked us and obscured our vision. The soft sand made us sink and stumble with every step. It took a Herculean effort to move the craft thirty feet.

By morning, we received word "Amy was moving out to sea" and the winds should be subsiding within twenty-four hours. Tension eased. The five pounds of sand, blown into our covered kayaks, seemed infinitesimally small in contrast to what could have happened to them.

By now, most of the folks, including the park Service people, had warmed up to us considerably. Even Royden, the three hundred pound maintenance man who had roared at us during our first morning on the island, opened up the dressing room so we could shower.

When late evening came, both of us witnessed a realistic showdown in the actors' apartment complex. When it was over and the "shootin' irons"—cans of Lysol—were put back on the shelf, all of us went out to the balcony for a breath of fresh air.

"Hey do ya hear it?" one of the "gunfighters," exclaimed. "I mean, it's what you don't hear; the wind has stopped!"

We were gone the following afternoon. Ridges of dunes, several hundred feet high, situated on the northern portion of the Outer Banks, were bathed in afternoon light as we paddled across seven miles of the sound. The huge monolith commemorating the Wright Brothers' flight of December 17th, 1903, was visible from our departure point, so was Nag's Head, where the ghost of a headless horseman, according to local folklore, rode along the sand dunes.

Jerry stood at the monument when the sun set, while I stayed with the equipment. Come morning, I took the same hike to the same place and watched the sun rise over the ocean. I went cross-country, through wooded areas and over sand dunes. Finally, there I was standing on the hill where powered flight began. There was a haunting loneliness about the area as the orange-balloon sun broke the horizon. I looked east at the glowing sky. For a moment, things seemed frozen. The distant breakers looked as though they were captured on an artist's canvas—motionless, frozen in time.

I thought of what Royden had told us about the area: "Out there lies the ghost fleet of the Outer Banks," he said. "The bones of over seven-hundred ships scattered up and down them shoals!" Wrecks caused by storms. Wrecks caused by pirates luring the innocent into the surf by lanterns tied to hobbled horses. Wrecks caused by blockade-runners and Union ships. Wrecks caused by World War II German submarines lurking beneath the waters of crowded coastal shipping lanes.

My gaze turned toward the monument and the busts of the two who opened the door to the world of flight. From there, my eyes moved to the small airport below the hill. The past and the present in a single sweep. There was no sense of time, only the vast endless eternity of now.

Chapter 29

Virginia

"I have never let my schooling interfere with my education."

Mark Twain

Coinjock was behind us and Pungo Ferry was fifteen more miles. To get there, Currituck Sound and part of the North Landing River would have to slide underneath our boats. The project was almost effortless. Everything clicked; both of us were supercharged with energy; there was no wind to speak of, our minds had reached a comfortable "paddling set" and the kayaks seemed to glide further than normal after each paddle stroke. A couple weeks earlier, Jerry and I had concluded saltwater was harder to paddle in than freshwater. Maybe the density had something to do with it, or maybe salt air just tired us out faster.

The rigs crossed into Virginia. Coaxed by anxiety induced from black clouds crackling with lightning, they sped down a reed-bordered river to the safety of the Pungo Ferry Marina. The marina wasn't our intended stopover, just like in so many other instances, it was just meant to be that way.

"Fourth of July, the three-hundredth day of the Trilogy. time and distance traveled seem to be determined by something greater than ourselves. A few hours ago, we didn't know where we'd sleep or eat. Presently, we are in a cabin and have just finished a flounder dinner—complements of Mr. Heart, owner of the Pungo Ferry Marina and Restaurant. Back at Albemarle Sound, we had a choice of paddling our present route—Virginia Cut—or altering our course slightly to the west, leading us past Elizabeth City on the Pasquotank River and through the Dismal Swamp Canal. Both routes are sixty-five miles long and both routes lead to Norfolk. Tonight we are quite glad to have chosen the former." rrb

Fourth of July weekend on the waterway was no place for kayakers. Jerry and I anticipated the crunch of boats and people and conveniently "lost" visiting friends in the Norfolk area.

While we were waiting, I attempted to fix my "waterproof" duffel bag with sheet metal tape—the life extender of most of our gear. By now, there was more tape on it than original material.

I was busily taping away when Henry and his wife Geraldine arrived. Henry was the brother of my father's friend. They had been waiting for us ever since I wrote them in Florida. Henry was outdoor-oriented and bubbled with enthusiasm about our travels. During our visit, they took us to the "Dismal Swamp"— now one-third of its former thousand square miles—to go grocery shopping and to a family Fourth of July picnic.

We walked around the grounds at Colonial Williamsburg and through the galleries at the Mariners Museum at Newport News. The museum captured the romance of the sea. It was interesting to see all the bits and pieces of ships' hardware lined up in neat rows.

The paint and glitter, though, could easily blind one to the other side of the coin—the sea's cruelness. I thought of the story we had heard, about an old fisherman who had no hands. His boat sank some hundred miles off the mainland during a winter storm, forcing him to row a small dory. When he was finally rescued, his hands were nothing more than dead weights frozen to the oars of his lifeboat.

The holiday weekend blew out two pole transformers at the marina. The crowds were gone, but the ladies in the restaurant were still cooking by candlelight while the electric company attempted to repair the damage. The power outage shut down the water pump and all we could obtain was one and a half gallons from a container in the kitchen. Our departure was aborted anyway when another fierce electrical storm rolled down the waterway.

One bolt of lightning hit the Pungo Ferry swing bridge, putting it out of commission for three hours. The incident created a waterway traffic jam that flooded the marina's bar with impatient transients and caused a major headache for the bridge tender.

Before the incident ended and the bridge was again "swinging," a score of maintenance people had become involved in an episode not unlike the Keystone Cops. Personnel scurried up and down and under the bridge while the tender pushed buttons and stood around with his hand on his hips. Warning bells sounded periodically, but nothing happened. At one time, Jerry and I noticed five people standing around, all with their hands on their hips, apparently waiting for divine intervention.

The episode inspired me to record: "Modern society—how easy we live, just a flick of the switch. Modern society—how vulnerable we are, just an overload or short circuit brings everything to a screeching halt."

Altogether, we spent ten days in the Norfolk area sleeping indoors. It hadn't been planned that way—it just happened. The *Ledger Star* carried a story on us and it had been released by the time we left Pungo Ferry. That afternoon, after paddling sixteen miles— divided equally between the narrow North Landing River and the Albemarle-Chesapeake Canal—we stopped at a marina near Great Bridge. There, the "celebrities" slept overnight in the crew's quarters of a yacht and left the next day with a new nautical library of books, charts and maps.

"I bet we got more charts here than most yachts," Jerry commented.

At least, someone didn't know we were coming through. It was the lockmaster at the Great Bridge Lock—Jerry had to wake him up. On the other side of the 2.5-foot drop, we entered the tidal Southern Branch of the Elizabeth River leading into Chesapeake Bay. As we cleared the lock gates, we were approached by a war canoe loaded with kids, armed with paddles flashing erratically in the sunlight. The counselor on board invited us to come ashore and "take a breather" at Camp Young.

"We saw you in the paper," he said.

"We saw you and your camp in the paper too," I added.

It was refreshing and important to see inner city youth being exposed to new experiences and positive challenges. The counselors, in effect, were liberating these kids by giving them a broader perspective on life. In essence, their work was just as important as the two hundred year old message on the sign at Great Bridge, only a few hundred yards away: "Thirty minutes of fighting, two hundred years of freedom."

The woman at Holiday Harbor Marina knew about the "kayakers." She offered us some money, but we refused.

"We don't need the money ma'am; just keep us in your thoughts," was our reply.

I could feel the acid gnawing away in the pit of my stomach as we untied the lines and crawled back into our rigs. The kind woman watched us depart and I'm sure waited till our kayaks grew to specks, then paddle flashes, finally disappearing amidst the giants of the harbor. Norfolk Harbor was unavoidable. In order to get to Chesapeake Bay, we had to pass through it.

The harbor lived up to its name "Home Port United States Navy, Atlantic Fleet." We yawed, pitched and rolled past destroyers, battle ships, troop carriers, tugs, freighters and fireboats. Traffic came from all directions and we stayed out of its way as best we could.

Harbors are big, noisy and oftentimes confusing places. On the other hand, they are also exciting and fascinating to be in. Jerry and I both agreed the highlight of our harbor "tour" was paddling across the bow of the U.S.S. Nimitz. The United States' largest aircraft carrier was moored to a pier. I remember waving to two tiny figures dressed in white leaning over the forward edge of the flight deck. I waved and waved; Jerry joined in, but the salutes were never returned. If the sailors saw us at all, I suspect they are still wondering what we were doing there.

Come late afternoon, we were at the Willoughby Bay Marina situated on a spit separating Hampton Roads from Chesapeake Bay. When the weather was right, we'd make our jump across the reach. From our vantage point, we could see Fort Monroe, our immediate destination, three miles away.

The fort was designed by one of Napoleon's engineers. General Lee, who was instrumental in constructing the fort. The fort was never attacked during the Civil War because he considered it impenetrable. During that same era, the fort's surrounding water was the sight of the 1862 duel between the Union's ironclad gunboat *Monitor* and its equally armed Confederate counterpart, *Merrimack*. The battle between the two revolutionary warships was indecisive and the Union's effective blockade of the Confederacy held. The stranglehold however, on February 12, 1864, did cause the south to use a little known piece of technology. This time, the *Hunley*, an experimental Confederate submarine, successfully sank the Federal ship *Housatonic*, off Isle of Palms near Charleston. But the war had been too long. The *Hunley's* crew perished after the tiny submarine was sucked into the breached side of the *Housatonic*. The South surrendered a little over a year later. Jefferson Davis was held prisoner at a fort that one of his general's helped build.

Our kayaks waited out four days of rain at the marina, while Jerry and I spent our time at an apartment. Chuck "discovered" us at the marina while he was working on his boat the *Liki-Tiki*. The time spent indoors made us very restless. My logbook commentary of the shopping mall next door captures my mood while in "confinement:

"An easy life spoils the mind and body. I walked to the mall. The noise, cars and confusion really bothered me. The place had all kinds of material things to pleasure the senses, but I didn't see anything that could bring happiness."

The weather wasn't settled when we launched. On the other side of the Hampton Roads Bridge-Tunnel, a squall hit. The winds came, waves quickly grew in height and both of us were scared. The advice given to us at Pungo Ferry echoed though my head: "If you're caught on the bay, dig your paddles deep into the water and quarter the waves."

"Let's land before they get any bigger!" Jerry yelled.

We edged toward the beach, Jerry fifty feet ahead of me. I saw his boat completely submerge in the breaking surf and then pop up again. Jerry was now out of his boat, past the surf and scrambling toward shore before the next wave broke.

Then it was my turn. The water grabbed the *Molly B.* like a powerful fist and pushed the tiny boat toward shore with uncontrollable speed. Somehow, I managed not to broach in the tumbling water and road through the surf, soaked but intact. It was our first taste of mid-afternoon squalls on Chesapeake Bay.

Warnings about Chesapeake Bay had been given to us even while we were on the Mississippi. Many mariners and pseudo-mariners frowned at us attempting the western shore of the bay to Annapolis.

"Too many big rivers to cross in those little boats!" they collectively said.

Someone even suggested crossing the mouth of the bay and traveling the east shore to avoid the James, York, Rappahannock, Potomac and Patuxent Rivers, as well as Mobjack Bay.

The comments and suggestions were taken with a grain of salt. Following them would have meant paddling seventeen and a half miles across the mouth of the bay and the open Atlantic. "Sure, we could just follow the Bridge-Tunnel across and get killed in the process," we said to ourselves. Our kayaks were on the western shore and that's where we'd stay until we got to Annapolis.

There, a four-mile jump would take us to the eastern shore.

The overload of static created by the layover was gone, in its place a sense of inner calm pervaded. While we watched a violent storm brew near the Poquoson River, the sea grass on York Point manifested my feelings. My journal recalls: "The waves washing rhythmically over the grass made it look like so much giant, green cilia—it was a very peaceful."

The storm never did hit us. There was no rain, just a strong east wind that lasted thirty seconds. A cool breeze then picked up from the west and faded into absolute stillness—allowing thousand of hungry gnats an opportunity of a lifetime.

One could easily spend several years exploring the rivers, hurricane holes and backwaters of Chesapeake Bay. We paddled over the slick waters of the York River in the evening—now and then bobbing over a glassy wave. If we used our imaginations, we could see silhouettes of packet boats bound to and from the colonial village of Yorktown.

The serenity of the York River melted into the waters of the Chesapeake. We crossed six miles of Mobjack Bay while morning light poured in from our starboard side. At first, we paddled toward a pinpoint on the other side that eventually grew into a lighthouse. The structure was abandoned; its sentry duty now taken over by a more sophisticated marker. The old structure was marvelous. The trapezoidal tower was made of large hewn stones and an osprey had made its nest atop the light cupola. The structure glowed in the morning light as we moved by.

We were again plagued by storms in the late afternoon. It was disquieting to constantly turn around and see the sky growing blacker as a storm front approached. The thunder grew louder and louder. Sometimes the storm hit and sometimes it didn't. I could smell rain when we finally decided to beach, but again, no storm—just a frustrating hoax followed by a wind shift, which prevented us from re-launching our kayaks.

The night was pure misery. The no-see-ems made sure we didn't sleep over five minutes at a time. "When the hell are we gonna get rid of these bugs?" Jerry asked, as we walked back and forth on the beach spooning down our granola in the sticky-wind dawn. The cloud of insects literally pushed us into the bay. By the time breakfast was finished, we were shuffling back and forth in the surf to keep our feet free of new welts.

The day began with bugs and ended on a swampy island covered with dead seagulls. There, two helpless kayakers watched a huge waterspout bear down on them. While we starred at impending doom, I thought of previous mariners who had battled storms, high seas and creatures of the depths. I thought especially of Gwynn Island where we had stopped earlier in the day and the wealth of seafarers it had produced. I thought of ships being broken to pieces by nature's forces and I thought of us—afraid and cold, unable to do anything but lie there with our faces next to the sand.

The spout was gray-white. It danced over the water—first straight down then twisting like an elephant's trunk. The beast grew closer and closer and then it VANISHED!

The passing storm left a sick feeling in the pit of my stomach, which remained until we crossed the Potomac the next day. For months, we had been told Potomac River horror stories. Of how small crafts had been caught in the chops of opposing wind and tidal currents. "Why, I remember crossing the Potomac—she was like glass and then like that, we were in six foot waves!"

The Potomac was calm as we stood on Ginny Beach and eyed it with binoculars. Before we made the decision to cross, Jerry and I got into a heated discussion concerning the crossing location. I wanted to paddle eighteen miles up the Virginia shore and cross from Sandy Point to Saint George Island Beach where the river was only four miles wide. Jerry wanted to make a straight, ten-mile shot across the river from where we stood.

"Randy, I have a gut feeling that we should make the jump now and go straight across. I just feel that it's the right thing to do."

I really didn't have a gut feeling either way. I did know I was coming down with a bad cold and felt tired and feverish, which probably added to my apprehension about crossing so much all at once.

"Oh hell, let's get it over with," I barked.

The three-hour crossing went without incident. After all we had heard, it was uncanny to breeze to the other side virtually without effort.

Chapter 30

Maryland

"I love to think of nature as an unlimited broad-casting station, through which God speaks to us every hour, if we will only tune in."

George Washington Carver

The Potomac divided Virginia from Maryland. It was our seventeenth state and the barns found scattered along the coves near Ridge reminded us of home. We spent the late afternoon at Trossbach's Marina, a friendly down home place where we were offered a "pile" of Spot—a common, tasty pan fish—for supper and a lightning bolt for desert. I kindly declined the fish because we had just eaten supper at a nearby restaurant. Jerry missed the lightning bolt because he was just plain lucky.

It all happened so fast. The storm rolled in. Jerry ran down to secure his kayak. KABLAM mixed with a blinding, blue flash and Jerry's body lay on the dock! There was a lifeless pause and then a voice: "I'm okay, just shook up; loud ringing in my ears; it feels like I been hit across the back with a two-by-four!"

"I thought you were dead! Burnt to a crisp!" I shrieked, as adrenalin shock propelled me to the scene.

Such power—electricity from the discharge between earth and atmosphere. Couldn't there be a way of harnessing it, instead of the atom? Jerry and I talked about energy alternatives while we sat perched high atop a thirty-foot bank made of rust stained sand and clay. It was the evening of the next day and Jerry could still feel the prickly static of the thunderbolt.

Somewhere around the corner stood two reactor chambers, not yet fueled. We had happened upon the spot quite by accident and were "filled in" by a guard as to the area's history. The place used to be a boys camp, now it belonged to Maryland Power and Light.

"Some people call it progress, I call it regression," Jerry said.

Our feelings were mutual. The dozens of new electrical generating facilities we had seen during five thousand miles of paddling were either coal or nuclear powered. The blossoming of "deadly flowers" where the living earth could eventually suffocate under a cloud of haze or fry in radioactive juices seemed too high a price to pay for electricity.

Periodically, I'd looked over the stern to see the reactor houses growing smaller. Neither of us spoke in the humid, early morning stillness. Jerry was now feeling lousy. The night had been constantly broken by his dry, hacking cough—he had picked up the virus, I was just starting to shake.

The colds stoked our displeasure over a marina we pulled into for rest after thirteen miles of nearly silent paddling. It was Sunday and the place, to us, was a mad-house.

"The complex should have been called the Human Zoo for the out-of-shape and overweight. People seemed to be taking their frustrations out on the water by madly racing around in powerboats. The whole place was un-believably crowded. Trailers were parked side by side and campers shared tent pegs. I'm sure neighbors would be able to hear each other snoring. The toilets were atro-cious—I would have much rather used the woods. The entire place had the aroma of a cow barn and music blared from the snack bar." rrb

Here was the contrast—the paradox: the crowd gath-ered to reach the sun and water, while Jerry and I stopped to seek refuge from it.

Oddly enough, out of the din, a man appeared and gave Jerry a couple of aspirins—who, by now, was lying flat-backed on the dock, legs up and face covered with one arm. The medicine helped lift the "hot iron" from Jerry's forehead and relieved his aching joints long enough for us to make our escape.

At least we didn't have to contend with the bugs. Somewhere along the line we had lost them. The puzzled looks of local residents when they were approached with the words "jaws," "no-see-ems," or "sand gnats" brought grins to our faces. Water salinity regulated their terri-tory and the bay's freshwater tributaries were erasing the scourge. It seemed too, from now on, salt film on our kayaks and barnacle covered dock pilings would be, for the most part, a thing of the past.

However, jellyfish were still prevalent in the bay. The morning of our Annapolis run, our paddles cleared a path before departing, after strong winds blew hundreds of the small creatures into the shallow water next to the beach.

The first four hours to Annapolis were equal to the effort put into the last two. It was so hot during our approach and entry into Annapolis Harbor, I feared the fabric on my boat deck would melt; my fingers would stick tight to the hot metal parts of the paddle shaft; and my hair would suddenly burst into flame.

Several weeks prior to our arrival, we made plans to stay with another army buddy of mine in Laurel, Maryland. By now, Chesapeake weather had pushed us into the "long overdue" category, while John and Hila waited patiently for our call.

"Is there such an obnoxious thing as a Randy Bauer around here?" a voice thundered across the Petrini Shipyard.

"It's the same old John," I yelled back. "Hell, I'd recognize your voice anywhere."

"Late again Bauer! We've been waiting for you," he replied.

The time at John and Hila's home was used as a springboard to visit Washington, D.C. We spent two days at the capitol, rummaging around monuments and poking our noses into museums and the structures housing government machinery. The ramblings took us to the offices of our Senators—Hubert Humphrey and Walter Mondale. Mr. Humphrey was at a committee meeting at the time, but Senator Mondale was available.

"Senator, Sir," I said. "We paddled all the way from Minnesota just to see you!"

In spite of our impromptu address and attire—Jerry wore his tank top—like Davy Crockett arriving in Congress with his buckskins on, the senator did leave us with a few words of wisdom regarding proposed legislation to protect five hundred miles of the Upper Mississippi River from the headwaters to Anoka, Minnesota, from "creeping uglification."

"The river needs to be protected. If not done soon, the opportunity will be gone forever," he said.

The senator's words made us think about the river and Tom—something we hadn't done for a long time. The Mississippi now seemed light years away.

"When I look back at the beginning of the trip Jerry, I see three little kids starting on a big adventure. Now, I see you and I as adults! So much has happened in between. Months of paddling had allowed us to grow emotionally, spiritually and physically

The Chesapeake Bay Bridge was a double-span structure nearly five miles long. Our kayaks bobbed alongside its numbered "legs." Annapolis and D.C. were behind us now, as we headed to the Eastern Shore. Logistically, the maneuver was to avoid Baltimore Harbor and Aberdeen Proving Ground. Instead, we'd swing around Love Point; go up Eastern Neck and past Rock Hall.

One night was spent on a sand spit guarding the harbor mouth leading to a place called Great Oak Resort and Yacht Basin. The spirit of the Chesapeake hung heavy over the water.

"I look out across the Bay at the rose twilight. The driftwood campfire, ringed with wet equipment, warms my feet and legs. The tea water is hot and grilled cheese sandwiches are frying in the pan. We expect the usual, heavy evening dew. The tent is up—it waits for us to sleep. We are hungry and tired. It will be cool tonight—somewhere in the sixties. Boats, black silhouettes against the sky, move slowly into the harbor with their running lights on. The marker buoys are black now. Small waves wash against the sand and pebble beach." rrb

Great Oak was the last night spent on the bay. Come evening, we stood on the littered beach line of Elk River. The next morning, a fifteen -foot speedboat had joined the debris. Presumably, strong southeast winds during the night pushed the craft to its new berth—right next to our tent!

"Hey, she has a Delaware sticker on the side," Jerry said. "Think she floated down the canal with all the other trash from Delaware Bay?"

Before leaving, we secured the "runaway runabout" and reported it to state park officials.

The Chesapeake and Delaware Canal formed a twelve-mile, sea level link between Chesapeake and Delaware Bays. The watercourse evolved from a narrow ditch with four locks and mule teams to an ultramodern facility complete with traffic lights and camera monitors

Jerry and I wandered around examining an historic stone pump house and water wheel mechanism used for filling old locks. Walking through a doorway, a barrage of screens, colored control lights and switches jolted us into the present.

"This is where it all happens," the man at the control board said.

He was a Corps of Engineers canal monitor. His monitoring equipment could look up and down the canal. He moved a few switches and a distant camera turned to bring a tiny speck into view on the screen.

"Now, I'll enlarge," he said.

We watched as the speck grew into a station wagon with a man standing beside it.

"Goin' through the canal?" he added.

"Ya, with kayaks," Jerry said. "Just waitin' for the tidal currents to switch."

"Well, I'll keep my eyes on you and make sure you get through."

We could feel "big brother's" electronic eyes peeking at us until we pulled into an abandoned side channel leading to Delaware City.

The water quality of Delaware Bay shocked us. It was muddy and polluted compared to Chesapeake Bay and made us uneasy when our paddle blades disappeared two inches below the surface. Fortunately, we didn't have far to go during our initial introduction—Pea Patch Island was less than a mile and a half from Delaware City.

The one hundred and seventy eight acre island held dark secrets. For one night, our kayaks joined the rubble on the trash-laden bank, while our tent sat amidst sumac in the front yard of the Civil War prison.

It was called Fort Delaware. It had been built in the mid eighteen hundreds to protect Philadelphia and its harbor forty miles upstream. The fortress looked and felt formidable. The combination of granite and bricks was well preserved and impenetrable. We followed the walls and old moat to the Sally Port where frenzied dogs, behind locked gates, barked and snapped. They seemed like banshees from hell screaming at us, or souls of the thousands who died of disease and neglect during their incarceration. Shrouded in fog and the gray mist of history, we were not alone.

"Here they come," I thought. "Ghost soldiers appearing from behind the trees and high weeds"

"Workmen," Jerry muttered.

The early morning spell broke. The entrance was unlocked and soon the cavernous fort swallowed all of the restoration crew, except one. Thirteen –year-old Wayne stayed behind and became our self-appointed tour guide. He led us through a honeycomb of passages—through restored room—to the top of ramparts and past gun emplacements.

"After Gettysburg, the fort and barracks on the island held over twelve-thousand confederate prisoners of war," he said.

Close quarters and filth-laden cistern water took their toll. Dysentery and smallpox ran rampant and one out of eight prisoners never lived to see the end of the war. Small wonder the Union prison was called the "Andersonville of the North."

Wayne took us along the island's east shore. The tide was out and fragments of Civil War and pre-Civil War china and bottles lie partially buried in the sticky, stinking river mud. Nails, spikes, straps and other metal objects littered the banks. With proper management and the hope of receiving a two million dollar bicentennial grant, the Fort Delaware Society planned for recovery of a wealth of artifacts and restoration of the fort and island.

The busy shipping channel bordered the island's east side. Freighters and tankers lumbered by throwing huge wakes onto the exposed shore. By 12:3O, the flood tide was ready to help our upriver paddle toward Philadelphia and we departed between passing ships.

The banks were heavily industrialized and the Delaware, itself, seemed more like a murky brew than water. Billows of bright green, just beneath the water surface near one factory, caught us by surprise. The fan of unknown chemicals surrounded our kayaks and slowly mixed with the surrounding homogeneous gray. Farther upriver, the burned out hulk of an oil tanker greeted us. A couple months earlier, we had heard of a tanker collision on the Delaware and the ensuing conflagration, but hadn't paid much attention to it. Now the tanker's vulnerability to catastrophe was all too real to us in the black, twisted metal—hardly resembling a ship.

When supper and finding a place to sit through the night began buzzing through our heads, we started looking at a low, brushy, trash-filled, spoil island near Essington, Pennsylvania. When night did come however,

Randy Bauer

both of us lay fast asleep aboard a moored cabin cruiser at the riverside yacht club, immediately across from the prospective campsite.

Jerry and I were treated like kings at the yacht club. It started with a conversation with "Murph," who happened to be working on his boat as we arrived. When we left—two days later—a deluge of reporters had picked our brains and our bodies were recovering from the hospitality at the club bar. Ginger flavored brandy and the folks at the riverside will always be inseparable in our minds. So will a man named "Red."

Late during our second night at the club, long after we had seen a ludicrous misrepresentation of our kayak trip on a television news spot, we listened and learned from Red. He had been born in a Philadelphia ghetto and had done the impossible—he had escaped.

"The ghetto is a trap," he said. "There's almost no way out. Either you're put in prison, crippled, or killed. You know, anyone can die! It takes guts to live!"

I kept thinking about Red's words while we paddled through the Philadelphia harbor. The smoggy, huffing-puffing city, sweltering in the late July heat, was far removed from the nation's birthplace we had seen the day before. Independence Hall, the Liberty Bell, Ben Franklin's Grave and the Betsy Ross House had been swallowed. They lie somewhere in the bowels of concrete, asphalt and glass. The waterfront, parts of which were in the process of being restored, revealed a rusty, sad looking, aircraft carrier. The ship was ready to be scrapped—its name, to my surprise, the *Shangri-la*.

Black children played amidst the roar of power plants, factories and traffic. One group, clinging to old wooden bridge supports, was using the river for a swimming hole. They kept yelling and waving at us as we drew closer. Finally, we heard them above the scream of a jet fired generating station. "You're on TV!" was what we could understand. We returned the waves and continued to paddle up the New Jersey side of the Delaware. Looking for a campsite at dusk produced a sandy no-man's-land of uneasy sleeping near Dredge Harbor. Once we were underway again, the pulse of the city continued to dissipate.

Trees screened the riverbank in many places. The historical Delaware, of two hundred years ago, was difficult for us to imagine, yet it was still there. The town of Bristol and William Penn's home appeared and disappeared. Bordentown wasn't far off and the incoming tide made paddling easy. A long, wooded bend was upon us now, so peaceful and then: "What the hell is that?" I yelled, as a gigantic steel plant revealed itself on the Pennsylvania side. The man-made complex, belching red smoke, was literally seething in its own wastes. To see it amid natural surroundings was an appalling sight.

People at the Bordentown Yacht Club were forewarned of the kayakers headed their direction. When we arrived, a burly man named Bob, his arms and shoulders full of assorted tattoos, greeted us. Inside the clubhouse, questions came from all directions: "How far you come? "Any mishaps?" "Where're you stoppin' tonight?" And the biggest crowd stopper of all: "You're going to paddle through the Raritan Canal?"

"Sure!" Jerry said. "That's why we come up the Delaware."

"Well you're going to need a hammer and chisel to go through the buildings," was the reply.

The problem was studied earlier. In our effort to avoid paddling down Delaware Bay and into the open ocean near Sandy Hook, south of New York City, we had gotten maps of the Delaware and Raritan Canal at Annapolis. Both Jerry and I knew at least ninety-five percent of the canal was navigable—at least for our kayaks. The only problem was at Bordentown—the old Delaware River entrance. For a few hundred feet or so, the canal poked through tree-lined banks, but then stopped abruptly when it reached some four miles of fill. The northern feeder, coming down the New Jersey side of the Delaware, was just as impassible—it went underground through downtown Trenton. After our last dam at Coon Rapids, Minnesota, over ten months before, portaging time was again at hand.

Our plan wasn't firm until two days later when we paddled through the cow lilies of Crosswicks Creek, intersected the White Horse Bridge and loaded our kayaks and gear for a three-mile ride to navigable waters.

In the interim, our kayaks sat idle on a floating dock while we explored our greater surroundings. We went up into the glacial drift area, to the Washington Crossing sight on the Delaware, where "smoke" over the countryside kept the fields and woodlands in soft focus. We passed a brownstone barn with rifle slits in it and a small cemetery where Continental soldiers slept in a land they helped set free. Names like "Poor Farm" and "Woosamansa Roads" stick in my mind, as does the decaying scenery of downtown Trenton.

Upstream from Trenton, the Delaware was bordered for miles by the intermittent Delaware and Raritan Canal on one side and the Pennsylvania Canal on the other. Bells tinkled on mules, as they were slowly led along the old trace. Lines followed and soon a wooden barge appeared from behind the shade trees lining the Pennsylvania Canal. Instead of tourists, we imagined the barge full of coal coming down from a Pennsylvania mine, bound for Philadelphia or New York City.

We had seen parts of both canals and now we floated in the one that led to Raritan Bay. It's century of commerce ended in 1932 and presently the canal was used primarily as a source of industrial and potable water for New Jersey. To us, the canal was an important link in our water highway. For a man in a rowboat, it was a way to prove self-worth. I thought he was fishing, or maybe just relaxing in the pseudo-wilderness, until he spoke: "My sister said I were crazy for coming out here alone!" The words were a short Sunday sermon for those who would listen and think about what he said. He only had one arm.

We chugged along for several hours in the heat, passed Princeton University founded in 1746, pulled over a chain of floating tires and stopped at our first spillway near Kingston. After 1932, when the canal was permanently closed to shipping, the swinging gates of the canal's six locks were removed and water level control gates installed.

Portaging around the structures was a devilish task. First, there was the job of securing a foothold on the steep bank. Then, the carry of a hundred or so yards, along the concrete lined lock chamber to a suitable launch site.

There was a lot of commotion on the first portage. We were on state park grounds and canoes were for rent. The fully loaded kayaks bent under the strain of carrying. Fire burned in my lower back and it felt like my arms and shoulder muscles would pop right through my skin. "STOP!" A two-minute breather and then off again. To our surprise, a worker at the site threw four cans of ice-cold soda into Jerry's kayak just as we set it in the water. The much appreciated cold drinks were gone before our kayaks had time to "rub noses" with their aluminum cousins.

By evening, we were at the Griggstown Spillway. It was the hottest day of the entire journey. The mercury had soared to one hundred and one degrees. We kept hearing reports about New York City's water pressure. Almost all of Manhattan's hydrants were turned on to help people living in sweltering tenements to cool off. It was hard for us to imagine the crowded, sticky, stifling city where there was no escape. A place where the low water pressure made flushing toilets impossible and city officials worried about a major fire and no pressure for the hoses.

A stranger walking into camp interrupted our supper. Charley worked for the New Jersey Resources Commission and was concerned about us camping on the overgrown mule trace. Since we appeared to be recreationists and since it was hot, he figured we were getting ready to throw a beer party. When we explained our motives and offered Charley a grilled cheese sandwich, he changed the subject. The canal, he said, was hand dug by Irish immigrants in the eighteen-thirties. And his concluding remarks were with us the rest of the night: "Hundreds of them died from cholera and were buried where they fell. You're probably camped on some of their bones right now!"

We ate breakfast at East Millstone, a village dressed in colonial atmosphere, and kept on paddling. Kids dove into one lock chamber while we sat on its concrete wall eating peanut butter and jelly sandwiches. At the spillway near South Bound Brook, it rained while we waltzed around broken beer bottles strewn along a steep bank.

Since we were no longer in commercial waters, bridges on the narrow canal appeared unusually low to us. We slipped under ever increasing numbers of conventional and old swing bridges, long since frozen from lack of use. Buildings flanked the shore in some places. I remember paddling past an office window and checking the time on a clock above a desk. Here and there were the marks of huge washouts. Several weeks before, during heavy rains, water along areas of the canal had risen six to seven feet in less than twelve hours!

Charley informed the tender at the New Brunswick spillway we'd be coming along. Thick duckweed, sticks and sludge bogged us down near the site but we managed to pole though the mat and land on the canal's west bank. Jerry left his kayak to explore and in five minutes came back with the tender and his wife. The headquarters of Johnson and Johnson bordered the park-like property of the canal's right-of-way. The whole area was surrounded by fence or water and the only way out, on foot, was through a checkpoint at the guardhouse in the Johnson and Johnson parking lot. We slept in a safe green oasis surrounded by the City that night. How very strange it was to be lulled to sleep by the periodic rumble of elevated trains.

The Delaware and Raritan Canal continued for another mile before emptying into the lower reach of the Raritan River. Since the river itself was now only a short walk down the bank and its last dam would be bypassed in the process, we side stepped the last portion of the canal and put directly into the river.

The marshy flats of the lower Raritan revealed a strange mix of factories, power plants, old piers and rusting barges of an industrialized river, as well as the boathouse for Rutgers University, founded in 1766.

Chapter 31

NYC—The Big Apple

"Travel is fatal to prejudice, bigotry and narrow-mindedness and many of our people need it sorely on these accounts. Broad, wholesome, charitable views of men and things cannot be acquired by vegetating in one little corner of the earth all one's lifetime."

Mark Twain

Both Jerry and I had been filled with uneasiness for several days. New York Harbor was our next task. "It's a place to paddle through as quickly as we can," I wrote. The "Big Apple" held no appeal for us, but it could not be avoided.

The night before our fourteen-hour New York Harbor nightmare was spent at the Raritan Yacht Club at Perth Amboy, New Jersey. After talking with many people concerning our plan, we finally determined our approach to worrisome tidal currents. We would avoid Arthur Kill, appropriately nicknamed "refinery row" and paddle the outside of Staten Island to the Verrazano Narrows Bridge. From The Narrows, it would be a straight shot up the Hudson.

As we bobbed on one of the floating docks trying to get some rest before the run, dozens of thoughts passed through our minds. Both of us tried not to think about the harbor and the city, but inevitably those thoughts seeped through the veneer of tranquility: Where would we stay if we couldn't make it to the George Washington Bridge over thirty miles away? What if the tides trick us? What if we swamp? Will ships be able to see us? And on and on and on.

Oddly enough, the people we met earlier at the club commented on our easy, slow paced life style and relaxed attitude. Of course, the gauge they used was one involving the city and, in comparison, the most chaotic, nervous moment of our life style would seem peaceful indeed. I told my logbook that night: "A relaxed attitude is something that apparently is hard to find in New York City, where the hustle bustle, noise, confusion, time schedules, smog and other evils are so great."

Earlier in the day, we had met Romando. He told us how he had watched his father work himself to death, dying at an early age of a heart attack.

"He was a Doctor," Romando said, "and I will never, never be like that!"

To Romando, we were "the answer;" to Sandy, we were an example. Sandy spent most of the evening with us. He lived in the city, was married and had a well paying job. His responsibilities, he said, allowed him to take only "small steps at a time," compared to our "big steps," as Sandy put it.

To ourselves, Jerry and I were two people doing what we wanted to do. But while I listened to the "grunt roar" of a fireboat breaking through other harbor sounds, I hesitated and really wondered if paddling through New York City was really what I wanted to do. Then, I looked at my hands, scabbed, scarred, calloused, aged and shining from the elements and grinned. I whispered: "Yes, it's what I want to do and we'll get through—we'll get through it!"

My stomach tingled and gurgled in the predawn light. We pushed away from the dock at six o'clock. Both of us were tired and uneasy. A feeling of paranoia prevailed—as if a giant sea monster was ready to explode from the depths and drown us. A warm light breeze from the Atlantic basted the starboard side of both boats. The tide was with us—I could see the ripples hitting my port side at an angle and could feel the slight tug of the current. A bell buoy nodded a dull clang. It was light enough now to tell the day would be cloudy.

If our timing was right, we'd hit tidal shifts about the time we reached the Verrazano Narrows Bridge and would follow the flood through the throat of the Harbor and up into the Upper New York Bay.

The bridge was high above us now. We were in the narrows and the water was fast against us. Partway through, we found some pilings to rest against for a few minutes. The current was less aggressive there than in the main channel, plus we'd have a point of reference to tell how fast we were being pulled back into the Lower Bay.

On we went. Ships and tugs were moving all around us. The current slacked and the bay widened. We were at the crossroads of two shipping lanes now—one heading off to our port side into Kill Van Kull and the other straight ahead toward the Statue of Liberty and the Hudson beyond.

The Staten Island Ferry ran past on our starboard side. It seemed to be the only thing of bright color in the harbor—a clay yellow. Everything else was gray, brown, green, or a combination of those hues. Tugboats and ships continually ran past and the Statue of Liberty grew closer. The New York skyline was clearly visible. The whole scene was unreal, ludicrous and ridiculous.

"If we don't take any pictures of us in this place, Jerry, no one's ever gonna believe us!" we snapped away.

We toyed with the idea of stopping at the Statue of Liberty, but there was no place to land our kayaks. Everything in the harbor was giant size. There was no choice but to keep going.

Near Ellis Island we could feel strong tidal currents again and both of us cursed.

"I thought this crap was supposed to stop, Jerry!"

I looked back and it seemed as if we were tied to the Statue of Liberty by an invisible rope. What had a few hours ago been a delight to see, was now a pariah

We kept paddling. The current increased and the weather changed. A northeaster blew in from nowhere bringing with it high winds and sheets of driving rain. Our ponchos were useless. They waved like flags in the wind and camouflaged us against the green, putrid water. We had a hard time seeing anything and, obviously, were impossible to see by anyone else. Refuse floated everywhere—garbage bags, railroad ties, logs, tires and light bulbs. It seemed we paddled through more oil than water. The wharfs were high and rusty. We inched along, pulling as hard as we could. I was worried, angry and becoming exhausted.

"The tide is a bitter enemy now. An adversary that's trying to kill us," I thought.

Again, we were able to stop for a few minutes near an abandoned railroad station on the New Jersey side of the Hudson. We tore through the water to the New York side. Chops hit us from all directions and, at times, it was hard to control the kayaks. One wave caught the stern of my craft and lifted it far into the air. For a second, I knew I would pitch-pole and be slapped face first into the water, but it didn't happen.

"Pier #27, #28, #29"—we counted off in our minds. I thought the pier numbers coincided with the streets, but they didn't. I saw a man standing near a fire dock and yelled over the roar: "How far to the Seventy-Ninth Street boat basin!" He yelled back, but I had him repeat it twice because I couldn't believe what he said.

"Five miles, Jerry" and I almost threw up.

We "hit the wall" in the chops near Pier #80. There was no boat basin; I was ready to cry. "Keep goin'!" I kept screaming at myself, while my body kept saying: "Stop, this is enough!"

The paddle shafts bent under the strain and mine broke in half. The starboard half fell into the water. I grabbed it, pulled a new set out and was paddling again in less than a minute. My voice was high, almost insane sounding.

"You bastard!" I screamed. "You thought you had me there, didn't you? But I fooled you!"

It was dark when our two kayaks pulled into the Seventy-Ninth Street boat basin. We were soaked, exhausted and relieved. There were at least two or three inches of the Hudson River sloshing around inside each craft.

I crawled from my boat, stood up for an instant on the floating dock and fell flat on my face. Jerry was still inside his boat—waiting. I stumbled like a man in a drunken stupor to a small building.

"Are you the dockmaster here?" I asked the person sorting mail.

"No," he said.

I explained what we were doing, expecting to get a negative reply. Instead, there were more questions: What college did I graduate from? What is your name? Still, I saw no facial expression at all.

How strange the whole encounter must have seemed to Dean. He standing there in a suit and me standing there in soaked clothes, ready to collapse from fatigue. Finally, the silence broke.

"I like your answers," he said. "I'm naturally suspicious."

Then he looked out the doorway.

"Once your friend shakes that charley horse out of his leg, why don't you come on over to the yacht over there? You can clean up, dry out and my wife will fix some food for you."

I couldn't believe what had just happened. It was a godsend! Maybe, the fact, Sue, Dean's wife, had the maiden name BAUER and was a graduate of the University of Minnesota had something to do with it.

As it was, the dockmaster turned out to be from Jamaica. When he finally came around, Dean himself had a hard time convincing him to leave the kayaks in place until dawn.

Safe aboard the yacht, after we were dried out and ready to fall asleep, I cracked open my logbook and scribbled: "This is fantasy, pure fantasy. It is a dream!"

At 6:OO a.m., we were part of the Hudson again. The wind still blew from the north, but it wasn't raining. The smells though, were still there—sometimes the odor of acid, other times the stink of gasoline, diesel, or the stench of raw sewage and now and then the waft of soap or burnt toast filled the air.

Our target yesterday, the George Washington Bridge, was a five-mile marker. The span hung two hundred feet over our heads and represented a gateway from the city. The land was changing. High bluffs bordered the side we were on. Originally, we had planned to camp someplace along Palisades Interstate Park. We were glad it wasn't to be. No overnight camping signs, ugly stone revetment, a road running alongside the river and steep cliff faces made it very unappealing.

Jerry and I paddled as long as the tide was with us. When it began to ebb noticeably, we were running along a swampy area near Tallman Mountain State Park.

"Let's hang it up," I told Jerry.

The Hudson had been very rough on us the last two days and all we wanted was some dry land to stand on. What we found, after paddling a winding stream through the swamp, was dry but steep. The slope, thick with poison ivy, became our home for the night. Long after the ebb tide had sucked the creek dry, we were both asleep. Saplings propped our sleeping bags and kept us from rolling into the mud.

By mid morning, the creek was deep enough to leave. Reversing our serpentine route, we charged into the wind and whitecaps of the widening Hudson. We were at the base of the Tappan Zee, a three-mile wide bulge in the river that extended some fourteen miles to the top of Haverstraw Bay. Crossing to Terrytown was impossible, for we'd have to broach waves nearly four feet high!

As a result, Dick and Judy would have to cross the Tappan Zee Bridge in order to pick us up. They did; at a place call Piermont, New York.

Three years before, we were soldiers in the same company. Now, the manager for a life insurance firm came down to meet a kayaker. Two different paths met on the Hudson. Dick summed it up as he loaded the trunk of his car with our gear: "Judy, look, this to me is just a jar, but for them it has a purpose, it serves an important function."

A new and final leg of the Trilogy was beginning. The anticipation and perils of New York Harbor were behind us and a feeling of euphoria prevailed. We would spend a few days at Brewster, New York—a quiet community of nearly two thousand situated near the Connecticut border sixty miles northeast of New York City.

The green Chevy with two kayaks on top and "bulging" at the seams with a life support system for two water gypsies, made a brief stop at Judy's parent's house.

"Everything these two guys own is in and on the car," Dick said.

"I can't believe they've been traveling like this for almost a year."

Judy's dad shook our hands.

"Your visit was foreshadowed by all your mail arriving at Dick and Judy's for the past two weeks," he said. "We've really been looking forward to you getting here."

The feeling of unconditional acceptance we felt from the entire family was wonderful.

Brewster was a major logistics stop for us, as well as, a place to sightsee, relax and laugh. We refocused our attention from saltwater and seaboard to freshwater rivers, canals and the Great Lakes. Our patched kayaks were re-patched, taped and scum and residue cleaned from their hulls and decks. Clothes and equipment were washed and repaired. We ordered charts and wet suits for Canadian waters and talked with reporters in Brewster and Minnesota. Saltwater and sweat-stained charts were sent back home, along with rolls of exposed slide film and the corroded remnants of Jerry's tape recorder.

Included in letters from home were assorted newspaper articles about our journey. Some stories emphasized the "excitement" of storms and waves, while others emphasized a humbling, people oriented experience. Sometimes, what we ate became a major highlight. A clipping from the Associated Press quoted: "Kayakers powered by peanut butter!"—Our whale-like appetites had consumed over one hundred pounds of the high-energy spread, well before we arrived in New York.

During our stay, we took a train back to New York City. Just before going underground, glimpses of run down apartments and laundry hanging on lines between trash-filled alleys flashed by. Through the train's greasy, dirt coated windows we caught the vacant stares of those looking out open tenement windows. "They all look so hopeless," I said to myself and then the scene went black.

The metal brakes screeched for a long time before the commuter train jerked to a standstill in the basement of Grand Central Station. We emerged into blinding daylight, into a man-made canyon of stale air, noise and seven million people. It was four o'clock and we had four hours to get a "taste of the Big Apple" on foot. We walked into Macy's, past Times Square, Rockefeller Center and ventured into Central Park. We found the Empire State Building and looked around in St. Patrick's Cathedral. Before our time was up, speed walking took us to the grounds of the United Nations Headquarters. There, we momentarily soothed our unhardened senses from the intense bombardment of city stimulation by reading: "They shall beat their swords into plowshares and their spears into pruning, hooks. Nation shall not lift up sword against Nation, neither shall they learn war anymore."

Preoccupied by the words, we walked past the U.N. Assembly Building guards at two different checkpoints. Needless to say, our inside "tour" came to an abrupt end with an official escort out the same door we entered.

A surprising number of business people got off the Brewster train. It was hard for us to imagine that for many of them, this was a five and oftentimes six day a week, 5:OO a.m. to 1O:OO p.m. routine.

Back at the house, we drank beer and related our adventures with Dick. Our evening began with a taped letter to army buddies holding a re-union in Chicago, which depicted madcap, every day life at our former army base in West Germany. While more beer was consumed, we laughed hysterically at old "You Bet Your Life" re-runs. And, finally, Judy found all three of us roaring over the comment that Jerry's billows of curly hair, bleached white by months of sunshine, made him look like Harpo Marx!

Our last day in Brewster was spent writing letters to people we had befriended along the way. It closed with us listening to the crickets and katydids. In the quiet, I remembered the story Dick told us about one of his college professors: "He'd stay up till 2:OO or 3:OO in the morning just so he could listen to and appreciate the silence."

The relatively cool, mid-August night dampened our weeklong euphoria. Both of us could feel fall and cold weather in the air. Both of us knew we were going north instead of south. And both of us, for the first time, could see, the flickering end of a journey fifteen hundred miles into the future.

Chapter 32

Birthday on the Water

"Wind you numb me so I can feel the gentle, sun you blind me so I can see further, waves you toss me so I can feel the softness, hunger you haunt me so I can taste you better."

James J. Bauer

The day before my birthday, we were on the water again. We celebrated it in Brewster, with wine and "kayak cake." We proudly wore our birthday bandannas while we headed north battling strong winds.

After so many months of relatively flat land and broad open horizons, the Hudson Valley topography was fantastic. High ridges and steep, tree-covered hills surrounded us. Towns and landmarks reflected an area rich in history. We passed Sing Sing prison, the towns of Verplanck and Peekskill . We camped on Iona Island in the shadows of Bear and Dunderberg Mountains. Both stood over eleven hundred feet high; the latter, according to Dutch legend, housed a goblin responsible for summer storms.

By our second day, we had paddled by Anthony's Nose and Fort Montgomery, where the Continental Army, in 1777, had stretched a heavy chain boom across the narrow 400 yard section of the Hudson to dissuade ships loaded with Hessian mercenaries. A little farther, at a narrow "S" curve stricture marked "Worlds End" on our charts, the Hudson reached a depth of over two hundred feet. It wasn't hard to understand why, in 1802, this dangerous to maneuver, section of river became the site of West Point.

We passed the impressive gray stone buildings of the military academy on our left and after a short break at a friendly marina at Cold Spring, chugged between the flanks of Storm King Mountain (1355 feet) and Bull Hill (1425 feet) on our east side. Near Marlboro, New York, we slipped underneath a railroad viaduct and found a suitable campsite in an abandoned clay pit before it started to rain.

The next morning, we rounded Danskamer Point. According to area historians, English navigator Henry Hudson named the point in 1609. While exploring the area on a "Northwest Passage" quest for the Dutch East India Company, Hudson and his crew happened upon

Indian people conducting a ritual dance in a cave near the point. Unfortunately, preconception and misunderstanding led to the name branding: "Duyvils Dans Kammer" (Devil's Dance Chamber).

That afternoon, another name was a harbinger for the troubled waters of the Hudson.

"Jerry, it's the sloop *Clearwater*—the one that Pete Seeger sings about!"

The boat was headed south under full sail. What a beautiful sight, the *Clearwater* with the green Hudson Valley and Poughkeepsie's huge suspension and railroad bridges as a backdrop.

People at the Rogers Point Boat Club, near Hyde Park, commented on the Hudson's water quality: "Five years ago you would have paddled through rafts of soap suds in some of these parts. Now there's even fish coming back into what used to be called a dead river."

Franklin Roosevelt's ancestral home was near the boat club, as well as one of the Vanderbilt's mansions, but they were closed. It was raining and we had seven paddling miles to reach an island just outside Norrie State Park.

Twenty minutes from our destination the rain stopped. In the darkness, if we didn't look at it directly, we could make out the island's silhouette. The air was calm, the river very still and the strong smell of rain soaked vegetation filled the air. As long as we kept the noses of the kayaks pointed toward the "shadow island," we'd get there. We paddled in silence, hearing only the dipping of alternating paddle blades. For a moment, we were captured in time; we were part of a bigger picture, one that artists for years had tried to capture on canvas. Then the boats crunched into the pebbles on the seven-foot beach—we were there.

Even though, industries, like the giant cement plant at a town appropriately called Cementon, dotted the shoreline here and there. The river continued to be a major shipping channel with the Port of Albany sixty-five miles upstream. The visible water quality of the Hudson continued to improve as we went north.

Twenty-eight miles from our island camp we found a tin roofed boat shed to sleep in at Hop-O-Nose Marine at Catskill. The town was gateway to the Catskill Mountains area of New York State and, like many others along the Hudson, was settled by Dutch farmers in the sixteen hundreds.

Perhaps a Dutch homesteader originally tilled the field we camped near on our last night in tidewater. I watched water slowly leave the channel we came in on, while Jerry torturously climbed through vines and underbrush to investigate the cornfield.

We had been on moon and sun regulated waters for seven months. In spite of the fact it was one hundred and thirty-five miles from the Battery in New York Harbor to our camp, we were still tied to their power over the earth's water.

"Corn's about ten days too old," Jerry said. "So we'll have to settle for grilled cheese!"

That night we sat in front of a campfire, something we hadn't done for a long time. Moonlight poured into camp while we listened to the radio announcer mentioning that Minnesota was expecting its first frost of the season. Jerry and I looked at each other, but we didn't say anything. We knew cold was coming—maybe a little sooner than we expected. Suddenly, the fire felt a little warmer in the growing coolness.

The lockmaster at the federal lock near Troy lifted us seventeen feet and then notified the paper we were coming through. The reporter waited two hours for us at Lock #2, immediately below Waterford—a little over two miles from our first lock—but we never showed up. Later, he found us parked for the night at the Trojan Marina. We had decided to take the stairway of five locks to the Mohawk River the next day.

Frank was very personable. He had lived in Colorado and supported our long ago established conclusion that people "out east" were quite friendly.

"Traveling has opened our minds a lot," Jerry said. "We have learned the east isn't nearly as bad as we had been led to believe. We hope to be back later."

We also got into a philosophical conversation and told Frank we no doubt would be doing similar things for the next five years. In a round about way, we were telling him and ourselves that we didn't want the trip to end. We knew the truth; it was expressed matter- of- factly in an earlier article about us: "One day in October, Randy Bauer and Jerry Mimbach will put down their kayak paddles, stand up and resume normal lives." The acknowledgment of that statement nearly scared us to death.

Earlier in the journey, we talked about going north on the Hudson through Lake Champlain, the Richeleau River, St. Lawrence Seaway, Ottawa River, Rideau Canal to Kingston on Lake Ontario and up the Trent-Severn Water-way to Georgian Bay. Now we stood at the crossroads. The freeway style sign had one arrow pointing right: Champlain Canal, Whitehall and Lake Champlain" and one arrow pointing left: "Erie Canal, Syracuse and Buffalo."

"It would be nice to do, someday," Jerry lamented. "But we just ain't got the time."

We turned left and headed east.

The chain of five locks, synchronized so a craft could take them one after the other, raised us over one hundred and sixty five feet in a little over one and a half miles. The "flight" bypassed seventy-foot Cohoes Falls and a series of dams on the Mohawk. The locks, run by the state of New York, were well used and their concrete walls deeply pock marked. Water boiled into the upper side of each chamber during the lockage procedure—something we were not used to. During our "flight" down the Mississippi, lock valves were always opened to drain the water out with no noticeable turbulence.

We were on the New York State Barge Canal. Our eight-day trip would cover one hundred and eighty-six miles. Nineteen locks would raise us a maximum of four hundred and twenty feet at Rome, New York and the remaining ten would drop us one hundred and seventy-six feet to meet the waters of Lake Ontario at Oswego.

We would be following, on and off sections of the Old Erie Canal built during the years 1817-1825. Originally, the waterway, considered an engineering marvel for its time, was forty feet wide and four feet deep. The one we were on had varying widths of forty-five feet at the locks up to two hundred feet in the river sections and a minimum depth of twelve feet.

The canal was either in or alongside the Mohawk River on its one hundred and sixteen mile run to Rome. We were cruising through a broad river valley on the southern fringe of the Adirondacks rich in history. During the first day, morning took us by the giant General Electric and Knolls Atomic Power Laboratories at Schenectady. Late afternoon, found Jerry waiting to buy us lunch at an Amsterdam supermarket while the man in front of him paid for eighty dollars of meat in one-dollar bills. Four miles later, we photographed a remnant of the past at Schoharie Creek, where an old Erie Canal limestone aqueduct solved the problem of the canal crossing creeks. The structure carried an artificial river over a natural one and, as strange as it looked, it worked quite effectively.

By evening, we were camped in a cornfield directly across the river from an historical marker that delved even deeper into the past. The shrine commemorated the deaths of Father Isaac Jogues and other missionary priests who died in North America in the sixteen hundreds. The edifice was huge and held a commanding view of the entire countryside. The martyrs gave their lives for what they believed in; yet, if they could speak, I wondered if they would advocate such attention to their deeds. I wondered if such a shrine, in a grotesque way, justified, for some people, the routing of Native Americans from their homes. I wondered if the shrine added to the distorted view of history that left us nothing more than a romanticized version of what really happened in the Mohawk Valley.

St. Johnsville was a storybook town for us. The rural community of two thousand was having a firemen's carnival when we arrived. Johnny, the caretaker at the marina, welcomed us. He was a likable person with a gift of gab, who squared us away with our domestic chores. Once we cleaned up and knew where we were going to camp, we walked across the tracks into a town with brick and wooden storefront buildings. Jerry and I stuffed ourselves with meat and potatoes, saw a dairy tanker parked on main street and walked past an old furniture-undertaking business before rolling our sleeping bags out on the soft lawn of St. Johnsville's Park.

The evening ended with fireworks from the town's carnival. The small display complemented our excitement. Jerry had just called home and found out his brother, Dennis, would meet us in Oswego in five days. Tempering the good news was also the word that it had snowed in Minnesota the day before.

The vertical gate hung open like a huge garage door slung between massive walls of concrete. The structure looked formidable as we paddled into the highest lock in the canal system just outside Little Falls. The lockmaster wished us luck on our journey and told us he would make the forty-foot elevator ride as smooth as possible. Once on the other side, the towns of Herkimer and Mohawk slipped by before we stopped at the Ilion Marina for an afternoon break. For a brief period, we found ourselves on a homemade runabout driven by a man named Frank. Frank remembered swimming in the old Erie Canal as a child. He took us back to a place where we had paddled by an hour before. There, just on the other side of the bank, was the remains of an old lock now filled in and overgrown with vegetation. The tight fitting, hand hewn gray stones were still held together in places by iron bands.

Here and there leaded pins poked out of hand drilled holes and, in one place, the rope burns from countless passes of tow line were clearly etched in stone.

"A buddy of mine was a mule skinner at the age of nine on the canal," Frank said as we motored over to the opposite show to visit Fort Herkimer.

The site was named in honor of General Nicholas Herkimer who was buried nearby. The general was mortally wounded at Oriskany on August 6th, 1777, after attempting to relieve British besieged Fort Stanwix at Rome.

Frank showed us the church, built in 1737 and then, excitedly, led us to his boyhood schoolhouse. During our brief walk, Frank's mood suddenly turned sullen.

"I don't believe it, I don't believe it! They tore it down!" he moaned.

A pile of rubble lay where the schoolhouse once stood.

Frank was wiping tears from his eyes, but tried not to show it, as he took us back to the marina. Once we landed, he said goodbye and walked away, clutching a schoolhouse brick in his hand.

The waterway hosted commercial traffic of barges, tugs and recreational traffic of all types. We did encounter a variety of watercraft, including sailboats with unstepped masts to allow them passage under low bridges, but not as many as we expected. Apparently, the damaged section of canal near Bushnell Basin, east of Rochester—which forced boats to take a long convoluted route through the Oswego Canal and Lake Ontario—was having an effect.

During the late afternoon, we did, however, meet a crew that came from Buffalo. They were facing backwards and rowing a two-person racing shell to Albany. From earlier conversations and the number of signs we had seen along the canal pointing out new community sewage treatment plants, their trip, just a few years ago, would have been miserable. In spite of the clean looking water, a youngster I met near our canal-side campsite gave us a stern warning: "Don't eat the fish from this canal," he said. "They're poison!"

Eventually, the waterway left the Mohawk and became a canal stretching fifty-six miles to Skinner's Marina near Sylvan Beach on the East side of Lake Oneida. We picked apples and grapes along the narrow portion of the waterway and found ourselves nervously noting other seasonal indicators:

"Fall signs are evident," I recorded in my logbook. "The days are growing shorter and periods of rain longer. We heard shotgun blasts in the surrounding countryside today, saw blackbirds and waterfowl bunching up, noticed trees with telltale signs of color, smelled burning leaves and the margarine doesn't melt in the jar anymore."

A couple at the marina let us sleep in the enclosed bridge of their yacht. As a result, their kindness allowed an early start on the lake.

"We woke at 4 a.m. and within thirty minutes, we launched into the darkness. It was black— a sticky morning with heavy cloud cover. We paddled past the streetlights of the Sylvan Beach Terminal. There were a few fishermen when we moved through—they looked surprised! We followed the flashing red markers past the breakwater and into the lake. We were able to see a few of the blinking, white markers far out on the port side—mist obscured them occasionally. At first, I thought a storm might blow in but the clouds moved out. Soon we were on a lake bathed in moon and starlight. A predawn breeze picked up but subsided with the sunrise. The beautiful sun—bright, orange, gauze draped ball hovering over the water. We glided through a green sea, a glassy sea and thick with thousands of insects. They nearly drove us berserk, crawling and clinging to every exposed inch of kayak and body. Dog days' green clouds of algae were everywhere."

We covered the twenty-two miles of Lake Oneida well before noon and were proud of ourselves. After a three-hour rest and a thunderstorm, we pushed on.

The second storm hit shortly after we left Lock #23. Lightning crashed all around as we sat motionless—powerless—in our poncho covered kayaks. Hugging the side of the canal, it was easy to imagine us and the tiny boats disintegrating into oblivion after each strike. With an earsplitting roar, one bolt exploded a nearby tree as my mind begged for our safety. When it was over, the strong smell of ozone lingered for a while, but steady rain lasted far into the evening.

We pulled into Pirate's Cove Marina at dusk and asked the restaurant receptionist if we could sleep in one of the boat sheds.

"Sure," she said. "As long as you don't smoke."

Jerry and I settled into our home for the night after drinking a half-gallon of coffee each—we couldn't afford the marina's food. The shed was ideal because it met a simple criteria—it was DRY. An added bonus was several dozen cement blocks stacked on one side of the sandy floor. Once rearranged, they became excellent mattress foundations for two exhausted, thankful and happy to be alive human beings.

We paddled two and a half miles and turned north into the Oswego Canal at Three Rivers—the Oneida, Seneca and Oswego River junctions. We had twenty-four miles to go, seven locks to negotiate and unfriendly winds, but it was Wednesday and nothing would stop us from meeting Jerry's brother.

On a three and a half mile straightaway, ending with a hook to the left and Lock #6, I saw Jerry staring at something in the distance. Later, Jerry said: "I felt Dennis' presence before I actually saw him standing by his car on that wayside pullout."

Dennis and reporters from the Oswego newspaper were waiting for us at Lock #8. In the excitement of reunion, the reporters were skeptical over our trip and refused to believe we had been out for almost a year. It didn't matter, Dennis had arrived with a carload of supplies and we'd have a few days off before venturing into our first Great Lake.

When the lock gates opened, we could see Ontario stretching endlessly beyond the harbor. Beyond the protection of huge breakwaters, the wind had whipped it into a frenzied mass of blue and white. The noise produced was incredible. Even inside the lock, we could occasionally see spray from the breakers as they shattered against the concrete barricades that we would soon venture beyond.

It took two trips in Dennis' Pinto to bring gear, the new supplies and us from the Oswego Harbor Marina to Fair Haven Beach State Park, twelve miles to the southwest.

Site #195 was our home for four nights and Dennis was our first official guest. He brought an assortment of requested supplies including camera film and new tennis shoes to replace the shreds of canvas we were wearing. Also included were items to prepare for the cold, short days and the Canadian wilderness: a plastic canvas tarp, to go over our sagging, leaking tent fly; gunny sacks, to be used for bear bags; fresh contact cement to insure against cold water leakage and a half dozen plumber candles. Our wet suits arrived at home the day after Dennis left for New York and would be forwarded to Port Severn on Georgian Bay. A badly needed spare kayak paddle blade, donated by our "kayak company friends" from Charleston, waited for us at the Oswego Post Office and Tom Anderson had given Dennis one of his blades to be used on the "home stretch."

"Our equipment, next to Dennis' shiny car and clean clothes, really contrasts. Our essentials look like junk compared to something new. The months of wear and tear, the effects of wind, rain, dirt and saltwater are very, very evident. Many things will be sorted out and left behind—several water jugs, an old can of glue and four cans of insect repellent. We will save the kidney bean can—it's a classic example of the corrosive effects of saltwater." rrb

One of our four compasses would also be going back with Dennis. The World War I brass heirloom was given to Jerry by his grandfather and had traveled with us for six thousand miles.

Our larder expanded to meet the needs of the growing cold and farther spaced food stops. Our new supplies included:

5 lbs. Sugar

4 tins Canned Luncheon Meat

5 lbs. Cocoa Mix

1 Pint Ginger Brandy

1O lbs. Granola Baking Power

4 lbs Powdered Milk Orange Crystals

5 lbs. Margarine Soup Mixes

4.5 lbs. Oatmeal

2.5 lbs. Baking Mix

5 lbs. Macaroni

6 lbs. Processed Cheese

5 lbs. Whole Wheat Flour

12 lbs. Peanut Butter

6 lbs. Honey

8 lbs. Rice

Food packing took place on railroad tie steps leading from the campground road down to our site. One of the people parading by asked if we were setting up a store. By the time we were done, food that had originally taken up space on six steps was consolidated on two.

Dennis left the Oswego Marina Harbor the end of August. In a week, we would be somewhere in Canada and he would be in the U.S. Air Force.

Chapter 33

Ontario Waters

"We did not build this place; it is not ours. A frozen vision, a stifling void, awaiting for the angels of daybreak. Ceilings without stars weigh me down, walls that divide never embrace. Together finding a round for tall place full of quiet voices builds softly. A house grows from within, tunnels line with secret thoughts join chambers filled with light, where we met stars in their fullness. No floors cut earth sky, mind from body."

Sim Vander Ryn

We followed the shore of Lake Ontario, rounded Stony Point, Point Peninsula and took the bay side of Grenadier Island, to Cape Vincent where we crossed into Canada. The eighty-mile run to Wolf Island, Ontario— gateway to the Thousand Island area on the St. Lawrence River —took five days.

Ontario water was cold and we quickly learned to be cautious paddling in waves where capsizing without wet suits could prove disastrous. The shore of the inland sea appeared remarkably sterile compared to the scenes we had been accustomed. The sand and glacial pebbles of beaches and the water itself all seemed so clean that the new environment prompted us to fill our water jugs from the Lake.

Our appetites increased with the cool weather. Corn bread, dumplings and fried rice were added to our menu. For more energy, our standard lunch of peanut butter and jelly sandwiches was replaced with peanut butter and honey.

Grenadier Island was the site of an early nineteen hundreds gambling resort, owned, from what we heard by a wealthy family from Oswego. Most of the buildings were still intact on the island, but they had been ransacked. We looked through the old generator house, ice shed, helpers quarters and stared at the remains of the old hall and gigantic fireplace. We found mattresses stuffed with Spanish moss and an old safe lying on the ground, with its door rusted open. The tongue and grove spruce flooring was still intact in a few of the buildings, as well as, the shake siding.

At Cape Vincent, while Jerry was buying a pair of work pants, an excited kid roared into the hardware store with a huge Musky dangling from a gaff hook. An old potato scale weighed the monster, unofficially, at thirty-two and a half pounds. A short while later, we saw the same person in the supermarket, but their scale only went up to twenty pounds. When someone suggested the scale at the lumberyard, he immediately headed that direction—fish tail dragging on the floor behind him. After the excitement died, Jerry disappeared for a few minutes and returned with a handful of rubber minnows, worms, assorted lures and hooks.

"Someday I'm gonna catch that big one in the sky," was all he said.

Wolf Island protected us from strong northwest winds while we crossed the St. Lawrence Seaway and the international border. Ocean-going freighters slipped by every fifteen minutes or so. The ships were easy to avoid; the only thing we worried about was the Cape Vincent Ferry, which, as we later found out, ran between New York and Alexandria Point on Wolf Island only on Sundays and American Holidays.

The Canadian customs man, who obviously didn't expect anyone, gave us a stern visual once over and then demanded to see our money. As we unloaded our traveler checks and what actual cash we had, he got a puzzled look on his face and asked how we entered Canada. In this case, a picture was worth a thousand words; we led him to our boats bobbing in the backwash of waves at the ferry dock.

"We've been out for a year now!" I proudly exclaimed.

"I see it, but don't believe it!" was his reply. "Enjoy your visit in Canada."

The charts showed an old canal cutting directly through the middle of Wolf Island. The three-mile shortcut would conveniently save us sixteen miles of looping around either end of the giant island and would also offer wind protection. After the first half mile however, the canal turned into a clogged ditch of cattails, reeds and waste deep muck. From a distance, horses, cows and sheep heard the curses of two underwear clad men, dragging and shoving their boats though an area normally filled only with the calls of blackbirds.

The day ended with us washing mud from our bodies in a place solid enough to portage a hundred yards to open water and the other side of the island. We were tired and could only think of setting up camp, when a woman rode by on a bicycle. She was on a road on the other side of the narrow inlet and we waved to her as she passed. In so doing, we came to the startling conclusion that we were nude! The cyclist never waved back.

Ontario was the first of three Great Lakes we would paddle. Lake Erie would be bypassed by the Trent-Severn Waterway and, of course, Lake Michigan was off our route entirely. We were on Ontario for a week. It was short compared to the time we would spend on Georgian Bay (Lake Huron) and Superior, but long enough to feel the Lake's power during a hundred miles of paddling.

The water was reasonably calm when we left Wolf Island and headed west. We were bound for the North Channel side of Amherst Island, ten miles away. As our kayaks passed Ferguson Point and rounded Garden Island, the mid morning sun lit up the City of Kingston immediately to the north. We could see historic Fort Henry, base of operations for the British Navy on Lake Ontario during the War of 1812. Immediately to the fort's left was the channel opening for the Rideau Canal—completed in 1832 to provide British North America with a secure alternate supply route other than the St. Lawrence River.

Our historical dreaming stopped once we cleared Simcoe Island, caught strong southwest winds and found ourselves in building seas. We quartered the waves and paddled as best we could. Half the time, I couldn't see Jerry or the shore. Both of us rode up and down the huge rollers and occasionally breaking waves that we estimated at nine feet. It was impossible to turn around for fear of broaching, so we kept on paddling. We were careful not to get too close to each other, knowing if one of us surfed a wave, one kayak could land on top of the other. Three long hours past in the dizzying ride. Both of our boats were filling with water from cresting waves and both of us worried about the consequences of increasing weight and inability to maneuver properly. In the distance, dead ahead, I could make out three tiny Islands called the "Brothers" on the chart—and that's where we wanted to be. It seemed we'd be caught in the giant washing machine forever before we finally felt the effects of eleven-mile long Amherst Island's lee side. Twenty minutes later, we thudded to shore on a crescent beach of the first un-named Brother—no bigger than a marker buoy symbol on our chart. Our kayaks held so much water they looked as if they'd break in half when we wrestled them out of the now small waves. The island was good to us. Firewood was plentiful; the tent was wind sheltered among a thick clump of trees; and we were safe.

"Jerry, I don't know if you were thinking about your brother, when we were out there today, but I was sure thinking about mine and whether or not I'd see him again!"

Ten miles from the Brothers we stopped at Bath, a small community situated in the protected waters behind Amherst Island. Little did we know the tavern just outside of Bath would be the site of a political rally, complete with fist pounding candidates, a live Pipe Band from Kingston and lots of Canadian beer! And little did the rally know, that two kayakers were close enough to their anniversary date to celebrate.

As the evening progressed, the candidates speeches grew louder and longer and the pipe band noisier and sillier. After five Canadian beers, Jerry and I were jigging around to the music of bagpipes, surrounded by the smoke of our anniversary cigars. After seven beers each, we were in the tavern laughing and carrying on with the pipe band.

"Is this live entertainment from the pub room at Bath or live entertainment from the bathroom at Pub?" I said in a loud voice, which was answered by the roar of laughter the BOOM, BOOM, BOOM of a drum and a ridiculous WAAAAA from a bagpipe.

As we sauntered off into the darkness to sleep on the grassy bank next to our rigs, I clutched the silver dollar, which I always carried in my pocket. It was one of three that my aunt and uncle gave Tom, Jerry and I at another party a year ago that night.

It was a short hop from Bath to Adolphus Reach and into the long arms of the narrow Bay of Quinte. Trenton was only fifty-three miles away—the start of the 240 mile long Trent-Severn Waterway—and by the end of the day we had nineteen miles to go. Over the next two days, however, paddling was replaced by walking. The wind closed the waterway door for us and at the same time opened the one to the Tyendinaga Reserve. We had just finished an eight-mile hike to Shannonville, when we stopped at 'Stella's house for water and to asked permission to camp another night on what we thought was her property. Before our water jugs were filled from the well bucket, we were invited in for tea and biscuits and only returned to camp to retrieve a few essentials to spend the night indoors.

"My Mother taught me that when a stranger comes to our door, we always give them half of what we have to eat—even if it's a slice of bread," 'Stella told us. "The good deed will always come back in another way."

'Stella was a woman who radiated peace and tranquility. She was born in the bush, near Napanee, some eighty years before and was a member of the Mohawk Nation. We listened and learned from her.

The Mohawk People were part of the Six Nations making up the Iroquois Confederacy. The Mohawk, Onondaga, Oneida, Cayuga and Seneca Nations formed a league in the late fifteen hundreds and, later, adopted the Tuscarora Nation in 1722. 'Stella's ancestors originally lived along the Mohawk River Valley we had just traveled through two weeks earlier. In 1777, after supporting British Loyalists, her people were forced to flee to Canada, leaving behind their burned homes and ruined agricultural land. Seven years were spent near Lachine, until finally the Mohawks were granted ninety thousand acres, which included the reserve we were now on.

"We woke to the smell of bacon and eggs—'Stella was cooking breakfast on the wood stove downstairs. The upstairs held the morning chill when I uncovered from the double quilts. A chamber pot sat on the floor next to a table holding a huge basin, towel and large pitcher of well water. I washed my face and walked down to breakfast. We ate thick sliced, home cured bacon, eggs from a nearby farm and all the toast and homemade preserves we could hold." rrb

John, a research field worker for the reserve, was at 'Stella's door at 9:OO and gave us a guided tour of the area. He was a decorated World War II veteran and had held the position of Council Chief twice on the reserve.

"Over the years like most places, the reserve, through land sales and dishonesty, has shrunk to a little over sixteen thousand acres—seventeen per cent of its original land size."

John, among many other things, was involved in treaty issues and the convoluted history of Indian land. He himself was caretaker of half the silver communion service given to his people by Queen Ann of England in 171O.

"Four of the five chiefs of the Confederacy, who at that time lived in the Mohawk Valley, went to England to show their support for the British," John said. "People over there called them the four Indian Kings! We still consider ourselves British subjects."

During our rambling, we visited the tribal headquarters, community center, school, a tribal run shoe factory, auto body shop, the Mohawk Church and passed hundreds of acres of prosperous farmland. At John's house, we saw ceremonial masks, old lacrosse sticks, a birch bark canoe, weavings, pottery, beadwork and a sign that hung from his living room wall: "Knowledge is the Discovery of Ignorance."

Late afternoon found the three of us back at 'Stella's house eating a late lunch.

"What I respect about you guys. Is your ability to listen," John said. "My people used to sit at council for days in complete silence before arriving at a decision. Each person said what they had to say and then everyone sat back and digested what they had heard."

Tippy, 'Stella's small dog, was lying on the floor staring straight ahead when we said we would be back again someday.

"He knows your going," she said. "He always acts this way when friends leave. I'll keep him inside, or else he'll follow you down to your boats."

I returned the comment with: "This is a place where we could and would spend the winter if we were forced to. I'm sad to leave."

We left carrying two baskets of food and, by late evening, we were cooking stew made from fresh vegetables out of 'Stella's big garden.

The night was clear and frost was predicted. Jerry sat on the water's edge watching the northern lights. One of us would be sleeping under the stars; the other one would be lying under the stars wondering why he was so sick. It may have been the unwashed vegetable I ate, or it may have been something else. Whatever it was, it struck with a twelve-hour vengeance of painful stomach cramps, vomiting, diarrhea, fever, chills and hallucinations. Between bouts, I was glad not to be in the tent and thanked God 'Stella wasn't around to witness the misery. Unfortunately, Jerry did know what was going on and suffered as much mentally, as I did physically. By next morning, whatever had been in my G.I. tract was soaking into the pasture. I was weak, but I felt better and forced myself to paddle a token five miles before exhaustion took over. I slept several hours in my sleeping bag while Jerry hiked into Belleville in search of medicine. When he returned I had been up for almost an hour, had started a fire and knew I was feeling better because I was now more worried over Jerry worrying about me than I was worried about myself.

The Alka-Seltzer he bought made me feel much better and the two new rolls of toilet paper—our supply was exhausted during episode—made both of us laugh.

The "scourge" was to return one more time in the next two weeks, but it would have a much weaker punch.

I woke up the next morning feeling great and appreciative of my health.

We made a fourteen-mile beeline to the Canadian Forces Base outside of Trenton and couldn't resist the hospitality. Before long, Jerry and I were giving our first kayak trip talk to a group of cub scouts at Frankford and were the guest of a CAF serviceman named Fred and Isabelle, his wife.

Frankford was on the Trent-Severn Waterway and we would paddle past it the next day. In the meantime, we participated in an evening water talk, with questions focused primarily on the next phase of the journey.

We learned our run would take us through the Trent, Otonabee and Severn Rivers, along with twenty lakes for a total of two hundred and seven miles. There would also be thirty-three miles of canal, forty-three locks and a marine railway. In the process, the waterway would lift us over a high section of the Canadian Shield to a height of four hundred and eighty feet above Lake Ontario. On the way back down, it would drop us two hundred and sixty-one feet to Georgian Bay (Lake Huron), leaving us two-hundred and nineteen feet higher than Lake Ontario.

Much to our satisfaction, the locks were free of charge to non-motorized craft—putting to rest conflicting reports we had heard in New York about Canadian waters.

As for its history, the Trent-Severn followed a water highway known to Indian people for hundreds of years. Samuel de Champlain was the first known European to travel its entire route in the early sixteen hundreds. The canal, itself, sputtered along for years before completion. Bogged down by red tape and disinterest, the canal started as a suggestion by the Duke of Wellington in 1819, shortly after the War of 1812. Finally, it became a through water-way for shallow draft craft in 1920. Its overhead clearance of twenty-two feet and a maximum draft of four feet and twenty-tons at the Big Chute Marine Railway severely limited the waterway's traffic to pleasure craft.

"Where are ya numbers? I can't lock ya through without yer numbers," the man in the captain's hat said.

We were at our first lock on the Trent-Severn and were dumfounded.

"What numbers?" I asked.

"All boats comin' through gotta have numbers," he repeated, while the cigarette, stuck to his lower lip, jerked even more.

"Okay, I see, well this boat's number is MN12345 and my buddy's is MN54321," I said.

The wooden gates opened, the wooden gates closed, we went up and then paddled out.

"I know we got Minnesota stickers for our kayaks, but those ain"t the numbers," Jerry said.

"I know," I replied. "We just gotta remember to 'keep the boss happy'."

We climbed one hundred and seventeen feet through six locks in seven miles. The areas around the locks were meticulously clean and many were beautifully landscaped with shrubbery and flowers. Our last lock of the day at Glen Ross had gates operated with hand-cranked capstans. Ten miles later, we found shelter in a small tarpaper hunter's shack on an island in Percy Reach.

In the open spaces between ash and cottonwood tees, gold colored steam rose from the water. In the reed beds, small groups of ducks swam back and forth while we silently packed. The smell of fall was definitely in the air. Later, cold rain fell at the flight lock at Ranney Falls.

The structure was an interesting arrangement consisting of two lock chambers and three gates. Once the first chamber raised us past the concrete sill supporting the middle gate, it opened and allowed us passage into the second chamber.

We had eight locks altogether that day and spent the night indoors for the third time in a row.

"We are at Lock #15," I wrote, "The sky is clear and the present temperature is thirty-nine and falling. It's supposed to freeze tonight. We are definitely falling behind our traveling schedule, but it cannot be helped. We have about a thousand miles to cover. Hard to say what will happen. We will surely go as far as we can. Presently, we are sleeping in a very spotless, ladies restroom at Lock #15. Bud, the lockmaster, gave us the key before he closed at 5:OO p.m. This place has electricity, hot and cold running water, heat and commodes. It's as good as any motel room for us." rrb

We waited for Bud in the morning and helped him raise the Canadian flag before the lock officially opened at 9:OO. While we were drinking hot coffee and eating jam covered toast in his office, we inquired about the peculiar color of the walkway going over the lock chamber.

"Oh that," he said. "Trudeau had some left over purple paint from his swimming pool, so we used it, eh!"

That evening we had our own camp and sat before a warm fire at the entrance to eighteen-mile long Rice Lake.

"We are slowly reactivating our winter clothes," I scratched into my log. "I pulled my mummy sleeping bag from summer storage and joined it with my light summer bag at Oswego. Jerry has his red gloves out and I have my wool ones on. Last night, I unpacked my insulated jacket."

Not far from the mouth of the Otonabee River, after we had paddled two-thirds of the way down Rice Lake, we pulled into a place called Elm Grove Camp for a break. The resort owners had been accommodating Canadian and American fishermen for the past twelve years. Surprisingly, in twelve minutes, it seemed as if Jerry and I had known them for the same amount of time.

We run the camp till mid October," she said. "Then we move to a camp farther north for the deer season. This used to be the only place on the lake. An old fella had it before we took over. Big recreation area around here; a lot of the fishermen are from the States."

Keith and Loreen were good to us. We left with pockets full of candy bars, two Peterborough anniversary silver dollars and ten dollars each! That evening, intruders set up at a cattle watering hole on the Otonabee and my logbook recorded the results:

"About 1:OO a.m., we woke to the sounds of thundering hooves and snorting. Jerry looked out to find tent and kayaks surrounded by fifty or so whiteface cows. We were afraid one of the beasts would trample the kayaks, so Jerry emerged in stocking hat, shoe and underwear. He growled, yelled, lunged and threw an occasional rock at our uninvited guests several times before the party broke up completely."

It was a ludicrous end to a good day. Before I fell asleep, I thought of a lock we had gone through the day before. It was another double lock and while I sat in my kayak in the first chamber watching the water streaming over the mineral stained, sunlit sill, I realized at that moment in time, I was perfectly happy!

A sixteen-mile day put as at the city of Peterborough. The first lock we reached, within the city limits, was #19. Commissioned in 1843, it was the oldest operating lock on the waterway system. It had slanted cut stonewalls and was unique to us because its valves were located in the gates, instead of the floor of the lock chamber.

Even more unique was Peterborough's third and last lock—the highest, hydraulic lift lock in the world. There were two such locks in North America. One was here and the other at Kirkfield, fifteen locks and eighty miles away.

The lift lock resembled two gigantic cake pans, measuring 14O X 33 X 8 feet, situated on two gigantic hydraulic pistons and rams. The two delicately balanced chambers were equipped with watertight gates to allow them to move vertically. Since both pistons were connected hydraulically in a closed system, the upward motion of one would allow displacement in the piston, lowering the other chamber. So, as we were going up sixty-five feet in two minutes, the other chamber was going down the same distance.

During the locking procedure, a recorded message told us construction for the lift lock started in 1898; operation began in 1904 and, amazingly, ninety percent of its original equipment was still in use!

We pitched our tent at the lock's picnic grounds alongside the canal and left in mild morning temperatures. Here and there, amidst the green, a few maples blazed orange and crimson. Three miles away was the Nassau Campus of Trent University. Its modern buildings were architecturally blended into the riverfront and easily accessible by kayak. We called the campus "a garden for the cultivation of thought, in a garden."

The woman in the map section of the campus library gave us four topographic maps to complement three others I had picked up the day before at a Peterborough land surveyors office. We now had enough maps to navigate to the west end of the North Channel on Lake Huron. The remaining four 1:250,000 scale maps, which included the north shore of Lake Superior, were ordered and sent to a G.D. at Britt.

We had been in the Kawartha Lakes area since Rice Lake and would continue to wind our way through its interconnected series of Finger Lakes until Lake Simcoe. The beautiful area was known for its tourism—and it showed. The day after we left Peterborough, the morning fog turned into a continual drizzle. We camped on Stony Lake on a small, wooded, cabin-free shoreline. Many of the red granite islands we passed would have made ideal campsites a dozen times over, but every one had a cabin. Jerry wedged the tent between two hemlocks and we spent the late afternoon and evening sitting under our tarp next to a campfire.

The following evening was the antithesis—rain in the morning, clear in the afternoon and evening. We had an island campsite bathed in moonlight on Buckhorn Lake. It was one of those odd days, ending with me covering fifteen miles and Jerry nineteen.

The discrepancy occurred at Lock #30 on the southwest side of Lovesick Lake. Preparing to lock through, we heard someone had forgotten their "Bible" at Burleigh Falls.

"It's my black, zipper case for my letters and journals!" Jerry said with a shocked look on his face.

In an instant, he was making kayak tracks and finished the round trip in forty-five minutes—a half hour faster than our normal traveling speed!

After eating a pan of hot corn bread soaked in margarine and corn syrup, we sat back to enjoy cigars the electrician had presented to Jerry on his return trip to the Burleigh Falls Lock. It was time to reflect and write.

"A loon just called in this nighttime—something we haven't heard for many months—the full moon, the forest and the quiet. Peace and contentment—it's everything I could possibly want from my existence."

On Sturgeon Lake I wrote: "I hope we are given the strength and weather to reach Duluth," Earlier in the day, rain, which we thought would turn to snow, forced us to stop at the Maple Leaf Marina on Pigeon Lake. Our trip reminded Mrs. Scott of her husband's time in the bush: "He spent a winter in northern Ontario on a survey crew. He had a tent with a stove and was warm as toast. He really loved it!" She also mentioned fall weather was two weeks earlier than normal and everyone expected what we feared the most, an early winter.

Between her musings, she presented us with duplicate, unrequested orders of hamburgers and coffee. Later, she gave us a plastic bag full of candy bars and another stuffed with matches.

Our climb down the waterway began once we crossed Balsam Lake at the Kirkfield lift lock. The height of land crossing meant we would be following whatever current there was. It also meant the waterway's marker buoys reversed sides—red was now to our port side and black to starboard.

The next lock had "our rooms" waiting for us again:

"The place we are staying at tonight is a real 'shithouse'. For the second time, we are staying in the ladies' latrine— this time at Lock #37. Clean latrines—our answer to cold, wet weather—would disgust some people.

The Kawartha Lakes Region ended at Lake Simcoe, a twenty-mile long, sixteen-mile wide body of water. Warning signs reminded us of the lake's unpredictable nature, but our thirteen-mile run on a northwest course to McRae Point was trouble free.

Since our charts didn't show it, we didn't know we were only sixty miles straight north of downtown Toronto. For the same reason, we didn't know we were camped in a closed provincial park. There were neither postings nor signs where our tent was set and our fire and kayaks were on the stone beach well below the high water mark.

It was dark. I had just finished baking corn bread, when a disembodied voice spoke from the bank.

"You can't camp here," he said. "This section's closed."

The caretaker seemed angry and kept threatening us with fines and calling the O.P.P.

"We get people like you all the time from Toronto. They break beer bottles, start fires and throw glass and trash all over. We can't have it! We just can't have it!"

When the sermon was over, I asked: "Where do you want us to go?"

"Over there," he said.

And we began a mile walk to where we were "supposed to be." En route, he started to listen about our journey and halfway to the campground he said: "Oh hell, stay where you are; just leave real early in the morning, so I don't get into trouble."

The caretaker watched us leave in the morning. He came running down in big rubber boots, attempting to speed up our departure by carrying on about Hurricane Eloise. We knew the fizzled out storm would give us more rain in a day or two, but other than that, it posed no threat. We told him we'd "watch it" and then reassured his job by waving goodbye.

Our twenty-four mile day took us through the narrows between Atherley and Orillia into Lake Couchiching and beyond. Hundreds of cottages cramped the waterway's shoreline. From previous experience, we could easily imagine the commotion in mid summer.

"People from the city drive up here for weekends or holidays to join the 'city in the country'," I told Jerry.

Scenery, in the evening though, was different. We found an uninhabited, rock island, immediately after crossing Sparrow Lake, just large enough for a tent and fire. Our perch gave us an east view over the water. Late in the night I rustled myself from the tent, to do what I normally had to do after too many cups of campfire tea. As I stood with bare feet hugging the rock lichens, I could hear in the stillness the barely perceptible honking of geese. The calls grew louder and louder and finally black silhouettes crossed the face of the moon.

A gray, canvas tepee appeared along the Severn River's birch lined shore in the misty rain. In an area where we had seen so many cabins, it shocked us. We passed Hydro Glen, Swift Rapids, Severn Falls and finally stopped for the night at the Big Chute "Latrine Motel."

The 4,000 kilowatt hydro plant at Big Chute had been generating power since 1909 and the Marine Railway had been shuttling boats around the fifty-eight foot drop since 1919. Now it was our turn.

"You're lucky to be traveling' this time of year through here," Jim, the operator, said. "Otherwise, you'd be portaging. It's not uncommon in July or August mornings to see thirty yachts waiting on the upriver side and the same number waiting on the downriver side. For some of them, it's an eleven hour wait."

The railroad flatbed car with a tilt bed was under water when we approached it. Once our tiny craft were situated between the support blocks on either side of the bed, Jim tilted it to a horizontal position and ever so slowly we rolled out of the water on top of it. The flatbed car rode on rails and was pulled, or let out, by a steel cable hooked to a powerful winch. Our downward decent was speeded up slightly and, as the car plunged under water, we sailed off with an extra push felt all the way to Port Severn and Georgian Bay eight miles away.

"Yabba dabba do, that's what you can call me too!"

His real name was Mike, a white-haired, crazy Hungarian, on a three-day boating holiday, who loved to drink beer and meet new people. We were introduced to him at Dunc and Betty's General Store and ended up spending most of the evening with him.

Duck hunters were all over the place. The season was starting in the morning and the sixty or so arrivals had swelled Port Severn's population by fifty percent. The activity was especially felt in the crowded, noisy, smoke-filled tavern where Jerry, "Yabba Dabba Do" and I were laughing and relaxing.

The evening was just what the doctor ordered. We had picked up our wet suits at the Port Severn Post Office and wanted to forget, for a short while, the grueling and dangerous task that lie ahead.

The next morning it was raining. After a light break-fast, we returned to the General Store and met John, who had stopped to purchase some nails to repair some knotty pine paneling.

"You're staying in the ladies room at the Lock?" he asked with an open-mouthed stare.

"For us, it's any port in a storm," Jerry answered.

"Well, if you're going to be around tonight come over to the Arrowood Lodge. Elsa and I'll take good care of you!"

John and Elsa, just like the folks at the General Store, had moved to Port Severn for a change. Whether it was the stress of urban living, or the need for open space and fresh air that precipitated the move, we didn't know. However, we did know the pattern was fairly common because we had seen it time and time again for almost thirteen months.

It was a blue-sky morning with heavy dew when we left. The gates of Lock #45 on the Trent-Severn opened and we entered the Thirty-Thousand Island area of Georgian Bay.

Jerry called the O.P.P. earlier, saying our checkpoint with them would be Snug Harbour, near Parry Sound—

hopefully, three days away. Our charts showed that we were now on the same latitude as Minneapolis and St. Paul. This bit of information, coupled with cooperative weather, psychologically, made us feel we had most of the "long hard climb out of the way."

The next two days of traveling were a treat. Small wonder why we encountered so many small boats our first day out as we threaded our way through the maze of islands in a "boater's paradise." Again, the congestion and "a cottage on every rock" became bothersome to us, as the beautiful weather gave us respite. The area was immense and quite pristine. The water and sky held were varied shades of blue and the bay often appeared green in shoal areas. Veins of quartz running through the pink granite were easily visible fifteen to twenty feet below the surface—but unfortunately, so were beer and pop cans.

The province and the federal government had made some headway into protecting an area on its way to being "liked to death." "Giant's Tomb," Beausoleil Island and other parcels we paddled by attested to their efforts, but it seemed to us, they still had a long way to go.

Our campsite the second day was in a small, uninhabited cedar cove on otherwise "cabin thick" Delhaven Island.

While we watched the sun sink into the bay, we also noticed the gnarled white pines near our camp. I called them the "frozen pines blowing in the non-wind." They represented the rule rather than the exception and talked loudly of what would inevitably come.

Our "honeymoon" with Georgian Bay was over. For two days we crept through back channels and the lee of any fragments of land, camping near Franklin and Shawanaga Islands. Our conversation with an Indian man at Parry Island added to our gloomy dispositions. He came into the marina talking excitedly about a bear he nearly ran over with his truck. However, once he picked up the tribal paper, things changed.

"I can't believe what's happening there," he said.

The paper covered a story about an Ojibwa community in western Ontario, not far from the Minnesota border. For years a local paper company washed its pulp with a mercury mixture. And for years, the mill's waste had contaminated the surrounding waters. The outcome: A Native community with symptoms of Minamata disease and a traditional food supply that could no longer be used.

Before we left, he looked out the window toward the bay and said: "I wonder how long it will be before we can't eat the fish here?"

Near Pointe au Baril Station, we talked with an Indian woman who, along with her three dogs, four kittens and "mama" cat, ran a combination general store, post office and gas dock. She was packing up and going into town in two weeks to spend the winter.

"It's scary to see seven to eight footers roll in from the gap this time of year, but it does happen, she said. "Last spring when I opened up, I found half the gas dock floating out there in the harbor. When a west wind blows anything can happen!"

We bought the last four candy bars she had and left with bits and pieces of her Georgian Bay experiences echoing in our minds.

For the next two days and nights the wind roared in our ears at an island camp.

"We are near Point au Baril but cannot venture beyond. The wind is our big enemy; we must show great patience and wait. We bide our time by the day—by the hour. I've seen my breath all day today. Jerry and I share our fears of getting caught in an ice storm. It seems as though winter will close in on us at any moment!" rrb

We shared the island with a cabin. It was boarded up and locked for the winter and prompted me to have a bizarre dream which may not have been too far fetched.

In the nightmare scenario, Jerry and I were in the cold water of the bay towing our kayaks to shore. Even with wet suits on, we were both suffering from hypothermia and needed to reach the safety of a shelter. Low and behold, the island we wash up on has a cabin. With a final burst of energy, we get to its door only to find it locked! I pound on the door with my right fist and then the dream ends. I explode into consciousness, to hear the never-ending wind and feel my skinned right knuckles throbbing from an injury earlier in the day.

The next morning we were able to pick up a marine forecast on Jerry's radio verifying we were waiting out a forty-knot gale.

We were now strongly contemplating a winter break at Sault Ste. Marie, some three hundred miles away.

"It's hard to say what will happen," I wrote. "I do not relish a November gale on open Lake Superior. We have tremendous respect for the water and we are not fools."

In spite of the weather and hardships, my logbook records:

"I love it out here. I love the natural world very, very much. I love kayaking. In the last thirteen months I have found communion with something much more powerful than myself. Again I must be reminded—we ride with the journey; the Journey does not ride with us!"

The next morning the water in our cooking kettle was frozen, but the wind had shifted to the east, making an escape possible. We had a twenty mile run—fifteen of it to the northwest around Point au Baril to Byng Inlet and then down the inlet, due east, to Britt and our mail. We spooned down rice made the night before, mixed with powdered milk, sugar, cinnamon and heated bay water. We put on our wet suits and gloves and were gone by nine.

One fella was looking at the "guts" of an outboard and the other had just gotten in from fishing when we tied up at Wrights' Marina to get directions.

Randy Bauer

"Britt's right over there by that white oil tank," the fisherman said.

"I'm goin' over there in a few minutes if you want a ride. Just let me get out of this bunny suit first."

From those opening lines, things began to snowball. The fisherman's name was Bob, a Canadian born, retired tool and die maker from Galion, Ohio. We shared supper with him at a truck stop on the highway and talked and talked and talked.

"I passed you guys when I was comin' in," he said. "Would you like to stay at my place? It's four miles from the marina—you paddled right past it. I got two empty bedrooms, no electricity or telephone and you have to get there by boat, but you're welcome to stay."

Bob parked his Vega at the marina, climbed into his boat and moved out. Jerry and I put on our kayaks and followed.

Bob's cabin was built in the thirties and its white sideboards and red rolled roofing could easily be seen from the main shipping channel leading into Britt. Its comfortable interior with spruce paneling and a stone fireplace, took our numbed minds off the weather, making it a good place to make an impending decision.

The next day Bob hit us square in the face with an offer.

"You know, this is Indian summer up here and the bad weather is just around the corner," he said. "Why don't you call it quits at my place for the winter and continue in the spring. You've come too far to have something go wrong now!"

That night the wind blew hard and strong. The back door banged continually and the cabin groaned in the strong gusts. I could hear the roar increase out on the bay as the night progressed and cringed at the thought of paddling a kayak out there in breakers that rounded the ends of logs to resemble the tops of baseball bats!

During the morning, Jerry and I took a walk and talked about our options.

" We probably could get to the Sioux, but it would be a battle every inch of the way," Jerry said. "I think it's either here or a few miles up the coast, Randy, before we have to stop. We got sixty-five miles of isolation between here and Killarney and a lot could happen in between."

I agreed with what he was saying and added: "I think this is a time when we have to bend with the breeze or break. My gut is telling me the same thing yours is. Common sense tells me to stop here. We have the time and we gotta play by nature's rules."

The decision was made and we told Bob.

In the afternoon, we were taken into town to tell the O.P.P. and the people back home our decision. En route, a commercial fishing boat passed by with a hundred or so seagulls trailing behind. It reminded Bob of earlier years and—cigar in mouth—he commenced to talk above the whine of the motor:

"Twenty-four years ago the Indians used to come down to Key Harbour, about twelve miles from here, during the summer fishing season. They would stay in tepees or wall tents and the kids would have their years worth of schooling in three months. For the other nine, the children worked just as hard as their parents, winter fishing and trapping for a living. There was a curfew bell that rang in the evening to get back to the camp and the kids would have to swim across the river from the general store—the 'hang out'. Now there were some Finish folks with the Indians 'cause these folks were fishermen too and it was quite a sight, when that curfew bell rang, to see all those brown little heads bobbing on the surface with the blond ones mixed in with them."

On the way, we pulled into a local resident's cabin so Bob could tell him of our plans.

"You'll like Joe," Bob said. "He's a trapper, fisherman, guide for the lodge and looks after my place over the winter."

Joe was French and Objibwe. His ancestors, in the late eighteenth and early nineteenth centuries, powered thirty-six foot Montreal Canoes for the North West Company. During their annual trip from Grand Portage or Fort William to Lachine, near Montreal, voyageurs departed or entered Georgian Bay twenty miles from Britt at the mouth of the French River.

He told us about the wrath of Georgian Bay and finding overturned boats, but never the people. He talked about running sled dogs, trapping for a living and the big beaver that chewed a hole in his boat. We learned that winters were long. The area normally received one hundred and twenty inches of snow and it took fourteen cords of wood to heat a small house like Joe's, in an area where minus forty degrees Fahrenheit was not unheard of.

At the marina, I headed to the phone while Jerry and Bob talked with an eighty-year-old fisherman. He made his own lures from spoons and before I was out of earshot, I heard the old timer say: "I have to experiment several times before I can get them to 'dance' through the water just the way I like."

Mom burst into tears and I almost did too, when I told her of our decision. We both agreed the homecoming would be a great gift for Jim and Molly who were celebrating their second wedding anniversary that day and also for Jerry, whose mother had just gotten out of the hospital.

Back at Bob's we started our "wintering process" by suspending the kayaks with slings in the storage cabin and loading our containerized, dry, food into an old ice block refrigerator.

The packing and preparation continued into the next day. We helped Bob with some of his annual chores and I found time for reflective writing on what was to come:

"I went for a walk amidst the rocks and fall leaves—a walk by myself. There's a lot on my mind. There has been too much to see and experience and winter has come too fast. I feel frustrated that we cannot move on—I guess we could, but we would be risking too much. I want to paddle into Duluth. I do not want someone calling home in the late fall saying, "lost on the lakes." I am a kayaker. Jerry is a kayaker. We are coming home and we are a little apprehensive. I really don't want to move to a world where the car and asphalt jungle are king. I am not ready for the change. I feel as if I'm a wild, free animal ready to be shipped to a zoo."

During our four-night stay, Bob fed us bacon, eggs, toast and grits for breakfast and a combination of fresh walleye, lake perch and small mouth bass for supper. The man who said "you have to acquire a feel for steel," sharpened all of our knives and told us how to make acorn tea. He talked lovingly of the bear and raccoon in the area, his friend "George," the seagull, and a family of flying squirrels he found one spring living under one of the wooden window shutters.

"We just didn't use that window till mama was done raising the little ones," he said.

He even liked the deer mice that frequented his pantry.

"They're pesky little critters, like to gnaw on about almost anything, but they're clean."

The last night at Bob's we saw the best Aurora display on the entire journey. We turned out the gas lantern and watched from the porch in the stillness. The lights had a tint of red to them as they shimmered and danced in a sky bright with stars. It was the land's way of saying goodbye to us.

The boat sped down the channel to the marina, to our appointment with the bus on the highway. Again, we stopped at a house en route.

"Here, take this fishin' pole and just set it by the door," Bob said to me.

He told us the rest of the story when I got back.

"For days I've seen a small boy fishin' off this dock with a broken fishin' pole. Just thought I'd make him happy!"

The bus ride took us from Britt to Minneapolis with transfers in Sudbury, Sault Ste. Marie, Mackinaw City and Duluth. It lasted forty-five hours, including an 11:OO p.m. to 6:OO p.m. "break" at the Sioux Station. Without money for a motel room, we spent a restless night there on benches that we concluded had been designed by sadists.

My pen "smoked" while we waited:

"Last night we watched the 'clean-up crew' sober up a drunk. Then at 6:OO a.m., when the station opened, an old codger came in, sat down at the coffee bar, looked another fella in the face that was already sitting there and said in a loud clear voice: 'You look worried.' I guess we looked just as strange to some of the riders. We were relieved to be on the bus at 6:OO p.m. The border crossing was no problem. The custom agents, I'm sure, thought we were nuts, so they let us pass through."

Finally, two tired, bedraggled and culture-shocked travelers arrived. "WELCOME HOME RANDY AND JERRY" and "HELLO TRILOGY CREW" banners were strung across my parents' house and garage. It seemed impossible to be back. Both of us wore our Trilogy dress shirts that looked strangely out of place with our well-worn clothes and general appearance. Our beards had been growing since New York and our hair hadn't been cut for months.

"Last Sunday night I woke up and felt tremendously relieved ... like a huge weight had been lifted from my shoulders," Jim, my brother, said.

"It's the same day, we decided on a winter layover," I told him.

The next morning I woke up thinking I was inside a cabin on an island. I could hear voices outside and immediately thought of the safety of the kayaks! As reality settled in, I realized I was in my parents home on a Saturday morning listening to them conversing over coffee.

For the next week I felt extremely guilty because the weather was perfect for paddling—warm and sunny. I remembered what the Indian Lady at Pointe au Baril told us: "If you do decide to winter over, you'll have two weeks of the most beautiful weather you've ever seen!"

Then I woke up one morning to reports of a huge storm on Lake Superior and Georgian Bay. The ore-carrier Edmund Fitzgerald and twenty-nine crewmen had disappeared in twenty-five foot seas and sixty-knot winds off Whitefish Point in eastern Lake Superior. Jerry and I both knew we would have been in the November tenth storm and, after the incident, I didn't feel guilty anymore.

We didn't see much of each other over the winter. Jerry worked as a janitor for a local school district at night and at a feed mill during the day. I took on the task of remodeling my Aunt and Uncle's house after a major fire forced them to relocate for five months.

Jerry and I wrestled with similar psychological adjustments. I remembered over and over again what Dave, on the sailboat at Apalachicola, had told us: "You'll get home and have the false expectation that everyone will have changed in the same way you have changed!" And Jerry wrote in his journal: "It seems like a lot of people around here are caught in a rut. It's not because they're not smart enough to get out, it's because they're not willing change."

As the winter dragged on, I began to worry about the safety of our boats and equipment at Britt. One night, I had a vivid dream where I went back to the 1906 cabin and checked the condition of our prized possessions. I woke up happy and relieved—the gear was fine and waited peacefully for our return.

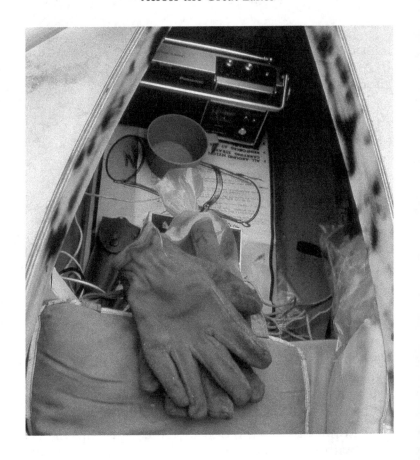

Chapter 34

The Return

"Life is either a daring adventure or nothing."
Helen Keller

Uncle Bob and his fifteen-year-old son, Greg, drove us back to Britt in early May. The orange suburban on the eight hundred mile "expedition" carried a canoe and enough food to last until Duluth.

It was late afternoon when we stopped at Joe's green-roofed house, which still had a huge winter supply of split birch piled next to it. Joe answered after ten minutes of pounding and invited us in for a beer. He was in good spirits, had gotten our letter and also a phone call from Bob, wintering in Florida, reaffirming our plans.

Before leaving, we agreed Joe would take all of us over to the cabin in the morning. He would leave Jerry and me off, unload our gear and then take Uncle Bob and Greg back to the marina.

The keys jingled as Joe unlocked the storage cabin and light shown on our kayaks and equipment. Everything was just as if we had left it an hour ago and returned. The five of us were together less than thirty minutes. Bob wanted to leave for Minnesota by noon and Joe had work to do at the lodge. The whine of Joe's boat faded into the sough of the pines and we were left to our own endeavors in the thirty-degree day with a steel blue sky.

Minor damage was quickly remedied. Strips of beef jerky with telltale gnaw marks in the ends were simply cut shorter and repacked. The brass bomb bolt trimming the front of the *Mississippi Queen's* cockpit was reworked after it finally succumbed to the effects of electrolysis. On the Mississippi, Jerry strengthened the bomb bolt—which slid through an aluminum cap—by screwing it into a steel plate. When wet, the combination became a homemade battery, deteriorating the cathode to the point where stress, from taking it down from its winter roost, broke the bomb bolt in half.

Our voluminous food supply included twenty pounds of frozen smelt given to us by Joe. Originally, we thought Greg and Uncle Bob would feast with us, but in the end, it was Jerry, me and "George," the seagull.

High winds prevented our departure for two days. Again we were relearning patience and I wrote: "We are weather dependent creatures—primarily WIND. We want to get to Duluth, but we don't know when!"

After freezing on Bob's porch the first night, we decided to bunk the next two nights in the storage cabin. We kept a fire going in the 1910 stove to fend off the cold.

"It will take awhile before we are again used to living outside in cool temperatures. The ice left the Inlet ten days ago and the ground is like a giant refrigerator. At least we don't have to worry about the flies for awhile." rrb

In a letter from Bob, we were warned about the hordes of black flies that made vast regions of the Canadian Shield pure hell in the spring and early summer. From previous experiences in northern Minnesota, we already knew about the pests, but didn't know about Bob's precautionary measure—twenty-five milligrams Vitamin B1, eight per day, decreasing to one per day after eight days. He had done it and said it worked. Since insect repellent bothered us, and the sweet smell of the ladies bath oil made us nauseous, we decided to experiment with the doses. In the face of stories about bug crazed individuals running naked through the bush, early explorers diving into the waters of Lake Superior to escape the insects and people turning into balloons after allergic reactions to the bites, it seemed like a prudent thing to do.

A note lay on the table telling Bob about our arrival and departure and thanking him for his generosity. For the first time in many months, we pulled on the paddle blades with fully loaded kayaks and were moving again.

We hid from the west wind for fifteen miles by ducking behind protected areas. At Key Harbour, we camped on a worn, pink granite island studded with gnarled jack pine and leafless birch.

Our bodies and minds continued to relearn. Sore muscles would be with us for a while and we would again have to readjust to the stress of cold water and wind chill.

"It's hard for land dwellers to appreciate the difference in land and water microclimates—especially on the Great Lakes. Wind and cold water create such a difference in temperature. I now understand why John Winkler said: 'According to Mark Twain, the coldest winter he ever spent was summer in Duluth!' "rrb

Both of us paddled with our shoes and socks on to keep our feet from contacting the water chilled fabric of our boats and, without gloves, our exposed hands became numb in seconds.

Things that had become automatic now required conscious thought. Packing the kayaks became a major chore and Jerry couldn't remember how the tent was rolled up. "It's unbelievable how much work is required in traveling," he wrote on our first night out.

A westward course took us through a fairyland of trees, rocks and water until the winds forced us to stop at the main mouth of the French River.

We were eating a late lunch in a warm wind protected cove and talking about Voyageurs when Jerry almost stepped on something he never expected to see.

"I don't know, Randy, but it sure looks like a rattler to me!"

Jerry was motionless—a three-foot rattlesnake was coiled in the blueberry bushes between his feet!

Ever so slowly, Jerry moved to open rock. As he did, the snake made a cicada-like sound very different from the sounds portrayed by its cousins in stereotyped Westerns.

It never occurred to us that we were on the extreme northern territory of the Massasauga Rattler. But it did occur to us that there may be more of the same around. The rest of the day and night we stayed away from brushy areas; kept the tops of the kayaks tightly sealed with ponchos and rocks; and made sure the tent was always zipped shut.

Voyageur Channel—the French River's most eastern outlet—passed by in the morning light. We paddled through a myriad of rock reefs and shoals, past azure, green and turquoise water and frothing sea castles built by the wind. Lunchtime found us on the Point Grondine Indian Reserve, near a two-mile wide shoal area of rock fragments called "The Chickens."

"We are eating peanut butter and honey sandwiches and drinking hot tea next to a huge pile of moose droppings. The Bustard Islands are about ten miles behind us. Jerry and I called them the 'Bastard' Islands because they were so hard to get to in this continual wind!"

Beaverstone Bay was our back door to seventeen wind free miles of paddling up and around a large island. The land was changing, the LaCloche Mountains, some of which rose a thousand feet above the bay were to the north and northeast.

The pink sky and quiet evening bespoke of a good run the next day. "Thirty-five miles and all kinds of smiles," I recorded. Our kayaks roared through cliff bordered Collins Inlet of Philip Edward Island and Jerry filled a water jug from melt water streaming from one of the numerous snowbanks and ice packs.

In my excitement to make meltwater tea for break, I horridly filled the kettle, started the stove and waited.

"Meltwater sure looks different," I said.

"That's gasoline!" Jerry yelled.

I had accidentally crossed the fuel and water look-alike bleach jugs!

The day was hot for us. The clothing under our wet suits was sweat soaked by the time we got to Killarney.

A waitress at a small cafe in the community told us the place was packed with tourists and sailboats during the high season. We were at the east side of the world's largest freshwater island, one thousand square mile Manitoulin Island. Its seventy-five mile long side formed North Channel out of the upper part of Lake Huron. The channel itself averaged thirty miles wide and was jammed with islands on its Killarney side.

Fossil-rich limestone rock now mixed itself with the granite. In some protected areas, leaves had come out and many of the hillcrests wore soft green haloes of bursting buds. The land was waking up and, in the still, we listened: "Last night Jerry and I heard Spring Peepers and the cronks, croaks, groans and cackles from the silent water and the swamp near our campsite. It sounded like a barnyard!"

Then the sounds disappeared in two days of heavy rain, mixed with thick fog, followed by strong north winds. The weather was testing us again and we were learning again. It became especially clear after we heard a quote from singer and songwriter Arlo Guthrie on Jerry's radio: "The more things you want—the less freedom you have."

When we did finally leave our campsite, it was done under threatening skies and cold temperatures. My journal gives a brief, but descriptive sketch of the day:

"We passed many streams and waterfalls roaring down from the high cliffs. Now and then we encountered small, sand beaches among all of the rock ones. Heavy north winds today. Very cold—in the thirties; ice cold rain, snow and ice pellets on and off throughout the day. During lunch we built a fire to warm up. I brushed my teeth next to a ten-foot deep, crystal clear rock pool. A sun bleached log, ground smooth by wave action, is nestled high up on our beach."

In spite of the wind, the following day we managed twenty-five miles by winding our kayaks between Great and Little La Cloche Islands, Dreamers Rock and past the landmarks of White Mountain, East and West Knob, Round Hill and Mount McBean. The paradise of gin colored water was lost when we cruised into the effluent basin of the Spanish River and were forced to camp on an island. The water turned brown from paper mill waste and reminded us of the Lower Hudson.

We climbed one of the island's steep hills with a cliff face and looked at the surrounding land and water. Beyond the partial protection of islands, North Channel boiled in the wind. On the way up, we noticed Canadian mayflowers stretching their green leaves and strawberries and some violets blooming. The temperature was almost seventy. Even on top of the windy precipice, we swatted black flies. It was obvious our magic cure for the "scourge of the north" was not yet working.

The average daily temperature was slowly rising, but the wind continued to blow. Again, after a twenty-mile day, strong westerlies forced us to stop.

It was nearing the end of the week and we were eager to pick up mail at Thessalon before the post office closed for the weekend. That evening in a protected cove of Turnbull Island, we cooked up a plan that seemed easy enough: We'd leave camp at three in the morning and paddle as much of the fifty miles to Thessalon as we could. Then we'd be in easy range of the post office to reach it before noon on Saturday.

In reality my log describes how the "plan" worked:

"We awoke at 2:OO a.m. in hopes of a pre-dawn launch. Prior to that time, I woke up about five times—checking the time and listening for the wind. At one point during the night the wind had died considerably and I could hear the frogs chirping. But shortly before the alarm went off, it began blowing again. A severe thunderstorm rolled by at 3:OO a.m. We caught the northern fringe of it. At first, Jerry and I thought the flashes to the north were coming from one of many mines near Elliot Lake. But when the flashes lit up the entire sky revealing a huge mass of purple clouds, we knew otherwise!

Randy Bauer

At pre-dawn light, we could see white caps. By that time, the storm had passed but the wind, coming from the northwest, was stronger than when we landed! "Robin Lee Graham, who sailed around the world, was a victim of the doldrums; we are victims of gales," I wrote.

Late that evening at the same place, we were hit by what we called a "killer wind." It blew with such force that we thought the tent would rent in half. Seven hours later well before sunrise, two kayakers, frazzled by violent weather, postponed their mail pick up at Thessalon until Monday and left for Blind River fourteen miles away.

We landed our kayaks in the small community park and immediately felt a positive feeling for the town. The only way to describe it—and we had felt the same feeling in other places and other communities—was, for whatever reason, Blind River "radiated goodness."

We took turns walking into town to buy almost anything with sugar in it to satisfy our cold weather craving for sweets. While Jerry was gone, a youngster came down to the shore looking for his pet turtle. From my conversation with him, I learned the community used to have a mill and wood processing plant, but both had closed. I also learned about last fall's weather, which reinforced again our winter layover decision.

"If you think the wind is strong now, you should have been here last fall. Cars were picked up," he said. "And a lot of trees were blown down."

The boy also told us of a good camping spot three miles away to celebrate Jerry's birthday. The site was a long beach strewn with pulpwood logs at the mouth of the Mississauga River. It was the first sand beach we had camped on since Chesapeake Bay. The black flies were pesky, but the setting, Jerry's canned meat stew, my fireside chocolate cake and the Great Blue Herons that flew in to join the celebration made the evening something worth remembering.

The earth is a sphere with longitude lines growing closer and closer together as they approach the poles. We forgot to take into account this fundamental physical fact while we measured our east-west progress to Thessalon. The particular topographic map we were using had longitude lines, degrees and minutes immediately under our line of travel. Therefore, we substituted minutes for miles that normally would be measured with a ruled compass. In calculating, we multiplied thirty-three minutes by 1.15 miles per minute at the equator, instead of .83 at our approximate position of forty-six degrees. For two hours we gloated over our fantastic mileage until the nature of things made us realize we had gone ten miles less. Regardless, from our campsite, we could easily see the trees on Thessalon's mile and a half peninsula and knew we would be there early the next morning.

Entering the harbor we added several thousand seagulls to a list of spring wildlife that recently included hundreds of northbound Canada Geese and a red fox. The fox drew our attention because it silently zig-zagged across beach drift near the rusted hulk of an old wreck in a vane attempt to reach ducks floating in the water. The seagulls drew our attention because we could smell their island fortress a mile away. They bombarded us, as Jerry puts it, with "heavy artillery" when we were within range.

Nothing however, stopped us from getting our mail until we read the sign in the post office window: "HOLIDAY LEGAL 24 MAY VICTORIA DAY."

We left a note for the postmaster requesting our mail be forward to Montreal River Harbour on Lake Superior and stopped at a nearby restaurant to forget about our "well laid" mail call plans foiled for the second time.

Situated on flat sandstone, our camp was well within cabin-infested St. Joseph Channel. North Channel was behind us and we were beginning our approach to Sault St. Marie. The course would take us around the east side of Sugar Island, Michigan, up Lake George, through

Little Lake George and down the old channel. The route would be longer than the main shipping channel running through Lake Nicollet on the west side of the island, but safer.

"Finally, no wind!" I wrote. "We covered thirty-five miles today and are in our twenty-second state. We are sleeping in what used to be a farm. The old farmhouse is south of us and the two outbuildings are roofless—their tops ripped off during the great storm last November when the Fitzgerald sank. A guy named Steve lives in a trailer about two hundred yards from our camp. He polled a johnboat in here a few minutes ago, while we watched a mink and gave us some sucker his Grandfather just smoked—delicious!"

The water was warmer than the thirty-three degree air and very calm. Fog, back lit by the rising sun, lay heaped like mounds of cotton on the surface of the old channel. The kayaks appeared and disappeared from each other's view, as did our view of the gossamer shore.

We passed a housing project and suddenly my kayak, grounding on an invisible object, turned to the left. Dreamtime was over. I flagged Jerry down, pulled to shore and emptied gear and ten gallons of bilge water out of a craft that hadn't had a severe injury for a long time. Instinctively, I repaired the two by two inch rip in the vinyl hull and counted the patches—there were over fifty now, each one bearing an invisible name as to where and when.

The patching routine broke an all time record. From time of impact, we were back underway in twelve minutes, bound for the Algoma Sailing Club and any nearby supermarket. Six loaves of bread, a pail of peanut butter, two pounds of margarine, canned meat and cookies were added to our larder, as well as a quart of cognac for evening salutes.

Friendship at the boat club delayed our departure. Fred and Maria drove us to their home where we cleaned up, washed clothes and ate supper. Before sundown, we were sailing with them on the St. Mary's River. It was a treat having the wind work with us for a change.

"I love it out here," Bill said, as the boat heeled heavy to the starboard side. "When the boys graduate from high school, we want to go on a year long sailing cruise. Kind of like what you guys are doing now."

Bill gave us a perspective of the city.

"Algoma Steel, who I work for, is the major employer of the Canadian Souix. I guess lumber would be second. Of course Sault Sainte Marie is a French name. The area was founded by French missionaries in the 1600s. The British North West Company built a fur post here in the late 1700s and the first primitive lock around St. Mary's Rapids."

Now, iron ore-carriers and ocean ships from all parts of the world pass through a mile long channel and modern commercial locks on their way to or from Lake Superior. We heard them the rest of the night, as their air horns periodically talked on an otherwise silent pilgrimage.

We tried to get some rest on board our hosts' sailboat, but it was difficult. The weather forecast was favorable and images of what THE LAKE would be like danced thorough our minds all night.

Twenty feet of turbulent water discharged from the tunnels of the Canadian pleasure craft lock. Once inside, the lockmaster asked us for our rope.

"Rope? What rope?" Jerry asked.

"Ya gotta have a rope to go through the lock," the lockmaster replied.

"We've been through over a hundred locks and you guys have always had the rope," Jerry answered.

"I can't let ya through unless ya got a rope," was the reply.

Then the young assistant spoke up: "Hell, give them the rope!"

And we were on our way up.

Both lock operators apparently didn't believe our story, or thought Jerry said sixty-five instead of sixty-five hundred miles. Once the upper gates opened, the lockmaster asked when we'd be coming back.

"We ain't never comin' back," Jerry yelled. "We're goin' home."

The kayaks were now at the same level as Superior—which was just around the corner. We held back at the sandy beach near Point au Pins and then started a twenty-four mile northerly course around Gros Cap, across Horseshoe Harbour to Goulais Point.

We now were on the largest surface area freshwater lake in the world—32,000 square miles of water! That's enough to easily swallow the entire state of South Carolina; or, more realistically, a taconite freighter and crew during one of its rages; or, if the lake decided, two small kayaks. We were specs of cosmic dust in the vastness of space, ciphers in the snow. The only words I could think of were BIG, COLD, DEEP!

Chapter 35

Lake Superior

"It is not length of life, but depth of life."
Ralph Waldo Emerson

The lake was kind and let us paddle the seven miles of rugged, no shelter, bluffs at Gros Cap and North Gros Cap without a problem. It was eerie to see lower cliffs, twenty to thirty feet high, with pulpwood logs stacked on top like match sticks—knowing full well how they got there. Just as strange, was the extreme clarity of the water. Oftentimes, we'd flinch as our kayaks glided over boulders that would suddenly disappear into green and then black.

When evening came, we hid our tent and kayaks deep within the woods, far from shore. Part of the reason for this was safety from a storm, the other was psychological. Lake Superior overwhelmed us and we needed to hide from it for a while.

However, we did come back to the stone beach at dusk. The day had been our first eighty degree day since last August, bringing us hope the below normal spring temperatures had ended. The water continued to be, uncomfortably, glass smooth. On the horizon line, I could see what I knew to be a giant ore boat. Against the vastness of sky and water, the ship looked like two tiny dots, a finger's width apart, separated by a thin pencil line. For an instant I had a flashback of a picture in a grade school science book comparing the earth to the sun. It was too much—I had to look away. As I did, I noticed Jerry opening our quart bottle of cognac.

"It's time for a toast," he said. "The magical mystery tour has begun!"

We poured three shots and saluted the lake for safe passage. Then, without hesitation, we downed two of the shots and gave the rest to Lake Superior.

While crossing Batchawana and Pancake Bays, Lake Superior heat mirages made the far shore seem closer than it actually was. We saw points named Rudderhead, Grindstone, Whiskey and Coppermine detach themselves from the mainland and float in a watery haze in the distance.

"Good weather makes us nervous out here," I wrote in my log.

We had gone thirty-three miles on a lake that wasn't supposed to give an inch, but we weren't complaining. Six and a half months earlier, the beach we were standing on received twenty-foot waves and flotsam marked Edmund Fitzgerald. Now in uncanny tranquility with a little imagination, we could hear the hazy, orange sun hiss as it disappeared into the water.

In spite of our Georgian Bay complaints of cold and rain, recent radio reports indicated tinder dry conditions in the bush. The haze we were seeing over the lake was from a major forest fire burning near Wawa. The stationary high-pressure system over this part of Ontario was beneficial to us, but deadly to forest resources.

We covered twenty-nine miles the next day and in the process stopped for mail at Montreal River Harbour. The water was so clear where we landed the boats it was hard to discern whether the beach stones were above or below the water. However, temperature wise, it was a different story.

"Jerry, take it easy. I can see my feet sinking in the gravel, but I can't feel them!"

My feet were numb after ten seconds, while I struggled lifting the stern of my boat.

Later, just before we were about to leave, a man who was staying at the Trail's End Lodge told us: "Lands and Forests told me a person could expect to survive no longer than five minutes in Superior this time of year!"

Bob's comment was verified an hour later near Agawa Bay when we lowered the Secchi Disc to fifty feet before it disappeared and measured the water temperature at thirty-six degrees Fahrenheit.

Bob was familiar with the area and had cruised the shore from Sault Sainte Marie, his home, to Marathon on the other side of what we called "the Big Bump"—a distance of two hundred and eighty miles.

"You'll notice the Pukaskwa area, or 'The Bump' like you call it, will have cooler weather than this part of the lake," he said.

Again, he was right. Later that evening when we checked a general vegetation chart of Ontario, we noticed a peculiar pattern. Since leaving Lake Ontario, we had gone through an area with a dominant mixture of red and white pine and white and yellow birch. Also present were red and sugar maple, basswood, oak and some jack pine. Of course, there were exceptions to the rule, but generally speaking, once we reached "The Bump," we'd see a change that would run all the way to Sibley Peninsula on the west side of the lake. The coolness of the massive body of water would pull down the Boreal Forest to its shores and we'd see dominance of white and black spruce, balsam fir and tamarack; along with white birch, quaking aspen and balsam poplar. Bob also talked about the area we had been through.

"About eight miles back near Point aux Mines, you passed an old uranium mine. It was active well before the ones at Elliot Lakes started up in fifty-four."

"The only thing I remember about that place was a huge boulder with pink granite and quartz in it where we had lunch," I said. "The black flies were so bad, we had to eat our sandwiches on the water in the boats!"

Jerry's ears were so bit up from the pests; he wore my white stocking cap over his ears to prevent any more damage.

"We have been taking vitamin B1," Jerry added. "But it doesn't seem to be working!"

"Well, you have about another two to three weeks and they'll be pretty well gone," Bob said.

Before we left, he gave us a binder full of detailed navigation charts, which would prove invaluable in pointing out safe harbor and dangerous cliff areas over the next week.

Finally, with his camera snapping away and our kayaks aimed at the far side of an eight-mile crossing, he said:

"Make sure you stop at Sinclair Cove on the other side of the Agawa Islands to look at the Pictographs!"

What we found on the cliff faces near the water's surface early the next morning was very special. There were faded red images of people in canoes, fish, bird life and serpents with and without horns. What looked like a caribou and a horned animal with a long tail and spikes running down its back had spoken to the lake for hundreds of years in a language unknown to us. We didn't speak during our visit and left as quietly as we came.

Farther up the road, near towering Cape Gargantua, we paddled in water over two hundred feet deep and past a forbidding group of rock islands shrouded in a mixture of fog and rain. The two hundred foot tall, Premier Island, labeled the "Devils Warehouse," didn't sit well with us. We were glad to clear it before camping in a narrow bay called Indian Harbour.

It was peaceful sitting around a pulpwood log fire throwing enough heat to relieve us from the cloak of dampness. The orange glow of the coals and flames contrasted sharply with the dark gray of cliff rock, scattered snow banks and the lingering pockets of blue ice we had seen during the day.

Beauvier Point, eight miles southwest of Michipicoten River, gave us a commanding view of the lake and a brief respite from the black flies and time to write:

"I'm on a bluff above camp. The tent is a green speck, the kayaks yellow and blue slivers in a cobbled cul-de-sac packed with pulpwood logs resembling scattered straw. A loon laughs while I sit here and a seagull flies by. This is their land —I'm only an intruder. They love it here and so do I. The wind is dying. It came in strong from the north-northeast this afternoon—that's why we're here. I only see wilderness around me—the water, the rocks, the forest and the sun. Superior stretches out to infinity. The water temperature is still thirty-six degrees. Heavy condensation forms on the inside of our boats from the cold water against the hulls and the warm sun warming the decks. My left calf was chilled to numbness today as it lay against the vinyl."

We passed cliffs of old volcanic rock; their beds highly distorted, twisted and convoluted. Some faces were broken and shattered, as if someone in a rage had smashed them with a giant celestial sledgehammer. Those with tops of aspen and birch were still not yet covered in a full canopy of leaves.

In the cleft of one of the lichen blotched cliffs, while floated quietly eating lunch, "great discovery" occurred.

"What's that down there?" Jerry asked. "Just below the water."

I looked and saw long yellow streaks running through a narrow vertical vein of white quartz.

"GOLD!" we both yelled at once.

Whether it was or wasn't we really didn't want to know. If it was, we'd never be able to find the place again anyway and if it weren't, we'd have nothing to fuel our imaginations around the campfire that evening.

Michipicoten River was a three-hour stop for us. We were sweating profusely from the temperature change after a two and a half mile uninspiring trek inland to a small ramshackle cafe on the highway. Once we called the O.P.P. in Wawa to verify a checkpoint, we walked back in a different frame of mind. We looked for moose along the backwaters and edges of the river and stopped briefly at a well-kept cemetery marked with dozens of plain, white crosses.

Twelve miles west of Michipicoten River, Jerry and I were well within the rugged, roadless "bulge." Consequently, it was quite a shock for us to see three canoes and six men coming from where we were going. The six-man group had been out for eleven days and had come down the Pic River. In passing, one of the men left us with something to think about over the campfire: "The western part of this roadless area has been designated a national wilderness park and the first thing they're gonna do is put a road into it."

It was all so strange to us. Lake Superior Provincial Park, where we had come from this morning, was doing just the opposite. They were in the process of reclaiming wilderness by tearing up many of the existing roads.

Whatever was going to happen, at least for the next three days we'd be in the largest roadless area of the entire journey. The night we slept on the sandy beach at Dog Harbour, we were thirty miles straight south of Obatanga Provincial Park. From a trip I made twelve years previously, I remembered the park vividly. The Trans-Canada highway had recently opened and I was a fourteen-year-old on a family vacation.

"You may be walking in areas in the park where humans have never stepped," the ranger told us. "Treat this place with reverence and respect."

I'll never forget those words.

The only discernible sound at four-thirty in the morning was the modulating roar of Dennison Falls less than a mile east of our camp. There, hidden by thick stands of spruce, balsam and green walls of alder, poplar and birch, the University River plunged headlong into the lake. By five, the sound of the falls was joined by the hiss of our gas stove. And by five-thirty, the beach was silent again. It was another cold dawn—forty-two degrees—before the sun cleared the hills. There was no wind, only the noticeable difference between locally circulating cold and warm air as it wafted over us. The calm morning gave us a few surprises. Several hundred yards of sheet ice an eighth inch thick greeted us after we were underway.

Five miles further, we cautiously ran a four mile line of continual cliffs, one-hundred and fifty, three-hundred, five-hundred and eight-hundred feet high! Shortly afterward, we startled ourselves and a young moose occupying a shallow backwater.

At Floating Heart Bay, we happened upon a scattered group of twelve loons communicating in all varieties of wales, hoots and yodels. Seven miles later, near Red Sucker Harbour, we stopped at a fish camp for lunch.

Unlike the cabins on Georgian Bay, this one was not locked and silently spoke of the camaraderie found in remote areas. "Make yourself at home; just close the door when you leave," is what it said to us and we liked it.

Again, our camp was in a deep cove ringed with a sloping, hard packed sand beach. I wrote without candle or campfire light until ten-thirty.

"The place we are tonight has no name on our charts, so we call it, at least for this evening, 'Forb Harbor' in honor of a small rock cairn we built on the east side—and the Far Out Rough Bastards that built it. Maybe, someday someone will find the note we left here in a well sealed film container explaining our trip."

The campfire had a southeast view of the lake, which was partially plugged, by a small island. Nevertheless, we could easily see the east half of Michipicoten Island, a little over ten miles away. For us, the sixteen by six mile island held an aura of mystery that had been certainly felt by many others passing this way.

The following day, mysteries generated on another island wandered through our thoughts while we talked.

"We were about the last people to have radio contact with the Fitzgerald," El, the lighthouse keeper at Otter Island, told us. "That storm was fierce. It also claimed the life of a pilot who tried to swim to shore and two fishermen whose trawler ran into rocks this side of Ganley Harbour."

The keeper, along with his wife and small son, were on Otter Island from April to December.

"Used to be we came here by boat, now a helicopter brings us. A food barge comes three times during the season. Nice and peaceful here, except when it blows."

The family had living quarters and a vegetable garden. We did see a television, but there were also many books. We learned the light had two back up generators and the diaphone automatically sounded when fog was detected a quarter mile away.

During tea, El showed us pictures that, at first glance, appeared to be young moose.

"These are some of the woodland caribou that come down here on the ice later in the season—where your boats are tied up. They're pretty rare now; but we still have 'em around. They're also supposed to be on some of the islands, inludin' the Slates near Terrace Bay."

Jerry and I looked at each other. We were both thinking the same thing. The rounded "moose" tracks along the beach at Dog Harbour and the "young moose" we saw maybe weren't what we thought they were.

A mile and a half northeast from Otter Island was the mouth of the Cascade River and it was suggested we go there before continuing our northwest journey along the "Bump." Following the sound to the source, we suddenly saw a huge waterfall pouring over ancient lava rock directly into the lake. Three miles later, we pulled into yet another quiet, sand beach at a place called Triangle Harbour. The variation of beauty over such short distance was wonderful. The shore was smooth except for the clear imprints of a cow and moose calf walking side by side. Jerry followed the tracks partway down the shore and stopped.

"Randy, come look at this," he said. A pair of wolf tracks joined the two where Jerry was standing.

We cooked whitefish given us by Nap, El's assistant and watched the sunset while listening to a special broadcast on Jerry's radio.

The director of natural resources was speaking about the tremendous fires burning all through Ontario. The government was considering using the broad sweeping powers of the Forest Fires Prevention Act to shut down all activities in the bush. Under normal conditions, a red sun slowly sinking in a hazy sky was a delight for us, but now the haze was a constant reminder of smoke and the problems we may encounter.

"Well, if they do stop activities out here, I hope it's not along the lake," Jerry said. "Otherwise, we might have another delay besides the winter one."

We paddled thirty-six miles on a north-northwest course to Pic River. Light zephyrs and a few ripples on the lake made the day into a long meditation. The shoreline was relatively straight, with only a few small points. Simons Harbour, Oiseau Bay, Player Harbour and nameless coves beckoned to us, but we kept on moving. The mouths of the White Gravel, Willow and White Rivers came and went as we wisely used the lake's tranquil mood to our advantage. Normally, we were told, a person could expect to be wind bound every third day on the lake, with moderate paddling conditions in between. In one day we covered a distance, which, as a general rule, should have taken four.

At the end of a twelve-hour paddling day, Jerry and I were enjoying the long twilight on the sandy shores of the Pic River. Both of us sat on partially buried driftwood logs digesting a huge meal of macaroni and cheese. Individual thoughts drifted through our minds like so many bubbles. Some we'd let drift by, others we'd capture and talk about. Now and then, I'd record a few:

"People ask us if we do any fishing en route. Usually, we're just too tired—like now—to do fishing. Our days are filled with paddling, setting up camp, cooking, keeping our journals up to date and figuring out our route."

"We heard on a Michigan station some town in Oregon reported a national low of thirty-six degrees—we had the same reading on our thermometer this morning!"

"A few days ago, while we swatted black flies on a Michipicoten River gravel bar, Jerry's radio picked up a program on 'How to Protect Yourself from the Blackfly'. The interview was hypothetical, inaccurate and really didn't speak from experience. However, the person was considered 'an expert' because he had a Ph.D. in bugs. I wonder how often we are influenced and lead astray by the 'experts'?"

Jerry and I shared the beach with an Indian family camped a couple hundred yards upstream. "Mom and Dad" strolled by our camp after dark.

"From a distance, I thought the two of you were the 'spirit lady' of the Pic River," I said.

"No," the man softly replied. "We're just out for a walk; gonna make love on the beach."

Before falling asleep, I heard the faint rumble of a train on the CP line four miles away. "We're out of the roadless area and past the Bump," I said to myself with a sigh of relief and a degree of sadness. The next third of Lake Superior, a two-hundred and fifteen mile trek to Thunder Bay, past a series of large islands peninsulas and bays would begin early the next morning. Our kayaks were packed and ready, when we walked over to our neighbors' tent to share in a meal of bannock. The breakfast invitation, however, would have to wait for another time. The family was asleep and we had thirty miles to go before we would do the same.

The paper mill town of Marathon was on our list for a mail stop, O.P.P. checkpoint, food supplies and a toque for Jerry's head. However, getting to the community was more difficult than expected. We roared around the high knobs of Peninsula Point, only to discover the town's harbor completely clogged with a gigantic raft of pulpwood logs held in place by a huge boom chain. Extremely frustrated, Jerry and I backtracked four miles before we found a semi-suitable landing place on a boulder field beach.

"Look at all these rocks," Jerry said. "They're all different sizes but all the same shape."

We were literally stumbling over the most interesting beach we had seen on Lake Superior. There were rock baseballs, softballs, cannonballs and bowling balls made from a vast assortment of multi-colored glacial drift, including granite, gneiss, basalt, diabase and gabbro.

In town, the temperature increased dramatically and talk of forest fires was everywhere.

"Even broken glass has been startin' them," I overheard one person say.

A short while later I heard the authorities were ticketing vehicles left idling alongside any roadway—the fear of fire from hot exhaust systems was great. Even when Nick who worked second shift at the Mill invited us in for a beer, the topic was the fire danger.

"It's been clear hear since May seventeenth and we ain't seen no rain. Some areas haven't had rain since Good Friday and they're predicting at least three more weeks of hot, dry weather,"

Continuing the trek, we logged eighteen more miles before setting our paddles down at 8:00 p.m. in Neys Provincial Park. We made the mistake of landing at the campground and were greeted by a swarm of shouting youngsters playing army at the former World War II prisoner of war camp. Sizing up the situation, we retreated to the picnic ground beach, nestled between smooth granite bedrock and proceeded with our itinerary.

The rangers at the park weren't expecting us, but we were expecting them. Last October, during our bus ride home, I had talked with an Ontario Regional Parks Planner at Sault Sainte Marie. Later, he sent me a letter indicating Jerry and I were invited to stay at Provincial Park staff housing along our route. In return, we'd share impressions of our journey to park staff members and the general public. As in most bureaucratic organizations, the ranger I showed the letter to didn't have the slightest idea what was going on, but nevertheless gave us a room for the night.

We shared our cognac and learned along with the Neys Park staff. What intrigued us the most was evidence of four thousand years of human activity in the area.

"Neys covers the entire Coldwell Peninsula," Chris said. "It protects the 'Pukaskwa Pits' archaeological site. "They're found on some of the lake's old cobble beach terraces and their function is still unknown. You passed by some of them coming in here. They might have been used as fish traps when the lake was much higher."

Prior to departing in the morning, I called home from a hand-cranked telephone at the park's main entrance a mile away. The walk reinforced again the microclimates of lakeshore and forest—foggy and cool near the shore, warm and sunny at the gate.

Chapter 36

Rail, Water and
Old Steamship Routes

*"We live in a wonderful world that is full of beauty,
charm and adventure. There is no end to the adventures
we can have if only we seek them with our eyes open."*

Jawaharal Nehru

For two and a half days the Canadian Pacific Railroad and the Trans-Canada Highway would be reasonably close to us. For two and a half days a triad of transportation routes spanning three centuries and uniting Canada would run practically side-by-side. Unstuck in time, Jerry and I could have been Northwest Company voyageurs at a sheltered camp in Victoria Bay in 1785; Canadian Pacific gandy dancers driving spikes at the ghost town of Jackfish in 1885; or truck drivers on the newly completed Trans-Canada Highway at Terrace Bay in 1962.

Eight hundred and fifty foot Mount Gwynne marked the entrance to Schreiber Channel. The water was remarkably calm, giving Jerry the chance to pose for pictures at its rugged base. For the first time, we'd have a comparative size record to remember some of the massive rock outcrops we were passing.

Where eleven-mile long Schreiber Channel met Nipigon Bay was a cluster of islands and the fishing village of Rossport. For commercial fisherman, it was the most protected deep-water facility on the northern part of the lake. To us, Rossport was the most picturesque community we saw on Lake Superior.

Our focus of attention was the Rossport Inn, where we were drawn for breakfast after "thinking" through six miles of early morning fog. It was built in 1884 by railroad laborers and now was run by three young people—John, Roger and Mary.

John cooked a lumberjack-style breakfast for us. He was a kind, considerate, interesting individual, who had black hair with matching beard and wire-rimmed glasses. Amidst the unique surroundings, we covered a wide variety of topics ranging from the pitfalls of television and the advertising industry, to the benefits of traveling and exercise.

"The dining room, pub room and sleeping accommodations of the Rossport Inn have real class. The dining room's windows give one a full view of the natural harbor and the Canadian Pacific track is only a few feet from the front door. A navigation map of Lake Superior hangs in the lobby in back of an old sofa. Beside it was an old clock with 'made in Canada' stamped across its face—not working of course. Nearby, a calendar reads May 20th, 1976—nineteen days behind. A black cat walks around its scratching post near the upstairs steps. Old pictures hang on the walls: a yacht wrecked on the shoals, a train derailment, 1956 ads. Odds and ends are in the pub room: fishing contest winners from the fifties; an old cribbage trophy; and a set of caribou antlers. A jukebox sits in the corner, wearing a yellowed, handwritten 'Temporarily Out of Order' sign. Out the back windows of the pub, one sees John's raised bed gardens containing black earth from a nearby lakebed." rrb

To us, the Rossport Inn was as comfortable and familiar as an old pair of shoes. It didn't need any glitter or polish. It was what it was and we liked it that way.

Just before we left, John asked us a favor: "When you guys leave, do you think I could paddle with you in my canoe just for a quarter mile or so?"

We obliged, but didn't realize our departure would be sidetracked nearly an hour.

At the government dock, we met a group of individuals eager to do their job. It seemed they spent a lot of time just riding around in their rubber boat. Now, they had something to do. The Coast Guard Auxiliary decided they would keep track of us from Rossport to the City of Thunder Bay—whether we liked it or not!

They also did something very beneficial for us by marking the location of fish camps and campsites on our charts. Again, we were entering a remote area of large islands and peninsulas—Salter, Simpson and St. Ignace Islands created Nipigon Bay's thirty-mile south shore. Part of forty-mile, coma-shaped Black Bay Peninsula formed its west side. Club shaped Black Bay with its seven-mile wide neck lie on the other side of the Peninsula and, twenty mile long, Sibley Peninsula created its southwest shore. From Sibley's Thunder Cape, thirteen miles of open water marked the boundary between the Lake and Thunder Bay. We appreciated all the help we could get and decided to take the lakeside after considering Nipigon Bay's limited shelter and steep shore.

While we poured over charts, Jerry saw John furiously paddling his canoe on the far side of the harbor. We hailed him before he disappeared behind a point, but he didn't hear us and continued to chase our non-existent tracks.

"Maybe we can still catch him before we leave," Jerry said.

We walked back up the hill and around the harbor to where our kayaks were docked. En route, we stopped at an old wooden white house that used to be a general store. Inside, seventy-five year old Ann Todesco interviewed us for the local paper. She was a retired school teacher and had lived in Rossport for years.

"The picture of the yacht you saw in the Inn was the 'Gunilda'," she said. "It was a millionaire's boat. It got stuck on the shoals here in 1911 and sank in two hundred feet of water while they were trying to pull here off!"

The story was different, but we had heard the same theme over and over again: Whether it be circumstance beyond ones control, carelessness, or just plain ignorance, the lake's power was something to be constantly aware of and respected.

Rossport, at nearly forty-nine degrees latitude, was the farthest north we'd go on our journey. By noon our kayaks were headed south through Wilson Channel and rounded the Lakeside of Salter Island by cutting through a sheltered passage created by Minnie and Harry Islands. We paddled a diagonal three-mile course down Simpson Channel and rounded Morn Point, to bring us to the open lake.

"I still feel bad about John," I told Jerry.

"He was trying to catch up to us, but we hadn't even left yet," Jerry answered. "Well, like so many others, he'll be with us in spirit!"

The weather changed. For the time being, our glory days of thirty and thirty-five miles were out of the question. During the next five days, we covered a grand total of twenty-one miles.

"Seven miles covered today in dense fog," I wrote. "We are at Pope Point. Stopped for a while in the lee of an island to let the fog blanket clear enough for us to travel. Got a bearing on Pope Point before the fog settled back in. Small rollers wash our gravel beachhead. A few minutes ago, the kayaks, only a few yards from where I sit at the fire, were shrouded in mist. The tent is tucked away in the black spruce and birch forest and sits on a soft bed of sphagnum moss. It is hard to describe the feeling of complete independence here. I love this land!"

An hour into an expected full day of paddling, dense fog made us backtracks to a sheltered harbor. Since the Coast Guard Auxiliary had so far mismarked all of the refuge areas and fish camps, we were delighted to find the harbor we were in had yet another tiny harbor with a gravel beach and small cabin.

The place met all of our fantasies as to what a fisherman's or trapper's cabin in the north woods "should" be like. Walls of spruce and balsam of varying sizes, beyond which lie misty green hills with bare rock outcroppings, consecutively ringed our "paradise". The reflecting pool of the inner harbor pulled the surrounding beauty a little closer. It also reflected the fog-soaked white blossoms of a shoreline Juneberry and the face of the bearded man who stopped to smell them.

I closed my eyes and, with a deep breath, drank in as much of the clean air as I could. Everything smelled like fresh strawberries and amazingly there were no blackflies to speak of.

The twenty by ten foot cabin was sheeted with weathered boards and a well maintained rolled shingle roof. A heavy logging chain hung on the outside wall. Inside, the cabin had a barrel stove, four bunks and a solid table where we sat and ate an early lunch.

Jerry left for a moment and then I heard him yell: "The kayaks!"

They were floating in the middle of the bay and slowly moving away.

"I'm goin' in after them, Jerry!"

I stripped to my wet suit, grabbed a life jacket and waded in. Fortunately, when we moored, I tied my kayak's towline onto Jerry's craft. So, when I reached his boat, I could tow both rigs. It was only fifty feet to shore, but halfway back I could feel the effects of the cold water. The body glove suit didn't seem to have much of an effect and I could hardly feel Jerry's hands as he helped me from the water.

Wrapped in a sleeping bag, I drank hot cups of tea and finally stopped my uncontrollable shivering.

"Well, I guess if your ship doesn't come in, ya gotta swim out after it," I bellowed.

"How in the hell did the kayaks get out there?" he asked.

After pondering the question for several minutes, we looked at the pool and noticed the water level was higher than when we came in.

"This place has a tide," I said.

The hydraulic effect of the lake and the small harbor created a four to five inch seiche every fifteen minutes or so. Our kayaks had merely floated away during the high water mark. We had heard about Superior's seiche brought on by strong winds or major differences in air pressure and now we had experienced it in miniature.

While trying to leave the harbor, we ran into the cause of the harbor's mad fluctuations—strong northwest winds. One navigation problem had been merely replaced by another. We turned around and headed back to the cabin.

During the night, annoying wind gusts played with the cabin door, until Jerry got out of the bottom bunk and latched it with a bent nail. Four separate thunderstorms, fierce with lightning but low on precipitation, roared through and made us wonder how many new forest fires had started in the interior.

The persistent wind shifted to the northeast, allowing us to depart at three o'clock. We crossed Blind Channel, skirted Flour Island and put up in a deep cove on Black Bay Peninsula. The ten miles we covered would be all we'd progress over the next several days, giving us plenty of time to eat, read and write.

"We're at the site of an old fish camp not far from Spar Island and the Lamb Island lighthouse. The tent is pitched in a grassy area directly in back of us. We sit at the water's edge on weathered benches next to an old table. The cabin is tumbled down and its former yard is full of European weeds—dandelions. A path leads from it to a trout stream. Such a long twilight compared to the Everglades. The spirit of the north is what lives here. It can never be captured and 'bottled' but it can easily be destroyed." rrb

"Our layover days have at least given us time to read the paperbacks we bought at the Soo. In between chapters, we take breaks for tea and look at the ten-foot waves crashing into the cliffs a mile away. We know the distance because it takes five seconds for the thunder to reach our ears!" rrb

"Strong winds, thunderstorms and fog have given us time to experiment with new recipes and foods. Since we've been here we've tried: bacon and fried mush, pancakes, rice pudding, tuna rice dish, corn bread made with whole wheat flour and dandelion greens salad with vinegar dressing. We are waiting for trout—Jerry hasn't caught any yet. Some of the food we'll try again, others we wish we could try and some we'll scratch off the list." rrb

For three nights and two days, we shared the dilapidated camp outhouse with porcupines—the first ones we had seen since North Channel. They apparently found the plywood seat quite tasty and continued to enlarge it all the time we were there. After our first surprise encounter, we made sure the throne was unoccupied and the size we wanted before sitting down.

"The Coast Guard's been lookin' for ya," Ron, a commercial fisherman, said. "They say you're lost."

"Well, tell them we're found," Jerry said sarcastically.

I showed him what they outlined for us on the map. Ron just shook his head and laughed.

"They gave ya the old steamship route, eh?"

We told him about the cabin we stayed at in the small bay.

"That's a real nice spot—the Squaw Bay cabin," he said. "We fixed the roof on it last year. If you guys want, why don't you stop at our camp on Magnet Island? It's about thirteen miles from here; right on the tip of the Peninsula, eh."

"That'd be fine," I said. "If the weather goes out on us again. My buddy's gotta be at his sister's wedding in five days and we figured we'd get to the fish camp on the mainland at Squaw Bay."

"Oh, the Ronquist's place," Ron replied. "That's a little over twenty miles from here. They're nice folks. They'd let you put up there."

We also asked Ron about the two round hills we could see seven miles to the southwest.

"Oh the Paps! That's supposed to be the Sleeping Giant's girl friend, eh!"

His reply perplexed us.

"The 'Sleeping Giant'?" Jerry asked.

"It's a thousand-foot rock sill on the end of Sibley Peninsula. Don't worry, you guys won't miss it. Ya gotta go right around it."

Before he left our small island camp in his open boat, Ron gave us a four-pound speckled trout.

"Here," he said. "You fellas look hungry."

We reached Ron's camp the next day just as heavy fog set in and were pleased to see chimney smoke coming from one of the shacks. Inside, we met Arvil and his buddy who was polishing an eight-inch trout spoon when we arrived. Arvil had blue eyes and a round, red face, weather beaten but not leathery and his buddy looked like Captain Bob down at Horseshoe Beach, Florida. Both wore wooden shoes with leather straps and both had hands that spoke of years of net handling.

We drank coffee with the two fishermen and communicated as best we could through a thick Finnish accent. We learned they had just returned from setting twelve by three hundred foot nets in one hundred feet of water. The shoals they worked were sixteen miles out in the lake and their open boat had ridden eight to ten foot waves on the way back.

The camp, patrolled by geese, had a well-kept garden and sauna. The log structure, with door handles made from sapling crotches, was definitely from the "old country." Arvil fired it up and we poured water on the rocks once the temperature reached one hundred and fifty.

Arvil laughed when he saw us rinse off with buckets of ice-cold lake water. After a second load of wood, a twenty-minute wait and the temperature now over the boiling point, it was his turn to go in. Some time later, we saw a pink flash exit the sauna followed by a tremendous splash and water plume.

"Dat's how ya take yer sauna," he said.

Ron was back on the island in the morning. We talked with him while he attempted to hook up an ice machine to a power generator.

"It used to be we'd just cut the ice from the lake during the winter, but there hasn't been ice out here for two years and it's hard to get people, like Arvil, to cut ice anymore."

Once hooked up, Ron's machine would produce six hundred and fifty pounds of cubed ice from lake water per day. But there was another hassle: "The government says the lake water isn't good enough for iced fish, so we got to mix a special chemical with it. Every year there's more and more restrictions and red tape put on us commercial fishermen."

Our conversation also included stories of the lake and its environs. Ron talked about the white haired hermit on a nearby island, who was found in his chair with a death grin on his face and a can of Sterno in his hand. He also mentioned," Ramona" paddling her ghostly canoe through the bay on moonlit nights and reports of giant sea serpents near Lamb Island. Once again, the ferocity of Lake Superior resurfaced when Ron told of mariners ducking popping rivets as they walked the cargo hold gangways of iron boats during heavy seas.

Chapter 37

Real Lake Fishing and Naniboujou

"When we show our respect for other living things, they respond with respect for us."

Arapaho Proverb

"There it is! The Giant!" Jerry shouted. "I can see the head and the chest!"

It was in the distance off to our port beam, a series of blue ridges fifteen miles away. Little did I know I'd soon be climbing the eleven hundred feet to The Giant's chest while Jerry recovered from a wedding celebration.

Once we convinced the O.P.P. and the Coast Guard Auxiliary to drop their concern over our welfare—which was being aired over Thunder Bay radio and television stations—we made arrangements for the business at hand. It was Alf and Edna's shopping day in Thunder Bay the next morning and we were invited to ride along. Jerry would stay overnight at a motel and take a bus to Minneapolis the next morning. In the meantime, I'd ride the fifty miles back to Squaw Bay with the Ronquists and sleep in their net shed until Jerry returned.

I learned Alf piloted supply boats and rafted logs for the lumber camps in his younger years. The rafts of sawlogs covered hundreds of acres. Boom logs held them together five feet in diameter and four deep, which in turn were fastened together with one and a quarter inch steel chain.

"The booms were so wide, you could have easily driven a car around it," he said.

The rafts were towed to Ashland, Wisconsin, on a five-day trip with a top speed of two miles per hour.

"We'd usually tow the rafts in July, before bad weather would set in. At night they'd be lit with coal oil lamps with colored glass in them—looked real pretty."

That was thirty years ago. Large-scale logging was now gone from the area along with the woodland caribou. I wondered if the dwindling number of commercial fishermen in the area and the profession Alf had learned from his father would follow the same path; I hoped not.

Back at Squaw Bay, Alf was preparing to go out with his sons to pick herring nets. I watched him eye the water as his mind interpreted clues and transferred them to likely conditions on giant Blackwater Bay. Likewise, I watched him eye me the same way, when I asked to go with him. Nodding his head, he handed me a pair of rubberized, yellow bib overhauls.

The thirty-foot, wooden fishing trawler pitched and rolled as we charged the waves. Alf didn't use too much power. He said if he did the waves would break over the bow. Realistically, I think he was being kind—he grinned a few times as I periodically lost my balance.

The nets were in Black Bay about two miles out and Alf spotted one of the red flag markers after a short search. By then, Brian and his thirteen-year-old brother, Carl, had gotten the winch ready and in short time were hauling in three hundred and fifty feet of net and herring from the forward starboard door. The net's twelve-foot width folded together as it was brought up and made a ninety degree turn off the winch onto a long wooden table. Three hundred pounds of herring slid down the table, between Alf's legs while he guided the boat along the plastic and aluminum float line.

The boat's wheel had several turning pegs missing from years of use. Its dial compass, its gimbals resembling a bowl within a bowl, was sturdily secured to a wooden frame. Alf said the compass was reasonably accurate except in areas marked magnetic disturbance on the charts.

"She'll swing in a hundred and eighty degree arc near Magnet Island and do nearly the same by Silver Islet."

I pointed to an ice scraper lying next to the window.

"Sometimes we go into December or until ice starts forming on the nets," he said. "Some of the best fishing is in the fall."

The net would be set another time and we headed back to the dock. By the time we arrived, Carl and Brian had tossed most of the herring into fish boxes. The boxes in turn were stacked on a dolly and rolled to the shed where the whole family cleaned and iced the fish.

When the processing was over, I headed back to my sleeping quarters.

"I sit amidst a potpourri of fishing gear most of which I have no working knowledge: floats, wooden buckets of lead weights, raincoats, boots, shoes, spools of heavy nylon line and thread. An assortment of nylon and cotton, three inch, hearing nets hang next to, larger sized, whitefish and trout nets The "Empire" coal-wood stove has a pot on it with the remnants of melted lead and a 1955 calendar hangs from the wall. There are glass jars stuffed with net needles and awls, coffee and tobacco cans full of nuts and bolts and assorted cardboard and wooden fish boxes. Kerosene lanterns hang on nails and a grocery store scale sits by the window. Gunnysacks of unknown hardware, one of which is soft enough for a pillow, lie piled to one side." rrb

Amidst the paraphernalia was my sleeping bag, rolled out on the flattest spot in the shed. When I looked up I could see the open ceiling and where the roof rafters tied in with the squared log timbers. The entry way was insulated with yellowed 1936 newspapers talking about Dizzy Dean, the Boer War and twenty-dollar suits.

What I saw outside was just as interesting: Net anchors shaped like grappling hooks, more wooden fish boxes and a net wound around a drying wheel. The south wall of the shed had hundreds of headless nails sticking out of its side in neat rows.

"They were used to hold cedar floats," Alf said. "Dad and I'd put linseed oil on them and they'd dry in the sun there."

I had seen a glob of tar on the end of a stick at Magnet Island, but I didn't see any around the Ronquist's place. Alf said the tar could have been used for sealing, or may have been left over from the old pound net days.

"We'd soak the cotton nets in tar—a very messy job—and then hang them up to dry," he said. "No fish could break them."

Except for half of Squaw Bay, the area north of it and the village of Silver Islet, eighty percent of Sibley Peninsula was Provincial Park.

Its geology was different compared to the preceding part of the lake we had traveled. Sibley and the surrounding area had an abundance of layered siltstones and sandstones. Millions of years before, molten magma squeezed between the layers of sediment creating sills of fine-grained gabbro called "diabase." When centuries of erosion eventually caused a landscape of diabase caprock mesas, the Sleeping Giant or Naniboujou was formed.

Since some of the sedimentary rocks were rich in calcium, the peninsula and surroundings had a greater diversity of plants and animals compared to other areas of the Canadian Shield we had seen.

"What a wonderful place to be in for a few days," I said aloud as I walked the road to park headquarters. On my trek, a dump truck hauling sand to a project in the park stopped and gave me a ride. The driver and I bounced along as he shifted gears every few seconds. Tom's truck was beat up and heavily used, but it was made for its type of work, just like Alf's boat was made for the lake. Both machines were noisy and powerful; they radiated the harshness of the surroundings they were in—the bush and the lake.

During the next week, I'd meet nearly all the park staff and then some. Appropriately, my introduction began with a four-hour walk to the top of Naniboujou, accompanied by the park naturalist.

It was the "weekend" for Dale and he was finishing a three day fast. Nevertheless, he felt a twelve-mile hike would further add to his quest for greater self-discipline.

"Fasting also helps cleanse the poisons from my body," he said. " It allows different types of sugars to reach my brain and, as a result, I can think more clearly. It is surprising how little the body actually needs to function normally."

"For seven-thousand miles of kayaking, Jerry and I had eaten large quantities of food just to function 'normally'," I thought. "Maybe, Brian meant many people—because of relatively sedentary lives—could cut down on quantity and increase the quality of what they ate simply because their metabolism wasn't demanding as much as they were shoveling in."

I continued to wonder about his last statement all the way to the chest of The Giant. But, because of the view, forgot to ask Dale about it once we finished the exhausting climb.

"This is like seeing the lake from an airplane," I yelled.

With the added height of the twenty-five foot observation tower, we were nearly twelve hundred feet above Lake Superior. I wondered if Alf had ever been to the chest of The Giant? And I thought of the ministry man who had given Alf a complete map of Lake Superior.

"Alf poured over that chart for nearly a half hour," he said. "His eyes never lifting from it. Well, that's where that is, he kept repeating."

The lake was Alf's home and, with the map, he was seeing it in a different perspective. Likewise, the effort of eight and a half million paddle strokes and the efforts of a half million more were put into perspective on The Giant as I looked where Jerry and I had been and where we were bound.

I was standing on more than a diabase-capped sill. Naniboujou, traditionally the great trickster-hero of the Ojibwa people in the region, now slept as a great mountain overlooking their home. If I closed my eyes and was quiet, I could almost feel his heartbeat reverberate through the rock.

The hike down the steep slope went quickly and soon we were back at the Sawyer Bay trailhead. Ironically, I would have supper at Silver Islet Village, a place indirectly related to Naniboujou's present disposition.

Dale and I were walking back to staff headquarters when Arne Maki stopped by and asked if I wanted to join him for a naturalist club meeting and potluck. I had met Arne briefly in the morning while he was issuing camping permits and learned two important things about him: He was 100% Finn—born in a log cabin just outside Thunder Bay—and, as Arne put it, "A professional photographer in an amateur status." He and I drove two and a half miles down the Sibley Peninsula road, which ended near an abandoned general store on the shores of Lake Superior.

"This is the old mining town of Silver Islet," Arne said. "The old silver mine is just over there."

He pointed to a chunk of rock barely above the surface of the lake, three-quarters of a mile to the southeast.

"People now use the houses for summer cottages. They don't have hydro down here; neither does the park. It makes it more like a wilderness area."

We drove up a short gravel road past a few cabins and turned in.

"This is the place where the meeting is going to be."

Inside, I was flooded with information about Silver Islet. Tom and his mother, Gertrude, spent the majority of the summer months in one of the few remaining company houses and both were walking encyclopedias about the village's history.

A long, gray vein of silver was discovered accidentally by mining company employees in July 1868, only a few years after treaty negotiations opened the area to prospecting. The event was historically significant for the Indian people living in the area and was one of many

Naniboujou stories. Briefly: Naniboujou created a storm on Lake Superior, drowning greedy silver prospectors and, as punishment, Gitchi Manitou turned him to stone. The story again revealed the clash of values between two very different cultures—the intrinsic value of the land vs. the value of exploiting land for personal gain.

Needless to say, a silver mine resulted from the discovery, as well as a town complete with two churches, company offices, various shops and stores, over one hundred resident homes and a jail. During the mine's fourteen year history, over three million dollars worth of silver was extracted from the thousand foot shaft on an island eighty-five feet in diameter!

In November of 1881, ice on Superior prevented a thousand tons of coal from arriving at the mine. As a result, steam driven pumps were no longer able to keep the shaft from flooding and the mine closed four months later.

"In a way, Naniboujou did win," I said to myself and then proceeded to paint a picture of Jerry and my trip in the minds of the naturalists at the house.

The trip to the top of The Giant re-reminded me of how dry conditions were away from the microclimate of the lake and it bothered me all night. The following afternoon, I happened into the park maintenance office and heard what I didn't want to hear: "Fire over by Squaw Bay!"

I joined a group where nervousness was expressed by glances at the walls and ceiling, finger and foot tapping, tuneless whistling and wondering aloud about what might happen.

"With this wind, Sibley might have to be evacuated." "I don't smell any smoke yet!" "I wonder if we'll get home tonight!" "I might of figured somethin' like this would happen," drifted through the air while we waited.

Finally, the phone rang and we learned the fire was under control. It had started in the dump and was about ten acres in size. A water bomber was on its way to aid the fire fighters.

"Let's drive over there before I take you back to your camp," Brian said. "They're just puttin' out the smudge anyway."

At the scene, four helmeted fire fighters armed with mattocks and water bags had contained a potentially threatening blaze.

"We got 'er in time, eh?" I heard one of them tell Brian. "We were usin' our helmets to fill up our piss bags with ditch water before the tank truck pulled in, eh!"

The water bomber, a yellow, single engine Otter, was the operation's grand finale. It disappeared behind the trees five or six times, scooped up water from Squaw Bay in its pontoons and quickly returned to deluge the remaining hot spots. In spite of continued fire warnings, I slept much better that evening knowing skilled crews were protecting Ontario's resources.

I continued my exploration of the P\peninsula. When Brian went to a softball meeting, I rode along to the Pass Lake store, mailed postcards, bought cookies and, feeling adventurous, walked back to the net shed. During the first hour of the ten-mile hike, I periodically ran to escape clouds of hungry mosquitoes. The tormenters slowly eased in the growing darkness and soon I found myself settled into a pleasant walk thinking about the events of the past week.

I thought about the red fox I had seen one morning trotting down the Ronquist's driveway with a fish in its mouth. Suddenly, in a world of gray and black, the silhouette of a fox silently glided across the road in front of me without a sound.

I remembered the moose I photographed feeding in Joeboy Lake and the wildlife biologist I had talked with who said Sibley was special for big game animals because it was full of salt licks. Then, an electric shock went up my back, as an immense antlered form stopped in the middle of the road, snorted and bolted into a bog.

I turned onto the Bay Road and by now was feeling my way along the gravel surface. I hadn't seen one in the park, but recalled the story of the black bear local residents was trying to catch. The bear, hungry after a long hibernation and dry spring, made a nuisance of itself around a local farm. To "punish" the animal, the resident baited it with meat laced with lye. Now the suffering bear was on the loose and very unpredictable. Concurrent with my thoughts, I noticed a boulder-size mass disappear into matching blackness only to reappear when it swung into the middle of the road. I stopped in my tracks, waiting to see if the shape would wander into the bush. Instead, it started moving toward me! I shouted, as the shadow grew closer. Frantically, I felt around with my feet for something, for anything. I picked up several large size rocks and threw them at the growing "nothingness." I heard the first rock thud on the ground and the second made a watermelon like thump. Immediately, the stillness was shattered with the roar of snapping and cracking brush that ended as quickly as it had started. Whatever it was, I never saw it again and never wanted to.

Brian picked me up a hundred yards from my destination. It was nearly midnight.

"See anything on your hike?" he asked.

"Just a few shadows, Brian," I said. "Just a few shadows."

When Jerry didn't show up Thursday evening, the Ronquist's invited me for supper. Alf brought smoked whitefish and lake trout. Brian broiled fresh speckled trout on the grill and Edna made mashed potatoes, gravy, cole slaw and white fish liver with onions. Carl poured us cold glasses of fresh milk from a neighbor's farm and had the honor of dishing out ice cream for desert.

"We were going to have beer, Brian said. "But I left it in the freezer and it froze!"

Jerry did show up the following afternoon. I spotted his red toque a half block away as I returned from Thunder Bay with Mort, a fisheries biologist. The car was unloaded, everybody shook hands and then Jerry's family departed.

"They took off faster than the moose I saw the other night, Jerry"

"It took us eleven hours to get here from Brainerd," Jerry said. "If Dad was alone, he'd stay, but his buddy forgot his glaucoma medicine so they got to get back."

Maps, rolled in five-inch plastic pipe, were among the food and treasures Jerry brought back with him. My uncle was able to get them from work and they covered the Minnesota shoreline from the Ontario border to Duluth.

"There must be sixty or seventy maps here," I said. "We'll know the name of every rock on the North Shore."

"That ain't nothin'," Jerry replied. "My fishin' pole case is stuffed with maps for the Savanna Portage. They're so detailed we'll know the name of every piece of swamp grass before we're through with it."

It seemed impossible we'd be carrying enough maps to get back into the Mississippi. They'd be the last new maps we'd need for the entire trip and that meant—as impossible as it seemed to us—the end was coming.

Chapter 38

The Eye of the Wolf

"Humanity is a river of light running from extremity to eternity."

Kahlil Gibran

The next morning a map of Squaw Bay and Black Harbour was outlined on the dew covered deck of my kayak by Alf's calloused finger.

"That's how ya go to Tee Harbour," he said. "It'd be a little over eighteen miles from here."

Bad weather didn't keep us from our destination this time. Instead, a young kayaker and a stop at Silver Islet held us back.

Dave had been camped on the small island in Middlebrun Channel for over a month and planned to stay the rest of the summer. He'd paddle his ten foot, red fiberglass kayak to Silver Islet once a week or so and was alone for the rest of the time.

"I spent a summer as an assistant at the Trowbridge Light near Thunder Cape and liked it," he said. "I just need to be near the lake. It has a special attraction for me. Just like it does for a lot of people. The keeper at the Porphyry Point Light has been there over fifty seasons."

A blackened kettle set over a small fireplace of flat rocks, heated tea water for us. Afterwards, Dave decided to join Jerry and me for the three-mile paddle to Silver Islet and disappeared once we got there.

Two of the folks I had met during the potluck witnessed our arrival. Tom Dyke had seen us approaching the dock and greeted us when we arrived. Another summer resident, a bubbling, retired schoolteacher, named Joan, invited us to her place for late afternoon tea.

"There's been a note taped to the curio shop window for two weeks now," she said. "It says something about two kayakers are supposed to get in touch with the coast guard as soon as possible!"

"This is gettin' embarrassing," Jerry said. "Everywhere we go we're known as the lost kayakers."

We were thinking about contacting Arne Maki at the park when he pulled up to Joan's cabin.

"I heard you fellas were down here, he said. "The bush telegraph works pretty fast."

Arne had a polite, shy manner and finally got around to inviting us to his cabin near the Pass Lake store for the evening.

"Hey, this is the place marked 'school' on my map," I said. "I walked right past it a few days ago."

"Used to be. I got it all fixed up inside; but before we stop, I'll treat you guys to dinner in Thunder Bay. How about some Finnish food?"

We drove to the Port Arthur side of the city and stopped at the Hoito. It was originally established in 1918 to care for large numbers of Finnish immigrants moving into the area.

"Thunder Bay is the Finnish capitol of Canada. There's over nine-thousand Finns here," Arne said.

Jerry and I ate huge meals of meat balls, boiled potatoes, cabbage rolls and Kalakeitto (fish soup) and learned from Arne the majority of the citizens of Thunder Bay actually wanted the twin cities of Port Arthur and Fort William to be called "Lakehead."

"A few years ago a referendum for consolidation was called," Arne related. "Three names were on the ballot: Lakehead, The Lakehead and Thunder Bay. The vote was split and Thunder Bay won!"

Before going back to the Pass Lake cabin, Arne showed us a collection of treasures at his house a short drive from the restaurant.

"His living room is decorated with his own work," my journal recorded. "Fox, moose, beaver, mink, skunk, deer, bear and wild flower photographs representing years of work and hundred of hours of patience, radiate a special sensitivity Arne has toward the natural world. The prints of a moose licking salt off a winter road and a sparrow hawk with a mouse in its talons powerfully express the harsh realities of the natural world."

A one-in-million photo of a bull moose in velvet, swimming across Joeboy Lake, made a strong impression on Jerry and me. Arne had captured powerful feelings of relief and escape in the animal's eyes, as the cool water of the lake flowed over its body. There was also a subtler feeling, one of frustration and futility that beckoned for an answer from the viewer. Only upon closer observation could noticing dozens of biting flies holding fast to the moose's nose solve the riddle.

Tee Harbour was so easy to get to the next day it almost scared us. The water on Lake Superior was glass smooth and it carried Tom Dyke's voice like a conduit. He was a mere dot when I clearly heard him yell, "Godspeed, Randy and Jerry!" Later, we'd receive a letter from Tom expressing his concern for us that day:

"As mother and I watched you paddle to the rock called the Sea Lion and then toward the open horizon of the lake, you two looked like you were sitting on two by fours. You may rest assured, you will never see Lake Superior as calm as it was during the summer you paddled through here."

Threatening weather and heavy seas in the morning gave us two nights at Tee Harbour—a wonderful place to be windbound. We took photographs of the surf breaking against the rocky outside beach and walked the sandy inside one searching for sub-arctic plants normally found much farther north.

During our wanderings, the rear end of a moose greeted Jerry and me on the trail across the neck of the two harbors. We patiently waited until it allowed us to pass and, in a short while, we found ourselves on a flat, open area of lichen covered rock.

From our vantage point we could clearly see forty mile long, Isle Royale less than seventeen miles to the south. By now we had learned the island had a large moose and wolf population. So, I wondered how relatives of the animal we had just seen got over there in the first place. Since Tee Harbour was one of the closest "spring-boards" from the mainland to the island, perhaps the animals came from where we stood. In my minds eye, I could see moose swimming to the Island driven by the scent of fresh browse and spring hunger. Likewise, in my imagination, I could see timber wolves, driven by similar needs, crossing to the island over an ice bridge.

"Some people call Isle Royale the 'eye of the wolf'," I commented.

After a short pause, Jerry remarked: "And we'll be at the nose in a couple of weeks."

The evening was windless and the light from a million stars made it easy to walk around our camp area. Silhouetted against pinpricks of light, we could make out the black palisades of The Giant. Every few seconds the rotating beacon of the Trowbridge Lighthouse, three miles away, dimly washed across the cliff faces. The effect was quite eerie.

"It looks like Naniboujou is breathing," I told Jerry.

The eeriness of the evening stayed with us as we cleared Thunder Cape in the patchy fog. The Trowbridge Light was off, but in the distance we could now hear its diaphone.

"The sound of that horn would be good for a movie about Bigfoot," Jerry remarked.

As we paddled, I remembered some of the things people said about Thunder Cape: "Thunder Bay gets its name from the huge waves pounding against the cliffs at Thunder Cape." "The high cliffs around the cape create waterspouts during bad weather that can sink small boats."

Suddenly, Jerry raised his arm and pointed.

"Do you see that, what the hell is that?" he asked.

We were both looking at what appeared to be a tall watery column to the lakeside of Pie Island. It shimmered and changed shape from a column to something resembling the bow of a great battleship, to a massive square and finally disappeared into a watery haze. The lake was playing tricks on us again, just like it did on its east side and just like it did coming into camp before Terrace Bay where, I was positive, the oddly shaped tree line was the outline of a massive paper mill.

We knew, even with good weather, it would take us four hours to cross the open water of Thunder Bay. Consequently, after rounding the cape, we headed deep into the bay. We ran five miles of rugged shoreline along the west side of The Giant, had lunch in Sawyer Bay and continued for twelve miles to Keshkabuon Island. From there we'd make a short two and a half mile hop to the east side of the bay and follow it to the city of Thunder Bay's Harbor.

Keshkabuon Island represented a phase change in our journey. The days after our island camp would be marked with the meeting of more and more people, as we slowly drew closer to roads and towns. It was one of the last times we'd be able to write how our journey through wilderness had affected us:

"We have a panoramic view of the Sibley Cliffs, Naniboujou, the Islands and Lake Superior touching the horizon line. In the distance, I can barely make out The Giant grain elevators, antennas and smokestacks of the city of Thunder Bay and I really don't want it to get any closer. Jerry reads *One Flew over the Cuckoo's Nest* and I am reading *The Great Fur Land* while we sit on the beach. The timeliness for both books in our lives is quite appropriate. During our time of travel, our clothes have become faded and worn, our hands cracked, tanned and calloused; our faces taut and brown; our muscles lean and powerful. We are products of this environment. We radiate its spirit. What we have experienced is a Georgian Bay—Superior reincarnation. Just as we were reincarnated on the Mississippi and the ocean."

Chapter 39

Brush with Society

"Travel is more than the seeing of sights; it is a change that goes on, deep and permanent, in the ideas of living."

Miriam Beard

Randy Bauer

The writing reflected both Jerry and my strong identity with the wilderness and the journey in general. The city we could see in the distance and the society it represented posed a threat to an environment and life style we loved and embraced.

"We have been insulted and cruelly thrown back into a world of pollution. Yesterday we paddled in water we could drink—now if we did, we'd be poisoned." rrb

Our thirty-mile journey put us into a city of one hundred and eleven thousand. We didn't like it, but had to pass through Canada's third largest ocean port in order to reach Old Fort William eleven miles up the Kaministikwia River. We paddled by wood facilities, grain elevators, a huge ore dock, ocean ships and great lakes freighters before turning up a slow moving waterway.

The river continued to shrink and we finally stopped at a bridge much too low for the Fort's "welcome" boat to go under.

"How much farther to the fort?" I asked the clerk at a nearby root beer stand.

"What fort?" he replied, with a puzzled look on his face.

"Old Fort William—the living history fort," Jerry said.

"Oh, that's way out in Neebing about ten miles from here" and he started to rattle off road directions.

"No, no, how far by water?" I interrupted.

The clerk got even a more puzzled look on his face and just shrugged his shoulders.

"Let's go, Randy. He thinks we're nuts, Jerry said.

The correct route lies a mile farther down the harbor and we found it without incident. As we started up the brown waters of the Kaministikwia, it never occurred to us the railway yard on our starboard side was where Fort William stood from 18O3 to1821. Where we were going was a reconstruction, not on the original site, but so authentic that a person waking up to its parade grounds would be hard pressed to think otherwise.

The air and river were tainted with the smell and outfall from a paper mill we descriptively nicknamed the Great Lakes Pollution Company. We made sure we were well upstream from it before camping on a hard-to-find fern and nettle flat spot, sandwiched between the river and a thirty-foot mud bank lined with houses.

Shortly after first light, we were on our way to a fort we had never seen. Our attitudes reflected the fresh morning air as we came around a bend and spotted the picket walls with building roofs poking up from behind. Like any voyageur, we paddled directly to the wharf in front of the main gate, expecting to be greeted with nothing short of a twenty one-gun salute. Instead, we received a somewhat less cordial welcome:

"Ya can't dock here! This area is only for the reenactments," the watchman said. "And besides, we don't open till ten."

He directed us to the welcome boat landing two hundred yards downstream. Then after several hours, we bought our tickets and entered the fort via the parking lot path—the way everyone else did.

In retrospect, the wait was a golden bonus for us. We talked with another early arrival who, after the fort opened, stayed behind and talked with us while his wife and friends went into the grounds. Before he left, Larry gave us five dollars and said with a smile: "Well, I hope the this place is as interesting as you two guys."

As Larry was going his own way, Arne Maki walked into the gift shop with Bob Soper, a fellow photographer.

"I see you made it to the Canada Day celebration," he said. "But the big one will be your Bi-centennial they're going to celebrate here on the fourth."

There would be a large group of scouts from the states arriving by Montreal canoes the evening of the third. Likewise, a group of Canadian scouts would paddle north canoes down the Kaministikwia for a Rendezvous reenactment.

Arne also mentioned the Bi-centennial celebration would include speeches by many well-known historians and wilderness advocates, including Sigurd Olson from Minnesota.

Our tour of Fort William would be a warm up for what was to come, if we decided to stay—we did.

That evening we slept at Bob Soper's house in Port Arthur while Arne drove back to his cabin at Pass Lake. My head was swimming with thoughts of the North West Company Fort we had just toured and I wrote down as many impressions as I could:

"The nature trail to the main gate of Fort William is a time machine. Jerry and I suddenly found ourselves in the year 1815 in the midst of Ojibwe men and woman scraping furs, making birch bark baskets and cutting "babish"—rawhide line."

From conversation, we learned Indian people were considered trade partners with the North West Company and dealt with as independent Nations. Indian people supplied beaver pelts, which would be shipped to Europe, sheared and the fur processed into felt hats. In return, the North West Company supplied Indian people with desired trade goods including: iron axes, chisels, files, spears, muskets, kettles, gunpowder, tobacco and blankets.

"The voyageur in the Winterers' or 'Hivernant' Camp said the majority of all voyageurs were either French, Indian, or a combination. He didn't know what Jerry was talking about when he mentioned our kayaks. After all, it is 1815, the year before Lord Selkirk, from the Hudson's Bay Company, took over the fort for nine months." rrb

The occupation was in retaliation to a skirmish near the Red River of the North, where pemmican hunters working for the North West Company killed some of Selkirk's settlers. The Winterer, of course, knew about pemmican because it was his main source of food on the summer journey to and from the fort. He loathed the Montrealers or "Pork Eaters" who spent their winters in relative luxury in the Montreal area and ate meals of dried peas and pork.

"Inside the main gate, there are over thirty buildings including fur warehouses, shops, canoe sheds, sleeping quarters for the "big shots" in the Company and a large meeting hall." rrb

While the backbone of the company were the Indian people who harvested the furs and a thousand voyageurs that converged on the trans-shipment point every year, the North West Company was owned and operated by a group of Scottish partners. Their annual business meetings were held at Fort William in conjunction with the Rendezvous. It was the only time during the year the Wintering Partners and the Partners from Montreal were together as a group and, from all the finery in the Grand Hall, there was no doubt they had a very good time.

In the Canoe Sheds, it was hard for me to imagine any craft with a weaker hull than my kayak. Yet, here they were, canoes with cedar rib frames, birch bark hulls, sewn together with spruce root and sealed with evergreen gum, charcoal and bear fat. Twenty-four-foot north canoes were used on small rivers between Fort William and interior the posts and thirty-six foot Montreal canoes were paddled over a vast majority of the route we had just run. The canoes had to be repaired nightly at camps we had probably slept at. They were vehicles made from the wilderness to be used in the wilderness—a gift from the Indian people who had invented their prototypes years before.

By the time we got back to Fort William, it was the afternoon of July third. In the interim, we were exposed to the haunting beauty and harshness of Lake Superior, as seen through the sensitive camera eyes of Bob and Arne. We also revisited Thunder Bay Harbor by road and photographed Kakabeka Falls.

To us, the gorge and one hundred and twenty eight foot drop, where we could slow the shutter speeds of our cameras for a "melting water" effect, was beautiful. But for the voyageur, traveling the water route of the Kaministikwia, the same scene was formidable and meant several hours of portaging.

"I heard they burned up seven-thousand calories and paddled a stroke a second during a normal sixteen hour day—maybe stopping for a quick smoke once in awhile," Jerry said.

"It makes us look like a couple of mamby pambies," I replied. "Hell, the Montrealers could go from here to Montreal in three weeks, that's over twelve hundred miles and they were considered the weak ones compared to the Winterers."

Our conversation took place while we waited for the Elgin Brigade to break around the downstream bend in the river.

"There they are!" another onlooker yelled.

One, two, three, four, five, six, thirty-six foot Montreal canoes now formed a single line with Bi-centennial flags flying and paddles flashing in the early evening light. As they drew closer, we could see the Avant in the bow and the Gouverner in the stern. Some canoes had twelve paddlers wearing bandannas or knitted toques. Amidst the group, an easily spotted top hat, adorned with feathers, indicated the guide. Company partners sat in the middle of some canoes, while it appeared others were filled with trade goods. The group was paddling in unison, one stroke a second and broke into *"En Roulant Ma Boule"* a hundred yards from the wharf. As the last canoe came in, Jerry and I paddled upstream to an exposed gravel bar to camp. The Rendezvous festivities would begin the next day.

Mr. Lee, supervisor of Old Fort William, found us in the visitor center the next morning.

"There you gentlemen are," he said. "I insist that you do not pay to enter the fort this time and handed us two passes.

Mr. Lee then proceeded to hurriedly write down a few notes on our journey and then scurried off to a million other duties. Meanwhile, we wandered off to visit other parts of the complex not seen on our first visit: the counting house, armoire's shop, kitchen, apothecary, naval yard and farm. The men and women making up the fort's Native and Métis peoples, merchants and engages carrying on their jobs and life's routines in an early eighteen-hundreds wilderness setting was "living history" at its best.

At two-thirty, the tourists who had crushed into the parade grounds to photograph Ojibwa dancers, a bagpipe band and a folk group were stampeding down to the wharf to see the start of the great Bi-centennial Rendezvous. As Canadian scouts coming from upstream met their American counterparts from Elgin, Illinois, Jerry and I decided to take a break from the heat and crowds. In the Fort's "Cantine Salope," we dined on baked beans and bread pudding until a pause in the festivities opened the flood gates once more and a tidal wave of visitors poured in.

We forgot our journey-induced agoraphobia as afternoon speakers left us food for thought. Canadian author and wilderness advocate Eric Morse stressed the people of the United States and Canada's common heritage. He emphasized wilderness as a keystone in the fine qualities found in the citizens of both nations and ended with a warning: "Because of demand and overcrowding, a time is coming when only Lake Superior, the Arctic and the really tough areas will give us wilderness!"

Minnesota author and environmentalist, Sigurd Olson, reinforced what Mr. Morse said. He also emphasized the significance of one hundred and fifty young people arriving at the fort by canoe. The Bi-centennial Rendezvous in itself was a promise for the future because it silently stated the ideals taught by wilderness were not forgotten.

SIGURD F. OLSON
106 WILSON EAST-ELY, MINNESOTA 55731
10/25/76

Dear Randy and Jerry:

What a magnificent achievement that trip of yours, perhaps the only one of its kind ever made or that will be made. Yes I remember meeting you briefly at the Big Rendezvous at Old Fort William on July 4th but did not fully realize at the moment, which was so brief, just exactly what you had done or were doing. If I had known I would have crossed myself in veneration to two of the greatest voyageurs of modern times.

What a story it will make. School children will be fascinated as will adults for this shows what modern young men can do in the old tradition. I am very proud of you both and wish you all the luck in the world in telling your story.

You say "I see the worth of wilderness because I have lived it --- it gave us time to see life objectively and with perspective. My new book "Reflections from the North Country" just out will give you faith and courage. It is my philosophy after some 50 odd years. I am glad my books have inspired you in the past. Perhaps this last will tie it all together. You are so right "Man's spiritual quest is closely liked to wilderness."

Kindest regards.   Sincerely

Quite to our surprise, Jerry and I were introduced as two modern day voyageurs "somewhere in the crowd." We turned our heads from side to side, like everyone else and tried to keep ourselves from laughing as we witnessed a "where are they, I don't see them" version of whisper around the world.

Afterward, when the main program was over, we walked up to the porch of the Grand Hall to meet a silver haired man in a yellow shirt. To Jerry and me, Sigurd Olson was the "bourgeois" of all wilderness travelers and we wanted very much to shake his hand. It was a brief meeting, amidst all the clamor of festivities, but a special one. In a handshake came a common feeling, a common understanding without words of the shared love and respect for wilderness. Here was a spiritually powerful man that dedicated his life to an important cause—it was good just to be close to him.

Early evening closed the grounds to the general public. While the dust settled from the day's events, Jerry and I feasted with fellow voyageurs. We met Charlie La-Berge, master birch-bark canoe builder at the fort; Maurice LeClaire, leader of the Elgin Brigade; Ralph Frese, who built the Brigade's authentic looking fiberglass canoes and Father Chuck, the group's chaplain.

Some Elgin Brigade participants were involved in a major 1973 expedition, retracing the Father Marquette and Louis Joliet expedition of 1673. On a trip lasting months, the group paddled from Lake Michigan into the Mississippi, to the confluence of the Arkansas River and back again. Father Chuck, part of the expedition, had a different point of view of the journey compared to the restaurant owner we met on that now long ago stormy day at Grand Tower, Illinois.

"The expedition ended up being a pageant and we were always preoccupied with deadlines," Father said.

Consequently, the expected spiritual benefit of the journey was much less than he had expected. He told us he had gotten much more out of the present trip, even though the group had paddled a comparatively much shorter period of time covering one-hundred and seventy miles from Two Harbors, Minnesota, to Old Fort William.

We continued to talk and eat until forced to the shelter of our gravel island. Inside the insect-free splendor of our tent, I could not help but think of the voyageurs we had just left, preparing to sleep under mosquito filled canoes.

Chapter 40

Back to Superior

"Twenty years from now you will be more disappointed by the things that you didn't do than by the ones you did do. So throw off the bowlines. Sail away from the safe harbor. Catch the trade winds in your sails. Explore. Dream. Discover."

Mark Twain

We were on our way once more, headed down the Kaministikwia to Lake Superior. Our paddling muscles had hardly warmed up when a group of large canoes broke through the morning mist. We hugged the reeds as the voyageurs, followed by a low flying CBC helicopter, passed by. The group wore blinding haloes as the morning light bent around their images.

"Good luck and God bless you," Father Chuck shouted.

It was the only words we heard from the otherwise silent group as they disappeared around an upstream bend.

The intensity of the Rendezvous lasted two days and forty miles. It was wearing off by the time we approached Pigeon Point. The four-mile peninsula marked the Pigeon River and the International Boundary between the United States and Canada. The water had barely a ripple on it, so we were able to moor our boats and walk to a three-foot tall concrete benchmark covered with orange lichens near the end of the point.

It had been a few months short of two years since our kayaks had been in Minnesota and it was time for a ginger brandy toast. The event was supposed to be a happy occasion, but neither of us felt that way. It wasn't until evening while we were camped on a small point near the Susie Islands in Wauswaugoning Bay that we both shared what was bothering us.

"It's amazing how the lake pushes rocks far up on shore, arranging them in fragile piles that crumble under a footstep," I wrote. "Jerry, in selecting a level place for the tent, moved some old logs and found square nails! I got a fire going and by that time the fog had disappeared, Hat Point was clearly visible and the sky was blue. I bent down to gather more firewood, looked up and saw that the sky was threatening rain and the fog was rolling in again."

The log entry of events on the outside also reflected our feelings on the inside. Just like the fragile rock piles and the square nails, both of us knew that everything changed in time. And just like the weather, our feelings reflected similar changes—sometimes bright and sunny, other times, gloomy and melancholy. The mood around camp that evening reflected the latter and was finally expressed in our dialogue around the campfire.

"Jerry, have you ever thought about what you're going to do once the Trilogy is over?" I said. "It's winding down fast!"

"I've been thinking about it all day, Randy and I don't have the foggiest idea," Jerry replied in a sad tone. "I've been focused on this trip for so long now I really haven't thought of much else."

"What I do know is when it does end, things will be different." I said. "Both of us have changed so much during our time on the water, it would be impossible for us to return to where we left off."

We fantasized about things to come for a half hour until hoards of mosquitoes drove us into the tent. Both of us did know whatever happened after the journey, whether it be good or bad, would be our own decisions.

Pigeon Point also marked our entry into the 45,000-acre Grand Portage Chippewa (Ojibwe) Reservation. Tucked away in a cove on the east side of Hat Point and growing out of rock, was a three-hundred year old red cedar known to local Indian people as Ma-Ni-Do-Gee-Zhi-Gance (Spirit Little Cedar Tree). Indian and non-Indian travelers over the years had stopped at the tree to ask its inhabiting spirit for protection on the water. We were no exception; we gave thanks for the journey completed and asked safe passage on what was yet to come.

We rounded Hat Point and entered Grand Portage Bay, tracing the same path Montreal canoes did in the late seventeen hundreds. In the distance we could see the reconstructed Great Hall, Kitchen and Stockade of the National Monument.

Before Fort William, the British North West Company held their annual Rendezvous at Grand Portage from 1784 to1803. The nine-mile path leading through the gap in the hills and connecting the Pigeon River with Lake Superior was the preferred route to the rich fur lands two thousand miles to the northwest. However, after Benjamin Franklin helped draw the international boundary to the north of Isle Royale and up the interior water route and the young United States starting flexing it political muscle to protect its territorial rights, the British Company was forced to move to the Fort William site.

Like Fort William, Grand Portage was a trans-shipment point with the trail being the pivot and canoes staying on either side. Over the years, hundreds of tons of trade goods went up the seven hundred foot climb to a smaller storage depot at Fort Charlotte, while a similar tonnage of furs came down the portage. The path was beaten deep and wide by thousands of moccasined voyageurs who completed the trip in two and a half hours, carrying an average of two to three bundles weighing ninety pounds each!

What was different about the site, compared to Fort William, was obvious. It was situated in the middle of Grand Portage Village. To the right of the National Monument we could see Holy Rosary Catholic Church, the roof of a log school and a few houses poking out from behind the trees. To the left we could see the marina and the Grand Portage Lodge. The National Monument was truly living history because it was in a living community. Indian people had lived on the shore of the bay and used the ancient Portage, Kitchi Onigaming (The Great Carrying Place), long before the North West Company arrived. We were sure many of the people presently living in the community had ancestral links to the North West Company, either as trading partners or voyageurs.

We paddled past the Monument, parked our rigs at the marina and walked to the recently opened Grand Portage Lodge for breakfast. It turned out to be a hot day, almost ninety degrees away from the lake—a good day for exploring and reminiscing in an area I had visited before.

My thirteen-year-old cousin and I had camped at Grand Portage while I was on furlough from the Army in 1972. We also hiked the Grand Portage Trail, camping at Fort Charlotte and took the passenger ferry to Isle Royale National Park on a backpacking trip. The trail hike wasn't important, but visiting the captain of the sixty-five foot passenger boat was a priority.

We watched as the Wenonah unloaded Isle Royale passengers at the National Monument dock. Some people were day visitors, others, seasoned backpackers and some thought they were seasoned backpackers. One boy in particular came off the boat wearing a pack adorned with a hatchet dangling next to his head. Later I wrote: "The kid was lucky he didn't come out of the bush with the hatchet in his head."

We introduced ourselves to the skipper, Stanley Sivertson and explained what we were doing. He had heard about us through reports on the marine radio and applauded our accomplishment. Stanley, also a commercial fisherman, understood we were waiting out bad weather, just like anyone else would do, when the Canadian Coast Guard reported us overdue and missing.

He was the son of a Norwegian fisherman and made his first run to Isle Royale over sixty years ago when he was six months old! Stanley talked about the invasion of lamprey and smelt into the Great Lakes and told stories about the early days of the National Park when many fishing families were forced out of their homes as part of bizarre government condemnation procedures.

Like many people we met, Stanley and the lake were inseparable. He was a kind person, reflected in his willingness to help individuals or society in general. He remembered my cousin and me from 1972, but he forgot about the dinner he bought us at a nearby restaurant. Commercial fishing was more than a way of life for Stanley; he thought of it as his personal contribution to the food supply of a hungry world.

A quote on the bridge of the Wenonah reflected Captain Sivertson's values: "You can tow a battleship with a silk thread if you start slow enough!"

Stanley talked about shipwrecks in and around the shoal areas of Isle Royale and personally recalled several he had witnessed himself. Ironically, the diver we met at the marina now saw what Stanley had seen on the surface under the surface. John was in the process of repairing a bent shaft on his 1955 Cristcraft dive boat when he invited us to sleep on board for the evening. Like us, he had a strong respect for Lake Superior's ice-cold water and a fascination for its mystery.

"It's fun to dive on the shallow wrecks, but the deeper ones become much more tricky," he said. "We can look, photograph and show other people around, but we can't take anything—they're protected by the Antiquities Act."

The next morning, Stanley hailed us with the Wenonah's air horn as the ship chugged east to Isle Royale's Washington Harbor. Even thought it appeared to be moving at glacial speed, the boat would still cover twice as many miles during its round trip than our twenty-two mile run to the mouth of the Brule River.

On our way, we saw the first sea arch and caves on the journey. The "Hollow Rock" had a large enough opening to slip our kayaks through. And, one of the large sea caves—in spite of the strange "glugging" sounds made by small swells brushing against its interior walls—was a welcome place to escape from the sun for a few minutes.

At the Naniboujou Lodge, directly across the river from our camp, we met people reflecting an attitude toward the journey of life that Jerry and I liked. Mr. Wallace, along with his wife, Susie, moved to the North Shore of Minnesota for reasons expressed in an article I found written about them in their Lodge:

"One day I looked around at the people in Los Angeles and they looked like zombies, robots and I felt like one myself. I realized I never really fully enjoyed a single day I'd lived there. So we got out. We'd just had enough."

Jerry and I understood them and they understood us. They ran a lodge unique and special to the area. We learned the building was originally constructed in 1927-1928 as an exclusive, private hunting lodge, covering 3,300 acres and a mile of Lake Superior shoreline. The high ceilings of the dining room were brilliantly decorated in Cree Indian designs and at one end stood the largest stone fireplace we had ever seen.

We came in for coffee and left stuffed—after the Wallace's told us to order anything off the menu we wanted.

We spent an additional night at the mouth of the Brule, just below the first set of rapids, when morning rain and afternoon offered an opportunity to hike four miles into the interior. A state park trail followed the Brule to a place where the river split around a Basalt Island. There half the water crashed over a seventy foot falls, while the other half disappeared into a huge pothole called the "Devil's Kettle."

Maybe it was the name of the place, or the fact that we couldn't see the familiar horizon line of the lake that made us feel uneasy. Possibly, our subconscious minds saw the Kettle as a kayaker's worst nightmare. Whatever, we both felt a strong feeling of relief hearing the roar of the Kettle fade as we headed down to our camp.

At Grand Marais, we picked up mail, ate home cooked food at Mabel's Diner and tried, without luck, to convince the clerk at a local sport's shop that a journey as long as ours didn't have a "catch" or "gimmick" attached to it.

"Well, what do you expect for a tourist town?" Jerry asked. "They've seen too many people coming through here thinking they're 'Daniel Boone' or 'Jim Adventure'. After all, Grand Marais is the gateway to the Gunflint Trail and the Boundary Water Canoe Area."

Ten miles from Grand Marais both of us continued to ruminate over our non-existent "gimmick" as we landed on a sloping shore east of the Cascade River. It was an ideal, isolated site, decorated with patches of azure and orange colored lichens, light blue harebells and wild roses blooming on the forest edge. The camping area was small, but large enough to explore its miniature points and numerous outcrops while confidently hopping around on the unusual non-skid rocks.

When the moon broke the lake's horizon line and climbed into a sky washed with thin, pastel colored clouds, the scene was almost too good to be true.

In spite of the surroundings, we had our second knife injury of the trip. Jerry was feverishly working on a wooden spoon replacement when he accidentally ran a filet blade over his left thumb. The injury could have been more serious than it was. We bound the inch long slice tightly together with band-aids and spent the rest of the evening wondering if smoldering frustration over the store clerk a few hours before or the full moon had anything to do with the accident.

We accepted Mr. Bruce's offer for a break, which turned into an overnight stay at his jointly, owned retreat near Lutsen.

"This place was originally called the Gitche Gumee Lodge. The main log cabin was built around 1924," He said.

The day was interesting and busy: "The name of the town we are near is called Lutsen—not 'Lutsem' as the title of a youngster's drawing at the art fair indicated.

A brass jazz ensemble played during the annual event. Their music was good except every once in a while the speakers made a disturbance not unlike someone giving a 'watermelon cheer' or the end results of too many beans. The fair exhausted us, partly because we are not used to the heat and partly because of the concentration required talking with so many different people. Nevertheless, it is still a privilege to be invited into such a comfortable place. I wonder if my parents spent part of their honeymoon here twenty-eight years ago?"

Mr. Bruce took pictures while we carefully maneuvered our fully loaded kayaks from their overnight nest, down a lava slope, into a protected pool of crystal clear lake water.

"The rocks under the water have a lot more algae on them than they did a few years ago," he said. "I don't know what it's from, but it's from something and it bothers me."

The Minnesota shoreline revealed its first taconite loading facility at Taconite Harbor. Two lake freighters were loading pellets bound for lower Great Lakes steel mills when we passed. The concentrated ore came from interior mines, which supplied raw material for the United States' industrial might and helped wage two world wars. Two days later, we'd see a small part of the socio-economic impact of iron mining in the community of Silver Bay. Three days later we'd see, first hand, the environmental impact of the nation's vital resource.

"PEDDLERS, CANVASSERS, AGENTS, SOLICITORS, PHOTOGRAPHERS MUST REGISTER WITH THE POLICE DEPARTMENT AND SECURE A LICENSE FROM THE VILLAGE COUNCIL," was written on a piece of paper Jerry pulled from his pocket. He had just finished a fifteen-mile hike down Highway 61 to Silver Bay and back.

"You can sure tell those people in town are upset about the taconite plant," Jerry said. "Everyone burned holes right through me with their stares—that's never happened before. I'm glad to be back!"

"Did anyone give you a lift into town?" I asked.

"No," he said. " That's why I got a big hole worn in one of my moccasins. I think everyone is too angry and paranoid to give a stranger a ride."

The people of Silver Bay were caught in a bad situation. Three thousand of the community's thirty-five hundred residents worked for Reserve Mining's taconite processing plant. The facility had gone into operation in 1955 and, under a permit, granted by the State of Minnesota, was allowed to dump 67,OOO tons of tailings into the lake per day! Residents, environmentalists, the state and the general public went about their business until 1973 when cancer causing asbestos fibers were found in the water supplies of communities, including Duluth, using the lake for drinking water. The ensuing court battle threatened to close the plant and Silver Bay's residents were caught in the middle.

The breakers rearranging the shoreline, along with a grassy bank covered with yellow trefoil, a few purple lupine and white yarrow, made us forget about the Reserve Mining uproar momentarily. We were windbound and coaxed by a second day of biting flies, decided to launch at 3:OO a.m. the next morning—weather permitting.

"The voyageurs did it, so why can't we?" I mumbled to myself while we packed in hazy moonlight.

Jerry noticed a closing ring around the moon when we left the stone beach but didn't pay attention to it.

The storm rolled in from the west. Hidden by the hills, it caught us off guard. A great wind, accompanied by lightning and peals of thunder, attempted to push us far into the lake. We fought the invisible hand with every paddle stroke, beating into the wind with all our strength. The feathered end of the paddle seemed like an airplane wing and was forced up or down with the slightest tilt. The wind sucked the words from my mouth. I could only think what I wanted to yell to Jerry: "I hope it doesn't get any stronger and I hope we're not by the Palisades!"

We were tiring, but so was the heavy hand that held us in place. Suddenly, it lifted and our kayaks tore through the water toward what turned out to be a stone beach just before Palisade Head.

Four hours past while Jerry and I slept in poncho-covered boats pulled far up on shore. By seven-thirty we were on our way again. The wind was gone and the rain came only in occasional bursts. Ancient, lava cliffs plummeted three hundred and fifty feet to the lake on our starboard side.

We were almost in Silver Bay. The dismal morning complemented the upcoming scenery, which in turn made a mockery of the town's name. A large canal about two hundred yards from us fed a river of gray water that poured over a delta of taconite tailings into the lake. The main outfall surged and poured into Lake Superior and surrounded our boats with a gigantic effluent plume of murky water. Both of us were stunned, hurt and outraged at what we saw.

"Why did the state allow them to do this to the lake in the first place?" I thought. "This is awful—disgusting! I can only imagine where the current is dragging all this crap. We encounter warm and cold surface currents every day. God only knows what the underwater currents are like."

We found respite at a Beaver Bay cafe a few miles on the other side of our nightmare and I recorded my anger.

"Maybe the public psyche of viewing Lake Superior as a universal sink—just as oceans and the atmosphere—had something to do with what we paddled through. After all, it does seem incomprehensible something with an average depth of nearly five hundred feet, a maximum depth of over thirteen hundred and containing almost three million cubic miles of fresh water could ever be contaminated! So here it is. The end result of legislation saying we could desecrate the lake. And the policy would have continued save for the discovery of agents linked to cancer in human. Shouldn't the lake be treated with love and respect, simply because it exists?"

In the next booth, we heard fragments of conversation between two elderly gentlemen looking back on the warp and weft of their lives. One was gloomy and negative and faced old age with regret; while the other was cheerful and positive and looked at old age as if it were a time to sample the vintage wine of his past experiences. Of course, we didn't know the background of either person, but it did remind us of the importance of maintaining a positive attitude, in spite of what we just experienced and in our growing concern with "life after kayaking."

The sun came out and the temperature neared eighty when the Split Rock Lighthouse appeared. It loomed atop a hundred and thirty foot cliff face almost directly overhead. I had seen the lighthouse as a youngster and remembered staring down at the blue, green and turquoise water of one of Lake Superior's dangerous reef areas. Not in my wildest dreams would I have thought I'd one day be doing the opposite. For me, a small circle in my life had been completed. I looked at the same beautiful structure from a different perspective and, in the process of completing the circle, had grown older and wiser.

Cliffs became lower after Split Rock Point and we found ourselves paddling through an area with numerous gravel beaches. At the same time, the frequency of people increased dramatically. We encountered dozens of large and small powerboats loaded with sports fishermen and at the mouth of the Gooseberry River, curious campers surrounded me while Jerry went on a reconnaissance mission in the state park.

I found it impossible to reconcile the crush of tourists seeking the beauty of the North Shore with the lingering images of the taconite plant using the lake for a garbage can. When Jerry got back, he had news of a campfire program starting in two hours, but both of us knew we couldn't bear the stress of all the people.

Back on the lake, I wondered how many times the rocks at Gooseberry Falls State Park had been grabbed and climbed over by tourists. I understood the importance of the wonderful state parks system along the North Shore, but, like in so many other places we had seen, it was being "loved to death."

The day had been an emotional roller coaster for us. Only time would tell whether or not wise legislation, fostered by a change in values, would allow this special place called Lake Superior to live.

The folks thought they were looking at two buoys as our kayaks approached from the northeast.

"We were plannin' on checking out Encampment Island to stay for the night when we heard you yelling at us," Jerry said. "We were just about out of range and could barely hear you."

The group of us talked till two in the morning, covering topics including: Protecting beehives from bears—as the neighbor did with an electric fence—and Lake Superior in winter.

"One December weekend we came up to the cabin and found an ice castle. The lakeside was completely encased and icicles hanging along the eaves had frozen at a forty-five degree angle from the northeast gales. Makes marvelous insulation."

During a cold winter night, Bob counted all the light points on the other side of the lake in Wisconsin, twenty-five miles away. The same evening, he and his wife, also saw distant car lights and those of freighters far out in the lake.

"One below zero morning, I looked out the window and saw a large chimney on the horizon. It must have been at Port Wing or Herbster, but I never saw it again."

What he saw could have been a real chimney, or it could have been similar to many of the "chimney" mirages Jerry and I had seen. The air quality and visibility over the lake, especially in winter, was something we had also heard about a few days earlier. A person we talked with in Grand Marais mentioned an experience similar to theirs: "On a clear winter morning looking south over the lake, I could clearly see the tops of the Porcupine Mountains in Michigan seventy miles away!"

Bob and Nancy's hospitality was the beginning of five nights we didn't have to bother with camp chores.

Duluth was a little over thirty-five miles. On July nineteenth, a Minneapolis/St. Paul television crew would document our last miles on Lake Superior as they closed out a series of reports on us. Jerry and I called Don Buehler's interviews the "Minneapolis to Duluth the Hard Way Mini-Series." We were more than happy for Don to broadcast eight, short, illustrated segments of our journey because it helped defray the processing cost of photographs we took en route.

The problem we now faced was not whether we would get to Duluth, instead, it was how to keep from getting to Duluth before the scheduled date of the film crew. The answer to our topsy-turvy dilemma was solved eighteen miles later at the Knife River marina when Roger Drill loaned us a sailboat to sleep on for two nights and a car to run some errands.

The Kellys ran an art gallery at the village of Knife River and watched as two weathered kayakers looked through their Lake Superior display. The prints and paintings had the ability to capture a dimension of the lake that the camera could not. The artwork evoked feelings in us ranging from peace and tranquility to fear and powerlessness.

"Wow, look at this one! This one is great!" Jerry and I repeated.

We didn't realize we were being overheard and we didn't expect a gift, but a pen and ink sketch of the Split Rock Lighthouse was given to us before we returned to the marina. On the back was penned: "To the power of Superior—Lots of luck to both of you, John and Barb Kelly."

At the marina, we met two men discussing the intricacies of overhauling a wooden fishing tug. It sat on blocks in the boat yard and belonged to the younger man; the older one had worked for years on Great Lakes freighters.

"There, in Two Harbors where you boys stopped for lunch, is where the first load of iron ore went out of the State in 1884," the older man said. "That coal burnin' tugboat, you saw, is the 'Edna G.' She was built in 1896 and the Coast Guard says she's still good for another forty years! She wheels them new thousand foot ore boats around just like a match stick."

He talked about riding the ore carriers and described how the steel decks of the long ships rippled during rough water. He was the younger man's source of advice and inspiration as he readied his boat for a long voyage somewhere in the future.

We ate supper on board Jerry's fishing tug, the *Crusader II*. The three of us were an interesting combination. Jerry was preparing to live his dream, while we were preparing to complete ours and in between lay the common denominator of the water and travel.

In the final analysis, Jerry's own words said much about his character: "If you never tell a lie, you don't have to remember what you said!"

My mom and dad expected to meet us at Lester River, six miles from Duluth's Aerial Lift Bridge, but neither party expected to meet simultaneously! As we approached the shore, I saw my parents drive across the Lester River Bridge. Before I could react by shouting "It's them!" we heard a three-second blast from their truck horn

Jerry and I quickly unloaded our boats in the heat and tied them to the truck's—hot to the touch—aluminum topper. We were surrounded by droves of tourists seeking relief from the inland oven. I thought most of them were staring at us when Jerry said: "Look at all these people coming down here to touch and see the lake." It was fair to assume many of the people had never seen Lake Superior before and others had been drawn back again by its mystical attraction. We saw children clap their hands, while parents stood silently gazing at the lake's open horizon. Camera shutters clicked in an effort to capture a fragment of the inland sea's vastness and now and then people carried off beach cobbles—possibly in an effort to bring home some of the energy they felt.

We checked into a motel and drove downtown to reconnoiter our "official" entry into the port scheduled the following morning. En route, cars honked and people waved as they read a homemade sign Dad taped to the rear window of the topper explaining our journey. At Canal Park, near the Aerial Lift Bridge, a tourist snapped a picture of our backs. I thought it was a curious thing to do until realizing Jerry and I were wearing identical shirts his sister made for us with "Trilogy Crew" embroidered on the back.

"They think you're off one of the ships in the Harbor," Dad said.

"Well, tomorrow we will be," Jerry replied.

Chapter 41

Destination Duluth

"Nature and books belong to the eyes that have seen them."

Ralph Waldo Emerson

It was a hazy morning and sixty degrees. Mom and Dad already left for the Lift Bridge and Canal Park to meet my aunt and uncle, as our kayaks waited offshore at Lester River.

A dirt speck appeared on my sunglasses, which slowly turned into what looked like a seagull and then an airplane.

"It's Colonel Buehler!" Jerry said, choked with excitement. "Let's paddle!"

The plane made six low passes over us and headed back to Park Point. Again, it was quiet. All we heard was the familiar, rhythmic dipping of paddle blades into the glassy ripples.

We paddled without wet suits—bare chested—into a day that would easily reach ninety degrees on shore. The green hills of Duluth lie off our starboard side. Straight ahead and to port stretched a barely perceptible thin line of land beyond which lie the harbor of Duluth/Superior. Huge grain elevators and harbor facilities appeared as tiny gray blocks of varying sizes. The lift bridge itself looked like a child's erector set.

Jerry and I were within a few miles of the western terminus of the St. Lawrence Seaway, stretching over 2,300 miles to the Atlantic Ocean. Along the route, Thunder Bay had the largest collection of grain elevators in the world and the port we were about to enter had the tallest. Superior, Wisconsin's elevators topping out at two hundred and ninety feet!

A large powerboat appeared from the opening leading into the Lift Bridge Canal and bore down on us. On board were the U.S. Coast Guard, Don Buehler and his film crew

"Morning, it's a beautiful morning!" he said. "Well, this is Gitche Gumee—the land of sky blue waters!"

"The lake has been kind to us this summer," I said.

"Compared to last November," Don remarked. "When the Fitz sank!"

"And the gale blew the windows out of the control house on the Lift Bridge," I added.

"You guys just keep on paddling, we'll film and then get shots of you taking the boats out of the water when you dock," Don said.

The Coast Guard escorted us the final mile of lake to the concrete jetties and into the canal.

"Almost two years out and seven thousand miles!" I yelled to an onlooker who asked where we came from.

I knew my parents, my aunt, uncle, cousins and brother were some of the images standing on the break-water cheering and waving, but they didn't register individually. When the bridge tender announced our arrival, we joined hands, raised our arms and let out a loud "Heehaw!" Then, before slipping around the bend to the boat basin, we turned our kayaks a final time to the lake and thanked it for letting us pass. We had learned much and, in the days to come, we would miss it.

"Mrs. Bauer, you must be quite a logistics officer to keep shuttling all this gear ahead of these fells," Don said.

His comments gave credit to our strong support network and underscored the fact that everyone surrounding us was as much a part of the journey as we were.

"No fanfare, no brass bands, just a quiet reunion of family and friends," ended the interview. We'd be on the six and ten o'clock news in Minneapolis and St. Paul, but would never find out what we said. Perhaps, it was better we didn't. The interview could never capture the mixed feelings in our hearts and the swirling thoughts in our heads.

The commotion was over. It was Monday and those able to take off from work headed back to the Twin Cities. My brother, Jim, would help us celebrate the occasion in

Duluth as soon as we explained the circumstances to Mr. Johnson, the boat master of the marina:

"We tried to get hold of you last night but the place was closed when we stopped by," I said. "There's ten of you listed in the phone book and I didn't know who to call."

The situation was embarrassing for me, but Clarence found it humorous and told us the kayaks could be stored in the boat barn for the night. When Jim left us off at the marina the following afternoon, Mr. Johnson handed us a twenty-dollar bill while we prepared to leave. When we tried to refuse by saying his hospitality was more than enough, he tossed the bill into Jerry's boat and quickly walked away.

Our ten-mile day took us through the port of Duluth/Superior to a swampy, wooded island in Spirit Lake on the Minnesota-Wisconsin border. We were again by ourselves. The deep harbor with its ore docks, grain elevators, Great Lakes freighters and foreign ships was behind us. In the next ten or so miles, on the other side of St. Louis Bay and a short distance up the St. Louis River, was our first dam.

We were in transition and soon would begin a trip up the St. Louis River to a convenient place to portage the height of land into the Mississippi River drainage basin. We had several options in mind. The most likely was the swampy, seven-mile Savanna Portage, which historically linked the Mississippi with the Lake Superior fur trade route via the East and West Savanna Rivers.

What we gave up to lighten our load for the uphill climb and portage was replaced by the weight of water jugs. We didn't like what lie ahead. The Lower St. Louis had five hydro dams to portage in between the historic village of Fond du Lac and the paper mill town of Cloquet, fifteen miles upstream. Voyageurs called the region the Grand Portage—the water dropped almost six hundred feet in the stretch making most of the area impassable.

Likewise, the Savanna Portage also bothered us—its reputation for mud and bugs made it the worst voyageur portage in the northwest.

"As the smell of the 'victory' cigar smoke fades from our clothes, I feel a little lonely and depressed tonight. The process of completing the circle and the long wind down cycle is ready to begin in earnest," I wrote before falling asleep.

The rafts of suds, smell of lignin and the chocolate-brown water indicated we had entered the main channel of the St. Louis River. We could hear the hum of the hydro dam before we could see it.

"When we came around the bend we could see the power house. White froth spewed from the turbine discharge tunnels. We followed the left channel, rounded a bend to the right and ground to a halt. We faced thousands of round boulders and a trickle of water leading to the dam about two hundred yards away. All of the gates were closed—water hyacinth grew from most of them. The horseshoe structure was a formidable sight. We set the rigs on rocks, loaded our gear into duffel bags and gunnysacks and stumbled off toward the face of the dam in sweltering afternoon heat. I climbed the forty-five degree slope of the face, picking my way over cement talus, broken sticks and a half-standing cyclone fence to a concrete wall. On the other side of the concrete wall lies another cyclone fence, a pool of water for about a half mile—then rock. High banks, of course, are all over the place!" rrb

Three hours passed by the time our gear and kayaks were sitting to the extreme side of the dam. We attempted to drag bags of gear up the steep slope but failed. We were sunburned, our legs scratched and bleeding from the sticks and brush, our feet bruised from boulders and we were exhausted, dehydrated and depressed.

"I don't know how in the hell we are going to get through all of this," I grumbled. "And this is the easy part."

Our maps indicated a mile long underground diversion channel from the Thomson Reservoir through Jay Cooke State Park and we were sure, with the drought conditions, that section of river would be a long, dry boulder field.

"I've got an idea, Jerry" and I left with two water jugs on a mile walk back to inn where we had stopped for lunch.

Two hours later I returned with water, a special treat and good news.

"Mrs. Korkala didn't want us to starve, so she gave us a huge bag of brownies and strawberries," I said. "Plus, I got hold of Ken Peterson's brother-in-law from Saginaw. He'll be down at the dirt boat ramp we passed in Fond du Lac at eight tomorrow to get us around the rocks."

"Yee ha!" Jerry yelled. "We're going around the Grand Portage in style!"

Jerry was delivering Mrs. Korkala a card about our trip and I had started up the road to Jay Cooke Park, when a 1939 Dodge truck clanked and roared up to the landing. Our help had arrived.

We bought Rick and Bob breakfast at Cloquet after an easy portage showed us what we would have encountered on foot— rocks, rocks, more rocks, no water, dams, cliffs and more rocks—an easy four days of portaging, possibly five.

Our help dropped us off at the County 33 Bridge, where we spent five hours looking over topographic maps of the area.

"We got about thirty-five miles from here to Floodwood where the East Savanna River starts," Jerry said. "But we can't tell if there will be any water in it."

Earlier, we had learned a two-mile stretch of boulder field rapids below Floodwood was unnavigable due to water conditions, further complicating our upstream trek.

"It might be better if we took the portage we talked about from Paupores or Mirbat Creek on the river to Prairie Lake," I said. "At least it is below the Boulder field rapids."

Jerry and I knew and trusted the correct choice would reveal itself as we progressed. By evening, we were at a designated campsite on Pine Island, four and a half-miles from the irritating hustle and bustle of the city. We were in a quiet area at the upper edge of a long pool created by Cloquet's paper milldam. The tree-lined banks were much lower than we previously experienced and the water was dotted with remnants of past log drives.

Several factors, besides the "Grand Portage," added to our feeling of peace and tranquility that evening. The first two were obvious: We had eaten a monstrous sirloin tip steak from one of Rick's homegrown cows and drank enough liquids to finally re-hydrate. The others were subtler: We were away from the heavily polluted water of the lower St. Louis. And, although we couldn't prove it, away from areas producing electro-magnetic fields.

"At the hydro dam last night," Jerry said. "I felt the same way I did in some of the big cities we've been in."

"Maybe, Ed down at McClellanville was right," I speculated. "He said cities with their thousands of running motors and electric lines effect people in strange ways. The hydro-plant would have been producing the same type of energy."

"Maybe we're extra sensitive to it because we're away from it most of the time," Jerry added.

Jerry's sister and brother-in-law figured we would be on the St. Louis River somewhere between Lake Superior and Floodwood, but they didn't know where. Whether it was just blind luck or a sixth sense at work, a day of pulling, pushing and paddling our kayaks through large sets of unexpected boulder fields ended with a pleasant surprise.

The day had actually been quite pleasant for us. The whirlpool action of water, oftentimes waste deep, was therapeutic for our scratched legs and temperaments. We had traveled eight and a half miles and were in sight of the Highway #2 Bridge, when I saw what looked like two kids playing with an inner tube near the boulder strewn shore. Jerry recognized Duane and Diane before they noticed us and we joined them at their campsite for the evening.

Before dark, the three of them went on a reconnaissance mission while I stayed with the equipment. Jerry returned two hours later with the following report:

"If you think this part of the river is bad, you should see it below Floodwood—nothin' but rocks! And Mirbat Creek, from what I could see, is full of deadfalls and barbed wire fences."

That evening we ruled out the Savanna Portage and decided to cross the height of land at the three-house community of Paupores, ten river miles from Floodwood. There we'd haul our rigs over eight miles of road to Prairie Lake.

"I think we'll be able to do it in one long day because we'll be portaging on a flat, hard surface," Jerry said.

Before we left in the morning, Diane shed a different light on the situation: "I contacted Mom and Dad, we'll meet you guys in two days at Paupores," she said.

Still traveling upstream, we pulled our kayaks through two long sets of rapids and watched as the bridge at a much-needed coffee break approached ever so slowly. Two fishermen watched us from the bridge and their stares began to irritate me.

"Whenever you're doing something as dumb, such as paddling upstream, there's always somebody looking at you," I mumbled to myself.

My logbook records the rest of the incident:

"Jerry unhooked a fisherman's line at the bridge and he offered to buy us a beer. His speech was so slurred we declined—figuring he was three sheets to the wind. His buddy was on top of the rise with a similar outlook on life. When we walked into Brookston and entered the village tavern to fill our water jugs, there were the same fishermen. This time, they were making irrational, but serious, plans to sail a windjammer on a fishing trip to International Falls and Montana. The bar tender just shook his head."

On Sunday morning, we left the sandy beach of our isolated campsite and paddled a half-mile upstream to Paupores. Jerry's folks were unable to be in Duluth because it was a workday. Now, they'd incorporate a small family reunion along with helping us portage.

We rolled over roads and past farmers mowing hay in an area where a few feet determined whether the scanty summer rain would eventually flow into the Gulf of Mexico or the Gulf of the St. Lawrence.

Leaving the public landing on Prairie Lake, heading toward a big island, I heard Jerry's dad yell at the family's Irish setter: "Sam, get back here. Where they're going you'd probably never make it!"

His words echoed a singular truth that stuck in our minds as we slept in a tent pitched amidst thick poison ivy. It came from an old timer who lived in a house near the landing who responded with the words, "Bad, bad," when I asked him about the Prairie River.

Overland, Big Sandy lay fifteen miles due west of Prairie Lake—a distance that under ideal conditions could have been covered in less than five hours during a leisurely morning of paddle dipping. Our ordeal took five days!

"Monday July 26th—leeches, deer flies, rocks, bridges, small man-made dams, beaver dams, swamp, windfalls, otters and osprey. We have just pushed through a meandering swamp and now are camped on the edge of swamp and woods—I certainly hope things change."

The way it ended up, our first day on the Prairie River was our best day, considering miles covered and the wildlife we saw. The swamp had a wide navigable channel and the surrounding area was dotted with several active osprey nests. In the late afternoon, a family of curious river otters swam around our boats as we plied the surface. They reminded me of the youngsters we met at the "swimmin' hole" at the beginning of the river. The otters and the youngsters both exhibited a wonderful energetic attitude toward the water. As far as we were concerned, both groups had the right idea because the Prairie River, to us, had become an adversary. It was difficult, if not impossible, to appreciate it for what it was.

"What a terrible ordeal for our kayaks to go through after seven-thousand miles. I am entering this account while seated on a huge logjam over the Prairie River— which should be called Prairie Creek for it's certainly no bigger than one. We called REST after I finally tore a hole through the hull of my boat. It is an absolute miracle that the craft didn't start leaking long ago. We have dragged our rigs over logjams, beaver dams, rock bars, shallows, sand bars, more beaver dams, ad infinitum. The swamp has beaver dams and the wooded areas have logjams— plus hundred of yards of shallow water with, very slippery, exposed boulders. Jerry tore the sole almost completely off his tennis shoe this morning and now holds it in place with a shoestring wrapped around his entire foot. I don't see how the "river" could get any lower than it is right now. We paddle fifteen or thirty feet, straddling our kayaks and then hop out for one of the mentioned obstacles. Jerry can usually drag and pull his kayak over the shallow areas, but mine must be carried."

"We are bundled up, not because it's cold, but to ward off the deer flies, horse flies, hornets and mosquitoes. I pulled at least a dozen fastened leeches off me today. My feet burn from leech and bug bites. Now, a new beast, the wood tick, has added its name to the list."

By evening we faced a new problem:

"We used the last of the tea bags tonight. We are making two pots of tea from one bag. We are out of fresh water, so have started boiling river water, strained through our bandannas. Hopefully, we will be at Balsam tomorrow. We think it is a settlement—at least it is marked as such on our charts."

Chapter 42

The Grind Continues

"I learned this, by my experiments, that if one advances confidently in the direction of his dreams and endeavors to live the life which he has imagined, he will meet with success unexpected in common hours."

Henry David Thoreau

"We wore bug nets ninety-percent of the day in order to keep our sanity. We came through some of the worst logjams I have ever experienced in my life. Every single bend of the river had a log jam in it. We went over, under, around and through logjams. Presently, we are camped at a huge logjam! The pointed sticks are dangerous. The fallen balsam have branches like springs, so do the dead elms. Mostly mud today. The river, where we are camped has steep, mud banks—three feet deep in places. We walked through the bush to an old trail that intersected an overgrown logging road and then marched out to a drivable dirt road."

"We carried empty bleach jugs to the first inhabited house we saw. It had a 'Fire Warden' sign and a set of chainsaw-carved children's furniture outside. Burton Anderson and his family lived inside. He is a lumberman, like his dad was, keeps his own hours and hunts and fishes when time permits. Two big dogs were at his place; one slept at my feet, the other was outside. A black kitten kept hopping onto my lap."

Burt gave us a ride to the logging trail and backed his truck down it at least a quarter mile.

"You're the first ones through the river, this year," he said.

"And I can assure you," I added. "There will be no one else!"

We walked the last mile in the dark with Jerry dead reckoning a path through the heavy underbrush right to the camp. In the tent, we cooked oatmeal for supper and nursed the aches and pains of the day. I dug a long sliver from my left shin and another from one of my toenails.

My final evening log entry reflected an attitude change we both felt after experiencing the kindness of one individual: "The land here now seems more friendly since we've met someone that has lived in this area for years."

"We worked our asses off today and made a grand total of one mile. I picked off a couple more leeches, so I guess the muddy water doesn't eliminate them like we thought—the other leech bites itch like hell! We each ate a half-cup of honey mixed with peanut butter this morning for energy—we are out of bread. We hauled our boats overland for at least a hundred yards, carrying them past four major logjams and launched them into the water from a mud bank where we sank past our knees in muck. It was a treat to get into the water—the mud soothed the burning from the stinging nettle. Both of us now wear tennis shoes tied to our feet with ropes. Toward the end of our day's ordeal, Jerry finally pulled off his tattered shoes, finding it easier to walk barefoot up the mud banks."

We dragged, lifted and skirted snags, logs and piled up timber until I was ready to throw up. There was a jog jam every ten feet and where the "river" was clear for fifty to one hundred feet, there inevitably was a pile ten to sixteen feet high and a block long to make up for it. We were extremely lucky not to break an arm or leg.

Toward the end of the day, a huge logjam blocked our progress. Jerry crawled to the top of the bank and discovered the gigantic beaver dam that marked the general area of the old logging road we had walked the day before.

Enough was enough! We unloaded the boats, hoisted them to the top of the bank and carried them to the logging road. From there we hauled our kayaks and gear a quarter mile down the logging road to a place where a big ditch crossed and prepared to camp for the evening. Our new plan was to carry the boats overland, one and a half miles, to a bridge where the Prairie River would hopefully be deeper after the confluence of the Tamarack. In so doing, we'd avoid three miles of plugged river and most likely three more days of trials and tribulations.

Low on water, we again hiked the road to the house with the "Fire Warden" sign.

"Burton is off fighting a grass fire near McGregor, but he should be home pretty soon," Margie said. "Would you boys like to come in for supper? You look starved!"

Eventually, Burton's truck pulled up the driveway. He was covered with soot, smelled like smoke and looked more tired than we felt.

"It's gettin' a little late for you guys to head back to camp," he said. "You can stay here tonight if you want"

In spite of our fatigue, all three of us talked until half past one, while everyone else, including the black kitten and "Sam" the Golden Retriever, slept.

Burton enjoyed reading books on Minnesota history and the natural world. He talked in a slow, relaxed, direct voice and related a story which reflected his wisdom and outlook on life:

"A man found a gold mine," he said. "He kept digging out more and more gold and kept bagging it up. Finally, he thought, if he filled just one more bag, he'd quit. So he dug deeper and deeper, shored the tunnel up more and more. And just as he was filling up the last bag the mine caved in on him."

Early in the evening, I called home and had a conversation with my dad that made me feel I had walked into the Twilight Zone.

"You know that good friend of Jim Heggem's who you were supposed to look up near McGregor? Dad said. "Well his name isn't Burton Johnson, it's Burton Anderson!"

I woke the next morning and silently watched a hazy, orange sun break a flat horizon line of trees and spread light over a dew soaked field of freshly mowed hay. The event was a prayer for a day, which would be much different from the previous four.

Soon, I heard a rustle from upstairs and in a short while could smell perking coffee, bacon and eggs.

"I'll give you guys a ride to the bridge in the four wheeler," Burton said. "It's up to you"

On our way to the rigs, Burton pointed out a neighbor's farm.

"See that tiny one room place over there," he said. "An old farmer lives there. He might have a small place and lives quite simply, but he can beat anyone in chess if he can still see the board." There was a pause and Burt added: "Or if he can't see the board."

The transmission whined as we backed down the old logging road toward our equipment. Jerry and I were soaked with morning dew from walking the last fifty yards, but hardly noticed and didn't care. After what we had endured, I found it exhilarating watching saplings and brush futilely clawing at the truck as if to prevent our departure.

Our mile and a half portage was completed in less than twenty minutes and Burton was on his way back to the peat fire, which burned until the first snowfall.

The Prairie River improved significantly after the Tamarack came in. Under normal conditions, the serpentine course avoiding most of the log jams and shallows would have been monotonous, but now, we found it wonderful just to be moving. We passed the confluence of the West Savanna River and in our minds eye could see ourselves somewhere on the East Savanna River wondering where all the water went.

In what seemed like an instant, we were paddling the rice-filled flowage leading into Big Sandy Lake.

"Wow, it'll be a bumper crop this year," I said.

"If the lake isn't lowered to prevent ricing boats from getting into the paddies," Jerry replied.

His comment came from a heated debate we heard concerning drawing down Mississippi Headwater Reservoirs, Big Sandy Lake included, to help maintain adequate flow for navigation and river dependent population areas.

"I guess a lot of barges are getting stuck on sandbars down near Lake Pepin," I added. "And the Minneapolis water works is worried about the amount of sewage they're pumping into their intake pipes for drinking water."

The two elderly ladies running Taylor's Antique Store on Big Sandy Lake waited our arrival. We entered inquiring about directions to Libby and the Sandy Lake dam and left with directions to a cabin.

"You stayed with my son and daughter-in-law on Lake Superior," Ann said. "They sent me the article that appeared about you in the *Two Harbors Chronicle and* I gave it to the ladies at the antique shop."

Time slipped away and we found ourselves pitching the tent in Ann's yard instead of, as she put it, "a poison ivy covered island on Big Sandy."

The next morning as I was brushing my teeth, I heard an audible, but not discernible, voice and opened the bathroom door to see Jerry's dad standing there!.

"I don't know how you did it," I said. "But you just found two needles in a haystack."

We spent the weekend at the Mimbach's cabin near Cross Lake, eighty miles from Big Sandy. Sweat, bugs and mud from days on the St. Louis and Prairie Rivers were washed from our clothes. However, the stay couldn't do the same for the growing anxiety in our minds:

"In a couple days Jerry and I will again touch the waters of the Mississippi to complete a seventy-three hundred mile circle. We will paddle home to Minneapolis but we are not sure if we will stop because we don't know if we'll be ready to stop. I love my way of life now. I dread returning to society. I was homesick for open water over the winter. I am free now. I can feel now. I live simply and simply live. I could continue this way of life easily for the next ten years!"

My dad came up from the cities the next morning and drove Jerry and me back to our kayaks. En route he told us about the powerful effect that our entry into Duluth had on him and the rest of the welcoming committee:

"At first, we could only see the water and the long horizon of the lake. Then, the Coast Guard Cutter appeared. Bob was the first one to spot your paddle flashes with his binoculars. Soon, everyone could see the paddle flashes and then two black dots that slowly grew into kayaks and finally kayakers! It was like you came from nothing right out of the lake—it was quite a sight."

We stayed another night at Big Sandy Lake because the events of the following morning made it impractical to leave. Ann's pump broke down and Jerry and I volunteered to fill water jugs and a stainless steel milk pail at another cabin.

While we were there, enthusiasm over the journey made it paramount that an article be written for the local paper. However, the recorder had us meeting Ann's son at Jerry's folk's cabin and couldn't figure out our route even with the maps we showed him. As a result, he decided to drive us to the Aitkin newspaper office thirty miles away. Unfortunately, the office was closed while the reporter covered the peat fire. So, he left his telephone number and the four of us—including the dog, which seemed to always have a perpetual smile on its face—headed back. Finally, after we thought all the facts of our journey were in order, we were asked: "Did you follow the shoreline of Lake Superior or paddle straight across?"

The remainder of the day was spent patching our kayaks. The Prairie River had been mean to Jerry's craft. The hull fabric of his boat had aged with the elements and now, being brittle, was leaking. By the time Jerry was done, he had glued seventeen new patches on the bottom of his boat where only two had originally been. My kayak, on the contrary, was doing quite well; it now had fifty-two patches, only one of which had come from the Prairie River. The hull still showed no signs of brittleness, but was still easily punctured and had to be treated with the utmost care, oftentimes at the expense of Jerry's kayak.

Larry, the repairman, arrived in the early evening and Jerry and I helped him remove the pump from the well pit.

Finding out the pump required parts Larry didn't have on hand, he concentrated on our journey and seemed to understand the difficulties we had encountered over the past week.

"The Prairie River used to be full of logging dams," he said. "That's why you guys had so much trouble getting through it."

Whatever the reason, the Prairie River was now behind us and, in comparison, the miles ahead looked easy indeed.

We paddled three miles to the northwest side of the lake, portaged the dam and set our kayaks into the Big Sandy River. A half mile later, we met the waters of the Mississippi—the circle was complete. Later, we thought of a dozen things we could have done at that moment, but didn't.

We drifted for a few seconds, looking at a river we found hard to recognize. For some reason, we expected it to be stuck in time, matching memories of a Mississippi we knew almost two years before. What we saw instead was a river five feet lower than normal, with clay banks lined with thick greenery, on a ninety degree August day.

Signs of the drought were everywhere: Jerry and I passed exposed rocks and logs, well below the normal waterline. At Palisade, we had a difficult time pounding tent stakes into dry ground packed as hard as concrete. In the community's small cafe, we listened to exhausted charcoal-covered fire fighters talking about peat fires, which now burned all over the county.

The next morning, the owner told us she was planning to sell the cafe and move to her farm because Palisade's population of one hundred and fifty was getting too crowded for her.

We ate pancakes draped over our plates and talked with an elderly lady. To us, she was as much a part of the cafe's pleasant atmosphere as the walls richly decorated with newspaper headlines and movie placards.

"The memories of your trip will grow over the years," she said. "Every time my husband recalls his 1916 trip to Mexico, it's like re-living the experience over again!"

The town's fire whistle sounded for the fifth time since the previous evening. While we drifted away, both of us felt a tinge of guilt, feeling we somehow should be assisting the fire crews instead of paddling on the water. Our public service opportunity did, however, unveil itself ten miles downriver:

"Around a meander curve, we spotted a white object moving across the water. At first, I thought it was a sheep, but it turned out to be a dog. It swam to the other side, pulling a long chain. How lucky, I thought, for the dog not to get hung up on the drift and sunken debris. Then, it jumped back into the water, swam over to a high bank, got its chain wrapped in submerged sticks and slid back into the river. I managed to paddle to the panic stricken animal and, after a short struggle, I was able to unsnap its chain. It tried to 'thank' me by climbing onto the deck of my kayak, its front claws puncturing the hull in several places, but eventually swam off never to be seen by us again." rrb

That evening we camped in one of the many sprawling flood plains lying between lazy meander curves typical of the river's course through Aitkin County. Jerry pitched the tent between cow pies and I did repair work on my boat. Just as the mosquitoes came out, I made the announcement: "Finally it's happened! I've glued a patch over a hole in a patch!"

The next day we were in Aitkin, staying the evening at Harold Beecroft's house, while Jerry attempted to find the leaks in his boat by using the old Laurel and Hardy method of filling the inside with water. The test, however, was inconclusive and the only thing we could tell was the boat leaked somewhere around the front stern strip.

Harold was an interesting person. We met him at the Aitkin public access and he directed us by water to the wreck of the Andy Gibson. The one hundred and forty foot stern-wheeler we had heard about on our first trip through the area plied the Mississippi between Aitkin and Grand Rapids from 1883 to 1892. Now, unusually low water exposed the steamboat's grave for the first time in many years. Only the white ribs of the boat remained, but it was enough to give a hint of what the glory days of steam boating were all about on the Upper Mississippi.

Part of our evening was spent at Herman Pittman's place, a friend of Harold's who was retired from the state forest service. Our friendship was assured when Herman remembered my grandfather, who worked for forestry out of Grand Rapids, as being the biggest practical joker in the region!

He talked about the early days of surveying in the county when accuracy in the swamps was as good as could be expected:

"One survey crew in the northern part of the county lost all its notes in a river, so the head surveyor just recalled the field notes from memory and sent them in. A section marker we were looking for ended up being six iron stakes covering an area as big as this house. Apparently, whoever was surveying the area would just get frustrated and drive a stake down in the approximate location."

Herman recalled days of his youth when he and several other Eagle Scouts retraced the Savanna Portage back in the thirties.

"It was quite a chore," he said. "We found some of the old cedar pole markers and rest platforms. The area used to be dryer than it is now and, even so, I've read accounts of people hearing the groans of bug-covered voyageurs crossing the portage!"

Jerry added: "If you would have been near the Prairie River last week, you would have gotten an earful, sure to equal to that of any voyageur on the Savanna!"

Twelve miles below Aitkin, the early unusually cool evening dampened the normal drone of mosquitoes. Crickets chirped around our camp and in the distance I could clearly hear the voice of someone calling cattle in for the evening. I reminded myself how lucky Jerry and I were to have the opportunity to lead a life style we had learned to love. In my mind I could see Harold standing at the boat ramp and hear his final words to us: "You know, I wish I could go with you, I really do!"

Our journey was winding down and we were dragging our feet. We noticed noise and congestion more and more and were easily irritated by it.

Since the Highway #6 Bridge was only twelve miles from the Mimbach's cabin, Jerry's folks treated us again to a third weekend of hospitality. While we waited for the 1950 pickup to take us to the cabin for an overnight stay, the long lines of weekend vehicles on the highway nearly drove us mad. It seemed like the flurry of northbound traffic had been just let out of a huge cage. Faster vehicles passed slower ones while a mixture of tires on pavement, loud motors and distorted music filled our ears. The air stunk of exhaust fumes and a wheel from an ill-maintained boat trailer flew off during the rush, nearly hitting Jerry.

The short stay was well appreciated, but it was good to get back to our "own" environment, regardless of how tenuous it was becoming:

"The Twin Cities are only a hundred and fifty miles away as we close in on them. Cars can be heard on Highway #6, a mile overland, but they are not loud enough to bother us. The wind tonight pours over the trees and sifts into the tent. The past few evenings have hinted of fall and now the full moon, in a partly cloudy sky, echoes the same. The leaves have a late summer droop and their green seems to drip off the trees during the hot afternoons."

It was surprisingly pleasant to find the portage at the paper mill dam in Brainerd much cleaner than two year before and we had no *deja vu* experiences with falling rocks at the Highway 210 Bridge.

We again passed through our favorite place on the Upper Mississippi—the twenty-three mile glacial outwash section between the Crow Wing River and Little Falls. In many places, it looked as though we were paddling into a renaissance painting where the wide river, dotted with rocks and islands, lush green vegetation and rolling hills was washed by a bright, hazy sun.

Now and then, we heard the rumble of far off thunder, which turned out to be artillery fire from the military reservation bordering our starboard side. When two lay back reservists, running a portable drinking water plant, invited us to stop, we reluctantly accepted the offer. During our brief visit, we learned the facility could produce three hundred gallons of potable water per hour. The rest of their explanation was cut short by one of them announcing: "The sarge is coming and he's a real ass hole!" The man, however, seemed friendly enough, as he followed Jerry and me back to our kayaks and watched us leave. However, both of us knew his more descriptive qualities would be expressed once he returned to the soldiers' duty station.

"It's the driest its been since 1936," my grand uncle told us, while we loaded our kayaks into his trailer at the Little Falls dam.

Bud also mentioned it was the first time the rebuilt trailer had been used to haul anything. So, he was a little reluctant to let Jerry ride in his kayak, sunglasses on and radio blaring, while we rolled down the road in the dark.

At the house, Hazel accepted us with open arms as she had done nearly two years before. But Jerry and I still felt somewhat awkward and out of place. I tried to verbalize what we were going through: "We are coming from the land of lumberjacks and fishermen, so, we only have clothes that lumberjacks and fishermen wear, We are gradually being re-introduced into society and we are having a hard time getting used to it. It's all so strange to us."

Two nights passed before we left Little Falls and when we finally did, the pre-departure was quite dramatic:

"Jerry was doing his usual thing of furiously "paddling" his kayak when Bud's vehicle bounced over the railroad tracks. I heard a strange clank, turned around and, to my horro,r saw the trailer, the kayaks and Jerry rolling down the road under their own power! Bud pulled to the side, while Jerry, now running alongside the trailer, shot past us! I joined in hot pursuit and together we were able to guide the runaway trailor into the ditch just before a major intersection."

There was no serious damage, save for a few scrapes to the ends of the rigs, but Bud still felt terrible about the whole thing. He seemed to feel better after we explained the incident was just another of our journey's many "Laurel and Hardy" episodes.

"Besides," I said. "Jerry needs things like this now and then to keep him on his toes!"

"It's the fastest I've ever exited my kayak on the entire trip!" Jerry laughed. "And I hope I never have to repeat it!"

Chapter 43

Clear Paddling, Civilization and the Trilogy Ends

"I think you end up doing the stuff you were supposed to do at the time you were supposed to do it."

Robert Downey, Jr.

We paddled all day in the heat, portaged the Blanchard Dam and reached the Sartell Dam at dusk. The pool above the dam was crowded with large and small-motorized craft of all kinds, some of which cut dangerously close to our kayaks. One boat, in particular, a canoe drew circles around us and then buzzed up from behind. I could see its bow closing in on my port side, when suddenly its outboard motor rammed a submerged boulder nearly throwing its occupants into the water. The incident was one of the few times on the trip Jerry and my vindictive wishes came true.

For the next few days, Jerry and I stayed with a long time friend, Larry Johnson. Larry and I had become Eagle Scouts through the same troop and all three of us belonged to the *Coureur du Bois*—a dynamic senior patrol involved in high adventure activities. Now, we met as adults, sharing experiences scouting helped prepare us for.

In some ways we were different, but in other ways, we were very much the same. Larry was married and his fast paced life style made Jerry and me nervous. Likewise for Larry, our relaxed pace made him nervous. However, the common thread of past experience and the common need to find the element we felt most comfortable in bonded us together.

"Jerry and you have found it on the water," Larry said. "And I've found it in the sky!"

Larry was working toward a commercial pilot's license and he took us into his element one afternoon. It was good way to celebrate my birthday. We soared a thousand feet above the Mississippi at a hundred miles per hour. We saw where we had been and where we were going. The winding channel, filled with dark water, passed urban and agricultural land, jumped over dams and flowed under bridges and power lines. Whether it is sewer outfalls, drinking water intakes, irrigation lines, or power plant cooling systems, the lifeline of moving water was tapped every few miles with human-made umbilical cords.

The plane flew over a wide gravel bar that Jerry and I camped on the following evening. We were midway in a fifty-three mile run between St. Cloud and Champlain, well within range of a rendezvous with friends and relatives.

"This evening we sleep on a dry riverbed of a Mississippi fifty-percent its normal size. A hot, dry wind blows and our kayaks help hold the tent in place. Neither Jerry nor I are very excited about our entry into the Twin Cities. We will take a short break and continue to Winona where we will officially end the Trilogy. Our excitement now must be transferred to those that look at us as examples of personal striving and perseverance of the human spirit."

The wind and heat of a thirty-mile day was gone and we felt the wonderful coolness of a late summer evening. A Minneapolis newspaper photographer snapped away as we paddled under the Champlain Bridge and over twenty people waited for us at the landing. Jerry's family and my family were there—a powerful reminder of the communion of support both families had given us during our two-year journey.

Before the stay ended in Coon Rapids, Canadian friends who searched in vain at Old Fort William and Thunder Bay finally found us. Carol and Donna had driven down from Winnipeg on a shopping trip to Minneapolis in hopes Jerry and I would be around. The reunion helped Jerry and me temper the sadness of our journey's closure, which would now end in a week with the happiness and laughter of friends that thought a lot about us.

"Two voyageurs stopped by our camp," I wrote when we were underway again. "They, like us, are on the road to find out. We talked with them until dusk. I'm sure they would have stayed overnight, if it wouldn't have been for a rendezvous with their relatives two miles downriver.

Dan and Greg originally planned to start at Lake Itasca, but moved their canoe trip a hundred miles to Bemidji because of low water."

We camped five more nights in the one hundred and forty-five river miles between Champlain and Winona. Our third night, the Richardson family at Hastings let us stay overnight on their houseboat, even though they had to leave for home. The boat's marine radio broadcasting Coast Guard announcements of sunken barges, burnt out navigation lights and low-water sandbars, as well as river dialogue between tow captains, re-reminded us of the "strong brown god" we'd have the privilege to paddle on a few more days.

My last few journal entries before journey's end reflect a range of observations, feelings and insights ranging from ludicrous to serious:

During a boring half day at the Lake City marina, while we waited out strong winds on Lake Pepin, I wrote: *"From the data we have collected over the last few hours, Jerry and I have concluded: The bigger the boat, the fatter the person."*

"For the past two years, Jerry and I have led a simplified, uncluttered life style, close to the natural world. I love quietude and long periods of silence. I am fond of foods which are easy to digest and I prefer fish, stew, or macaroni and cheese, to a steak. This is the healthiest and happiest I've been in my entire life!"

"Tonight, our last night on the water, we ate Red Snapper at bass camp, just across from our sand spoil 'hotel'. It tasted good, but it wasn't anything like the Snapper we ate during our first night in Florida. Tomorrow we end our journey in Winona. It has taken five hundred miles and forty-three days to wind down from the trip since Duluth. Jerry and I have finally accepted the fact the journey is ending—and it will do so simply and without fanfare. Our journey is ending with a fall chill in the air—as it should. The weather was excellent and we paddled thirty-five miles today. In total, I figure we've gone about 7,500 miles and now have twelve left. The kayaks certainly show it. The paddles are splitting and falling apart. We are tough, brown, weathered and strong."

The gates of Lock 5A slowly swung open, revealing a game warden's boat.

"What are ya doin'? Loafin'?" a voice boomed over the bullhorn. It was Bill Gannaway. We had contacted him the day before and he said he would meet us somewhere on the river.

"The *Winona Daily News* and *KTTC* are coming out with a film crew from Rochester," Bill said in his normal, matter of fact voice. "Can you guys hold your horses while we get them?"

We waited on a sandbar, ate peanut butter and honey sandwiches for the last time on the journey and then paddled three miles with a small, official flotilla to Riverside Park.

"The journey has taught us a lot," Jerry said to one of the reporters. "It might take us years to understand all its aspects. Randy and I have learned about other people, the land and ourselves in a unique way and feel obligated to share what we've learned. The journey and the people we have met along the way have given a lot to us and, as we begin a new life style, it's our obligation to give something in return."

I gave another reporter a copy of the letter we sent out during the journey's second winter:

"The journey has been a 'rebirth' for us both spiritually, physically and mentally. We truly owe the success of our journey to the help and hospitality extended by the folks en route. Our adventure—the Trilogy—is was not just an adventure of Jerry and myself, it was an adventure of all who cared or thought about us."

As we headed north to the Twin Cities, we hardly spoke. There was no need. The past two years had changed our worldview and we would look at things differently for the rest of our lives. What we had experienced and what was now in our hearts could never be taken away. Both of us knew we had the courage and integrity to face the challenges that lie ahead.